MANAGING THE DESIGN FACTORY

A Product Developer's Toolkit

DONALD G. REINERTSEN

THE FREE PRESS

𝑓**P**

THE FREE PRESS
A Division of Simon & Schuster Inc.
1230 Avenue of the Americas
New York, NY 10020

Manufactured in the United States of America

10   9   8   7   6   5

Library of Congress Cataloging-in-Publication Data

Reinertsen, Donald G., 1950–
    Managing the design factory : a product developer's toolkit /
  Donald G. Reinertsen.
        p.   cm.
    Includes bibliographical references and index.
    ISBN 0–684–83991–1
    1. New products.   2. Design, Industrial.   3. Product management.
I. Title
TS170.R45   1997
658.5'75—DC21   97–20343
                                                        CIP

Dedicated to my brother

LEE ALAN REINERTSEN

Contents

PART THREE: ACTION TOOLS

Introduction

REVOLUTION IN THE FACTORY

Starting in the early 1980s an amazing revolution swept through America's manufacturing companies. It was not propelled by any consulting firm or academic gurus. It was initially ignored by all the leading business schools. Yet any manufacturing manager will tell you that Just-in-Time (JIT) manufacturing has probably had more impact on actual business economics than anything that has happened since the assembly line.

This revolution contained many specific operational lessons that can be directly transferred from the factory into the development laboratory. Central among these are the importance of achieving small batch sizes, increasing flexibility, and reducing variability. More subtle, but no less important, is the fallacy of focusing on efficiency and the need to fit product and process. Unfortunately, the development process in most companies has been slow at applying these insights. This book will show you how and when these lessons can be applied in product development.

By now, most of us are familiar with the primary effects of JIT. Cycle times in factories have dropped by factors of 10 to 100. We have reduced inventories by more than 90 percent, freeing enormous amounts of cash. We may also be aware of the secondary effects that improve quality, accelerate learning, and lower production costs. The JIT revolution is an example of the gains that can be made by questioning fundamental assumptions about how a system, in this case a factory, should work. JIT approached the problem of manufacturing as a fresh design problem. It ignored the doctrine taught by every major business school, and it ignored the shared beliefs of generations of manufacturing managers, accountants, and general managers. And in this case a breakthrough resulted. The development process is now ripe for such a change in paradigm. In the course of this book we intend to show you how many of our deeply rooted beliefs about product development may be incorrect and dysfunctional. To begin exploring this possibility we must make a brief visit to our product development process.

INTO THE WITCH DOCTOR'S TENT

In most organizations product development is a mix of black art and esoteric ritual. Most development processes have not been consciously designed, but rather have evolved along a bumpy path. Things are tried that work, so we keep doing them. Things are tried that don't work, so we stop doing them and never try them again. Our processes contain a record of these evolutionary adaptations embedded in our rituals and traditions. Some of these adaptations remain useful. Others become obsolete but persist as historical relics, just the way we carry around an appendix. Product development is a messy process, like the old joke about making sausages. You may want to enjoy the results, but you really don't want to know how they do it.

It is very easy to treat product development as a black art rather than a science, because so many of its elements are unpredictable. This unpredictability is inherent in doing things we have never done before. We are just guessing at how long it will take, how good the results will be, and how much money it will cost. This strong unpredictable element can cause us to falsely assume that product development is totally different than repetitive activities like manufacturing.

In this book we will strive to be much more disciplined in our thinking. We will take a careful look at what really goes on in product development. We will learn to apply some mathematical tools, such as queueing theory and information theory, to the world of unpredictable processes. We want to question some of the rituals, since many of them may have outlived their usefulness. By the end of this book, I hope you will be convinced that such an approach offers some useful insights.

THERE ARE NO BEST PRACTICES

The focus of this book is on tools, not rules. To some readers this will be disturbing. Surely some approaches work better than others. Why not identify the best practices, follow them, and live happily ever after?

After many years of working in product development I have concluded that the idea of best practices is a seductive but dangerous trap. Best practices are only "best" in certain contexts and to achieve certain objectives. A change in either the context or the objective can quickly transform a "best practice" into a stupid approach. For example, a dedicated prototype facility may be a superb practice in one business but an economic disaster in another. In some mechanical design businesses a dedicated prototype facility may provide the means to create reliable prototypes quickly. In contrast, for a semiconductor business a dedicated prototype facility could be outrageously expensive. The great danger in "best practices" is that the practice can get disconnected from its intent and its context and may acquire a ritual significance that is unrelated to its original purpose.

This distortion appears to arise because of our tendency to start believing the label "best" as an absolute judgment. Why would you choose not to do something the "best" way? It requires great mental clarity to recognize that the label "best" might be misleading. Abraham Lincoln once asked, "How many legs would a horse have if you called a tail a leg?" His friend replied, "Five." "No," responded Lincoln. "Four. Just because you call a tail a leg doesn't make it a leg!" Just because we call something a "best practice" does not mean it is our best choice to achieve a particular goal in a particular context.

The most effective way to deal with this problem is to try to retain a degree of thoughtfulness. We must continue to think about what we are doing and to avoid value-laden labels that oversimplify decisions. It is for this reason that this book focuses on tools rather than rules and rituals. A tool enhances our ability to achieve a certain effect in a certain context. A hammer is a good tool for sinking nails but a poor way to drive screws. We are much more likely to think clearly with this metaphor than when we call certain techniques "best practices."

The tools in this book can be divided into two basic groups. Tools that assist us in thinking about the problem of product development are called "thinking tools." They allow us to understand why we must do certain things. For the most part these tools have been borrowed from the worlds of engineering and finance. However, managers must do more than think about things, they must do things as well. To deal with the problems of doing, we have provided what we call "action tools."

While both types of tools are necessary to succeed, the thinking tools are most fundamental. They enable you to understand *why* you are doing things, not simply what to do. The great Japanese manufacturing engineer Shigeo Shingo commented in his book *Non-Stock Production* that he was constantly visited by Americans seeking know-how, but he rarely saw any interested in know-why. He observed that his visitors would never understand his success until they started asking him *why* he did certain things. It is only with the knowledge of *why* that you gain the ability to adapt an approach to a specific situation in a constantly changing world. In this book I hope to help you develop this ability to think clearly about why certain things work in certain situations.

WHERE IDEAS COME FROM

The most usable ideas in this book have come from practitioners. I am particularly grateful for the valuable inputs that I have obtained from my consulting clients and from participants in the product development class that I teach a few times a year at California Institute of Technology in Pasadena. They have helped me to find out what, among the vast flood of ideas that appears in management literature, is really working for people.

Several practitioners deserve special mention. Marv Patterson, author of *Accelerating Innovation*, first started me thinking about how information theory applies to product development. Dan Krupka of AT&T played a similar role in reviving my interest in queueing theory. The late Chris Lorenz of the *Financial Times*, and author of *The Design Dimension*, played a unique role. He grasped the business value of the economic analysis tools almost fourteen years ago, at least a decade before any other observer. I am firmly convinced that without his support I would never have been able to specialize in this narrow area of consulting, and thus I am deeply indebted to him.

As always, I am interested in the views of readers on these issues and can be contacted at:

Donald Reinertsen
Reinertsen & Associates
600 Via Monte D'Oro
Redondo Beach, CA 90277

Telephone: (310) 373-5332
Fax: (310) 373-5093
E-Mail: DonReinertsen@compuserve.com

THE ORGANIZATION OF THIS BOOK

Part One of this book proposes the concept of a Design Factory. Such a concept is only one model of the development process, but one that I believe is useful. As a model, it is a map of reality and not reality itself. Therein lies its strength and its weakness. As a simplified abstraction it will generate useful insights. However, we must constantly remember that the simplification is a veil between us and the reality of the process. It will be very easy to forget this.

Part Two will introduce some thinking tools to help us understand our model. These tools are borrowed from the world of engineering and finance, and they will help us treat development problems more quantitatively. Interestingly, as is often the case with quantitative tools, they will generate qualitative insights as well. The tools we will use are economic modeling, queueing theory, information theory, and systems theory. There is nothing particularly new about these tools, nor are they terribly difficult to understand.

In Part Three we will cover the action tools. These tools come primarily from the world of management and include organization design, process design, and risk management.

Finally, we will discuss what steps can be taken to intervene in and improve the development process. If you take no action with the new ideas you have wasted your time reading this book. Now let us begin by examining the Design Factory in more detail.

Part One

THE DESIGN FACTORY

1

Into the Design Factory

Imagine that you own a business with a large bank account that pays no interest. You would be unhappy. Now imagine that this bank account loses half its capital value every year. You would be outraged. Yet this is exactly the situation that most companies find themselves in as they try to manage their product development process. They have high levels of investment in partially completed designs, but these investments earn them nothing until the products are introduced. These investments are at risk, because a competitor's product introduction can make a partially completed project worthless overnight. In effect, they have a large non-interest-bearing asset that loses its capital value very rapidly. There is however one key difference. Most companies have no clue how big this asset is, or what sort of return they make on it.

This chapter introduces the concept of the Design Factory, the foundation upon which we will build when we introduce more powerful analytical tools later in the book. We will look at the goals of the Design Factory, its output, its inventory, and will examine its similarities and differences from the manufacturing factory. I have chosen the term Design Factory for our product development process because it gives us a useful context within which to view this process. By approaching the problem as a manufacturing problem, we can exploit certain tools and concepts that have proved useful for repetitive processes like manufacturing.

There is a good reason for viewing design through the eyes of a manufacturing manager. In general, more careful management thought and

9

more insightful review of experience have occurred in the area of manufacturing than in the area of product development. This is true in part because we have better accounting systems in manufacturing, which makes it easier to assess performance. It is also true because we spend more money in this area, causing it to receive a higher level of management attention and scrutiny. It may also be true because manufacturing is an inherently repetitive process and therefore more likely to produce learning than a nonrepetitive process, like product development. Whatever the causes, the net effect is that we have scrutinized manufacturing more carefully than product development. This careful study has sharpened our thinking and produced some useful tools that can usefully be applied to the development process.

OUR GOALS ARE ECONOMIC

We must begin by asking, "What is the objective of the Design Factory?" We cannot optimize the Design Factory unless we are clear about what we are trying to optimize.

The answer is quite simple. The Design Factory exists for one purpose—the same purpose as the manufacturing factory—to make a profit. I would argue that it has no important objective that cannot be quantified in economic terms. Furthermore, I would assert that it is only by attempting such quantification that we can objectively weigh the consequences of particular actions. We are only philosophers until we begin to use numbers.

This view is not as starkly mercenary as it appears. All profit derives from a single source: the ability to sell things or services for more than they cost to make or acquire. Our sales price is a measure of the value that people attach to our output. If we fail to create sufficient value for customers, then they will spend their money on something else. In this sense sales price is the customer's message that we have done something useful. Our cost, on the other hand, is a measure of how well we use time and physical resources. A manufacturer who is efficient at converting material, labor, and energy into products is rewarded with profits. When resources are squandered, profits drop. In this sense, profit is simply a measure of how efficient we are at converting time and resources into things people value. When we do important things for people, without wasting time and resources, we are rewarded with profit.

We will develop this measure of profit more completely in Chapter 2, where we will show how measures like time, expense, cost, and performance can be converted to a common denominator of profitability. For now, just remember that our objective is profits, not products.

PRODUCTS VS. DESIGNS

How does the Design Factory plan to produce these profits? Here is where we find a fundamental difference from manufacturing. Producing a design is a different problem from producing a product. As Marv Patterson has pointed out in his book, *Accelerating Innovation,* the purpose of a design process is to generate information. It is the difference between making food and making recipes. The manufacturing factory creates food for people to eat. The Design Factory creates recipes. Behind this simple statement are some interesting implications that we shall examine in more detail in Chapter 4 when we cover information theory. For now, let us make a few basic observations.

The recipes we produce in the Design Factory only achieve our objective when they are converted to our valued goal, which is profit. Thus, the *only* measure of the value of design is its economic value. Our designs are not important because they are new, or because they are beautiful, or because they are innovative; they are only important if they make money. Our designs will only make money if we create recipes to turn material, labor, and overhead into valuable functionality better than our competitors do.

The goodness of our recipe is important, but it is perishable. The ability of a design to make money is greatly affected by time. Our recipe is constantly measured against the recipes offered by other companies. The profit of the recipe is determined by its value, which takes the form of sell price, and its cost. Both of these factors vary with time. For example, the original Sony Walkman sold for around $150. Since it cost less than $150 to make, it was profitable. The same design today would make no money because the market price for this functionality is less than $30. Market prices have fallen because today's designs have different recipes. They have substituted plastic parts for metal ones and can be sold profitably at today's low prices. Thus, we need good recipes, and we need them before our competition gets them.

DESIGN-IN-PROCESS INVENTORY

When we begin a design we make investments in creating recipes. However, a recipe does not generate profit until it is completed. During the time that the recipe is incomplete we are holding an investment that is earning no money. We call this investment design-in-process inventory (DIP).

This is the Design Factory's equivalent of the work-in-process inventory (WIP) that we have in the manufacturing factory. Like the level of WIP, the level of DIP is a sign of the health of our process. When we bring our designs to market quickly, we can begin earning money quickly, which is good. When we are slow, we will have large levels of DIP which earn no money for us. Thus, the design process has inventory just as the factory does.

This DIP inventory is actually more important than inventory in the factory, because it is much larger and more expensive to hold. Manufacturing plants turn their inventory with incredibly fast cycle times. Modern plants can turn their inventory more than fifty times a year. In contrast, it is the rare development process that achieves more than one turn per year. Thus, DIP can be a much larger number than WIP in most companies. As the data in the Figure 1.1 show, DIP can easily be ten times bigger than WIP in many situations.

Furthermore, holding costs are much higher for DIP than for WIP. A traditional rule of thumb for the cost of holding WIP is about 25 percent of the inventory value per year. This takes into account the cost of storage, the risk of obsolescence, the cost of capital employed, and so on. The holding costs for DIP are much higher because the risk of obsolescence is high. In certain categories, a product that arrives to market two

FIGURE 1.1

Design-in-Process Inventory (DIP)

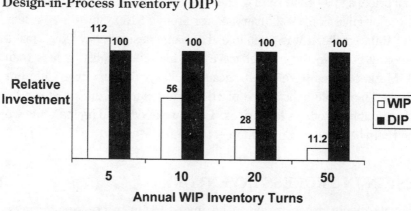

Note: Assumes 10 percent R&D-to-sales ratio and two-year development cycle.

years late will have zero value. Most manufacturing inventory does not drop to zero value nearly as quickly.

You would think that the high levels of DIP and the high cost of holding DIP would be incentives for management to measure and manage it. Sadly, it is ignored, due to a critical weakness of our accounting systems. For example, look in any annual report. Where is DIP? There is no evidence that it exists. But why?

The invisibility of DIP is actually a cruel trick played on us by Generally Accepted Accounting Principles (GAAP). Long ago, accountants agreed that R&D expenses should be recognized at the time the money is spent. They maintained that the value of a partially completed design could not be assessed with enough accuracy to treat it as a financial asset. They asserted that companies would inflate their balance sheets and overstate their profits by claiming that money spent on R&D was the same as deposits in a bank.

These arguments are sound, but the unfortunate consequence of such sound accounting practices is that DIP is invisible on our financial statements. Neither shareholders nor managers have any clue whether they are managing this resource well. Because we never show it on our balance sheet, we do not think of DIP as an asset to be managed, and we do not manage it.

Thus, an incomplete design is like an invisible non-interest-bearing checking account. You have invested the time and effort but you are not yet getting a return. Even worse, it is like a non-interest-bearing account that loses its capital very quickly.

The key value in recognizing the existence of DIP is that recognizing it empowers us to do something about it. If we don't know DIP exists, we cannot manage it. Later in this book you will see how development process design choices can minimize the magnitude and cost of this inventory.

RISING COST OF CHANGE

We have seen that the Design Factory has profit objectives and inventory just as the manufacturing factory does. There are, however, areas where the Design Factory can be quite different from the manufacturing factory. One such area is the way the cost of change behaves during the process.

The cost of making changes during product development rises expo-

FIGURE 1.2

Rising Cost of Change

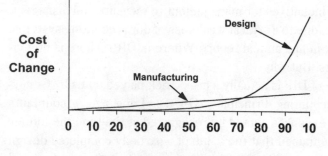

Percentage of Work Completed

nentially throughout the design process. This is quite different from a manufacturing process, where value-added rises more linearly through the process. In a design process, the cost of making changes early is exceptionally low, whereas the cost of late changes is very high. This exaggeration of economics will have important implications for how we need to manage the design process. Exponentially rising costs make it critically important to drive changes into the upstream portion of the design process, where such changes are hundreds of times cheaper to make. Figure 1.2 contrasts the cost of change in design and manufacturing processes.

Because of this rising cost of change the problem of managing changes becomes a very important one in the Design Factory. Late changes are very expensive. We shall see later in this book how this changes our approach to generating information and managing risk.

LATE-BREAKING NEWS

The irony is that while it is very easy to talk about driving all changes as far upstream in the design process as possible, it is much harder to make this happen. The key problem is that information becomes available later in the Design Factory than it does in the manufacturing factory. To see this we must make a subtle distinction between requirements information and information about execution.

In a manufacturing process, our product requirement is 100 percent complete at the beginning of the process. The requirements will almost never change during the process itself. At each manufacturing step, we try to get feedback about the effectiveness of our execution. If we have failed to meet an intermediate requirement, we take some sort of corrective action. For example, if we are machining a shaft we know the required dimensions the instant we start machining. When we perform individual operations on it we verify they have been done correctly, and fix them if they haven't.

Let us contrast this with what happens when we do product design. We think we have the requirements defined, but they always change in some way during the design process. This means that, unlike the manufacturing process, we receive some of our requirements after work has begun. We also get feedback from the customer about the suitability of our design solution after we make the design choices. Often this feedback comes very late, such as when we perform beta tests at the end of the design process. For example, we may design our shaft with a certain thickness. We may discover that the shaft breaks in field testing due to unexpectedly high loads. We now have to make changes very late in the design process. Thus, we are plagued in the design process with late arrival of information. Figure 1.3 shows the difference between the Design Factory and the manufacturing factory in the timing and arrival rates of information.

Interestingly this late information arrival interacts negatively with the rising cost of delay because a lot of information arrives when it is expensive to react to it. As we look at this problem more carefully later in the book we will discover that we do not have to passively accept

FIGURE 1.3

Information Arrival Profiles

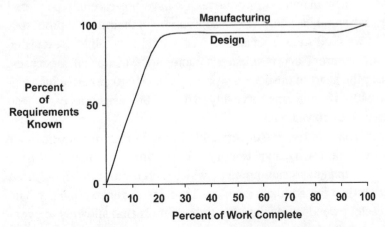

this late arrival of information. Instead we can actively manage the timing of information arrival and thereby have an important impact on our economics.

ONE-TIME PROCESSES

There is another important difference between the Design Factory and the manufacturing factory. The manufacturing factory usually does things more than one time in a row. In contrast, the Design Factory primarily engages in one-time processes. In the Design Factory we will never do the same thing, the same way, twice in a row. The design process produces information, or "recipes," and there is no value in creating the same "recipe" twice. For a manufacturing factory, which produces products, there is value in producing the same product twice. This means that in the design process we can only add value when we do something differently. If we change nothing, then we add no value. In contrast, in manufacturing if we change nothing we can still make money. You could say that while we make no money by reinventing the wheel, we can make money by manufacturing the same wheel many times in a row.

This constant pressure to do something new and different has important implications for how we have to manage the process. It means that we will see much more variability in the design process than we see in repetitive manufacturing processes. This variability is an indicator that we are doing something new in the design process, and thus that we are adding value.

Unfortunately, many managers schooled in the techniques of variability reduction in their manufacturing processes have not carefully pondered whether such variability reduction is appropriate in their design processes as well. As we shall show in Chapter 4, risk, and the variability associated with it, are inherent and *desirable* characteristics of design processes. They are at the heart of the design process's capacity to generate information. The path to eliminating variability in design processes can easily lead to a process with no value-added.

This difference in the role of variability has important implications for the type of tools the Design Factory inherits from the manufacturing process. The manufacturing process, which is repetitive, benefits from variability reduction, so it has developed tools to reduce variability. The Design Factory needs variability, so it needs tools that allow us to coexist with variability. If we blindly use manufacturing factory tools in the Design Factory, we may do more damage than good. For example, in manufacturing processes we create metrics, we set standards, we measure deviations, and we take corrective action. We shall see later how the same approach can be poorly suited for the world of product design.

Fortunately, the unsuitability of manufacturing tools does not leave us toolless. Our manufacturing tools are well-suited for dealing with predictable, deterministic processes, but in development we have variable, one-time processes. The good news is that powerful tools have been developed for managing variable, one-time processes. We will describe these specialized technical tools in Chapters 3, 4, and 5.

EXPANDING WORK

There is one final important difference between our Design Factory and the manufacturing factory. This difference arises from the one-time nature of the design process, which we just discussed. A manufacturing factory normally does things more than once. Whenever we engage in repetitive tasks we have some implicit standard for how long the work should take. In effect, the finish line is defined for a manufacturing process. We have either finished making the part or we haven't. For example, we machine a piece of metal and measure it to assess if we are done or not. If we have achieved the desired measurement we stop.

In the very different world of engineering our work perversely expands to fill the time available. Some managers blame this problem on the engineers. In reality, it is inherent to the engineering task itself because such tasks require solving a problem that has not been solved before. When we try to solve a problem for the very first time, we consider various options, some likely, some far-fetched. We usually rule out the unlikely options and proceed to check the likely solutions. The classic model of design is explained in Nobel laureate Herbert Simon's famous work *The Sciences of the Artificial*. Simon's observation is that we do not continue searching forever for a perfect solution but rather we stop searching when we find a satisfactory one. His design world is bounded by reaching a satisfactory solution.

In a certain sense, this takes a strange form in the real world of engineering. Here, we rarely stop when we achieve a satisfactory solution, because this will simply result in a satisfactory product. Instead, we stop when we run out of time. You can see this for yourself by looking

FIGURE 1.4

Task Completion Times (Theoretical vs. Actual)

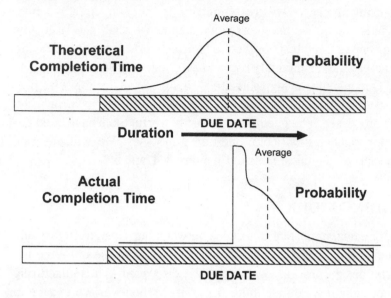

carefully at when engineering tasks are scheduled to be complete and when they are actually completed. In theory, if an engineering task was over when an engineer found a satisfactory solution, then some engineering work should be completed early and some engineering work should be done late. In practice, we see something very different: engineering activities are completed either on time or late. They are never completed early. When we do engineering, we stop when we run out of time. If we find a satisfactory solution early, then we use the extra time to find a better one, because there are always things we can do to improve performance or lower costs. We have little incentive to deliver our work early, because the next activity will probably not be ready to start early anyway. It is always more attractive to polish the design than it is to have it gather dust waiting for the next activity. Actual task completion times look very different from theoretical ones, as we can see in Figure 1.4.

This property of expanding work has important implications, as we shall see in Chapter 11. It means that the schedule will inexorably unravel on us unless we use a process that compensates for this expansion. Fortunately, there are ways to do this.

SUMMARY

We have seen that there are many similarities between the Design Factory and the manufacturing factory. Both are primarily interested in making money. Both use input resources to produce output, although the output in one case is products and in the other case is information. Both factories have inventories, although for the most part our design-in-process inventory is hidden from financial visibility because of our accounting practices.

At the same time there are some key differences. In the Design Factory the cost of change rises dramatically during the process. This will affect the way that we think about change. In the Design Factory we start the process with less of the information that we need to complete it. This means that information is arriving in the middle of the process, which has very interesting implications for our process design.

Our Design Factory processes are much less repetitive than manufacturing, and have higher variability. Moreover, this variability is central to their success. We shall see later in this book how this variability is our friend and not our enemy. This fact drives us to seek tools designed to allow us to live with variability, rather than tools designed to destroy it.

We also observed that the Design Factory engages in inherently expandable tasks. The finish line is made of rubber and can easily move away from us. This will have important implications for how we structure our control systems, as we shall see later on.

We now have a general concept of the Design Factory and some of its characteristics. However, we must penetrate a bit deeper to understand how we can manage it. To do so we need to equip ourselves with some basic tools. These are covered in Part Two, Thinking Tools. In Chapter 2 we will look at economic modeling tools that give us quantitative insight into project and process economics. We will then look at the field of queueing theory in Chapter 3. Queueing theory allows us to understand process design and capacity management issues in a quantified way. Chapter 4 will introduce information theory, a powerful tool for understanding how a design process should produce information. Finally, in Chapter 5, we will look at systems and feedback theory to understand their implications for the design of complex systems. The concepts in Part Two of the book are a critical underpinning for the action tools we will describe in Part Three.

Part Two

THINKING TOOLS

2

Making Profits Not Products

M any companies are trying to make some sort of change in their development process—make it faster, more accurate, or more efficient. Why are they trying to do this? It is astonishing how many companies cannot answer this question. Instead, when you dig below the surface you discover that most change programs are motivated by two forces: imitation and obedience. Companies imitate what other companies that they admire are doing. They replicate behaviors of these role-model companies with no real understanding whether this will change their own performance. At times this imitation will be useful, but it often will fail to produce the desired benefits. You may use the same golf club as a tournament pro, but it may not improve your game, particularly if your needs are different than his.

The second key force motivating change is obedience. Managers read articles about "good" management practices and adopt these practices simply because they have been labeled "good," without knowing how these practices might affect their economics. The great risk in behaving this way is that you are constantly being blown hither and yon by each shift in the managerial winds. Every fad, and every new magazine article, shifts you in a different direction.

There is a different way to make these choices, a way that is embarrassingly simple, but surprisingly powerful: Do more of the things that help you achieve your objective. If, as we discussed in Chapter 1, our objective is profit, we must determine which things in the infinite list of things we could possibly do will actually help us make money.

FIGURE 2.1

System Economic Model

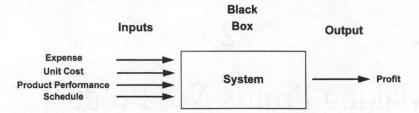

The tool we use for maximizing the profit of a complex system is an economic model. It is one of many ways to model system behavior, each of which focuses on particular properties of the system. We are interested in economic modeling because it describes a behavioral property that is fascinating to us as business people: that is, how we will make money.

As Figure 2.1 shows, we view the system as a black box with an output and inputs. The output we are looking for is profitability. The inputs are variables that influence the output. Our desire in creating an economic model is to identify how to manipulate these input variables to maximize profits. To do this, we must understand how changes in the inputs will change the output.

The technique we use to achieve this understanding is called sensitivity analysis. We change one input variable at a time and observe how the output changes. When this is done systematically we can identify relationships between input and output. These relationships may tell us that certain inputs have more impact than others on our goal of profitability.

This chapter will describe three types of economic models used by product developers. The first is a project-level model. Project-level models are useful to manage an individual project. Second, we will discuss models of application economics. These models are useful to understand feature tradeoffs at the product level from a customer perspective. Finally, we will look at models of process economics. Such models are useful to tackle the problem of overall process design. Each of these models serves a certain purpose. The type of model that we use will be determined by the type of decisions that we are trying to make.

PROJECT MODELS

The most common model used in managing the development process is a project-level model. This models the profit of an individual project and

FIGURE 2.2

Economic Modeling Process

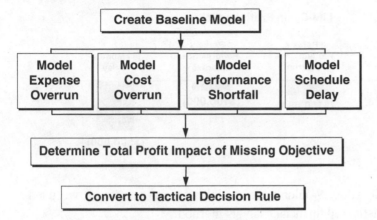

checks its sensitivity to key controllable factors such as development expense, unit cost, product performance, and schedule. Its output is a set of tactical decision rules that enable us to make tradeoffs between one parameter and another.

The project model is actually just straightforward financial analysis. As Figure 2.2 shows, we start by creating a baseline model. This is a life-cycle profit and loss statement that shows what will happen if everything goes according to plan. Then we independently alter four parameters: development expense, unit cost, performance, and schedule. This changes the life-cycle profits. We compute the total change in life-cycle profits and finally we convert this change to tactical decision rules.

A tactical decision rule is a tool that supports making the day-to-day decisions that occur throughout a program. It is created by translating the model output into a form that can be easily used by a team. We do this by normalizing the profit impact into factors for a 1 percent change in expense, cost, and performance, and for a one-month change in schedule. This provides us with a powerful tool to make tradeoffs between these parameters. The output of the model might look like that shown in Figure 2.3.

Let us look at the steps that we follow in developing such a model. The baseline model is simply a profit and loss statement for the project over its life. It would typically be constructed on a spreadsheet program. You may wonder why it is simply a model of cumulative profits instead of a more sophisticated analysis approach such as discounted cash flow or

FIGURE 2.3

Model Output

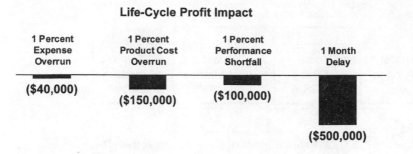

Life-Cycle Profit Impact

1 Percent Expense Overrun	1 Percent Product Cost Overrun	1 Percent Performance Shortfall	1 Month Delay
($40,000)	($150,000)	($100,000)	($500,000)

net present value. Wouldn't the model be more accurate if we used a more sophisticated financial analysis method?

Actually, it would, but there is a solid practical reason for not using a more sophisticated analysis: not everyone will understand it. The more complex we make the model, chasing after a bit more accuracy here and there, the more we create a formidable maze of calculations that will not be trusted by the team. In general, our practical experience suggests that the primary driver of model accuracy is the quality of the input data, not the financial analysis technique used. It is far better to choose a simple modeling technique and have 100 percent of the team understand the model than it is to risk confusing half the team with an elaborate technique that is 5 percent more accurate.

Our second step is to create the individual variations from this baseline. This is done by creating other spreadsheets to cover the variations. It is usually a good idea to use the graphing features of the spreadsheet program to depict some of this information visually, since team members can assimilate visual information far more effectively than pages of numbers. The variations require making assumptions about how the world would look if one of the input parameters changed. Let us briefly look at how we might model the four variations that we discussed.

The first variation that we model is a change in development expense. Because there is often a fuzzy line between one-time engineering and one-time manufacturing expenses, we will often group these two factors together when we analyze a change in development expense. We usually model a development expense overrun with an increase in sustaining engineering costs later in the life of the product,

FIGURE 2.4

Effect of Cost Overrun

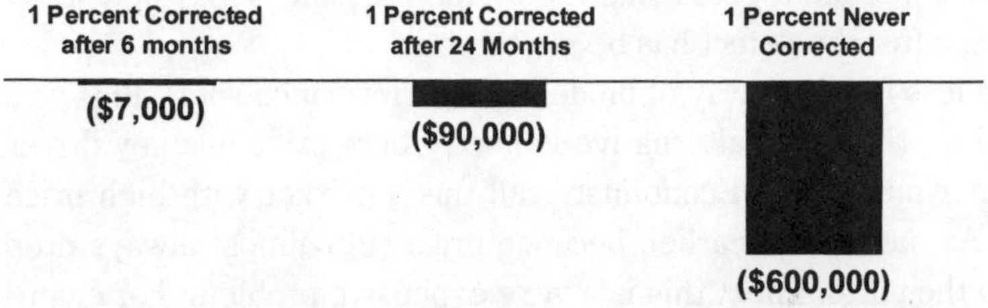

1 Percent Corrected after 6 months	1 Percent Corrected after 24 Months	1 Percent Never Corrected
($7,000)	($90,000)	($600,000)

because increases in product complexity during development usually lead to increases in support costs after development is completed.

The second variation is a change in product cost. This is modeled by altering the unit cost. The key trick here is to determine what portion of product life will be affected by higher unit costs. For example, a company that does rapid cost reduction of its products may introduce a high-cost product and very rapidly follow it with a cost reduction. Only six months worth of units may be shipped at higher cost. If the same company takes two years to do a cost reduction, then we raise the cost on two years' worth of units. Thus, the cost reduction cycle time is a key parameter required for this analysis. We also need to take into account the expense of doing the cost reduction. If the cost reduction comes from vendors it may come for free. If it requires extensive internal engineering work it may cost quite a bit. Sometimes it is useful to generate more than one scenario for cost reduction, to show the effect of doing it quickly versus slowly. This will establish a range of impacts that you can use for decision making. The output of such an analysis is shown in Figure 2.4.

Our third variation is a change in product performance. This can be modeled in two ways: either as a drop in unit volume or as a drop in sales price. A reduction in unit volume is the most common way to model a performance problem, because it is the most common reaction to such a problem. When most companies fail to provide the desired performance in a product they are more likely to accept a low market share than they are to cut their prices. They do this for the simple reason that price cuts do the most damage to profits because they drop straight to the bottom line.

When we model such a performance problem we need to recognize that the volume drop may or may not be permanent. For some products we can do a "performance fix" after the introduction of the product. In such cases, we model the performance problem as lasting for part of the product life. Nonetheless, we need to be careful because the market share impact of an early performance problem may be surprisingly persistent. Once a product gets a bad reputation customers may stay away from it even after the defect has been corrected.

A much less frequent way of modeling a performance shortfall is as a drop in sales price. This alternative is used where price is a key driver for customer purchases. Economists call this a market with high price elasticity. As mentioned earlier, because price cuts almost always drop straight to the bottom line, this is a very expensive problem. For example, if your profit margin is 10 percent and you cut prices by 10 percent you can reduce your profit margin to zero. This means that you have lost 100 percent of program profits.

Our final variation is a schedule delay. This is modeled by creating a new unit volume curve based on the later introduction. The four common shapes that this delayed volume curve might take depend on the characteristics of the market. They are shown in Figure 2.5.

Let us review these cases in order of potential impact. Case I, monopoly, illustrates a market where delayed introduction has very little effect.

FIGURE 2.5
Delay Scenarios

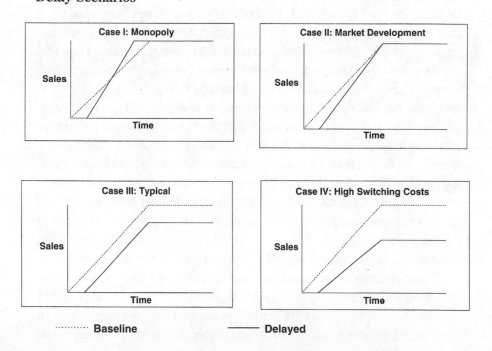

.... **Baseline**   —————— **Delayed**

All of the customers wait for your product and buy it when it becomes available. Such monopoly positions are extremely rare, so be very suspicious if someone suggests using this scenario.

Case II, market development, illustrates a market where delay is a bit more costly. In this case the late entrant is capable of growing sales faster than the early entrant because the early entrant must engage in missionary marketing to develop the market. This occurred in the personal computer market where later entrants were able to grow sales faster than early suppliers such as MITS and Radio Shack because the world had already become convinced that personal computers were useful.

Case III, typical, is the most common way to model a development delay. In such a case the sales curve is displaced downward by a fixed amount. This assumes that sales grow at the same rate, and peak in the same year. The logic behind this is that the sales growth rate is typically determined by factors like the amount of advertising spending and the rate at which sales calls are made by the sales force. For most companies there is little reason to believe that sales will build at a different rate if there are no changes in sales and marketing.

Case IV, high switching costs, illustrates a market where the early entrant will permanently lock in customers, preventing the late entrant from achieving the same sales growth as the early entrant. This will commonly occur in markets where customers do a lot of repeat purchasing and it is difficult for them to switch suppliers. For example, a custom semiconductor chip will get designed-in early in a chip user's design process. If you miss the design-in opportunity you may never have a chance to sell into that socket again. In such markets with high switching costs, it is extraordinarily important to get to market early. This scenario usually has the highest costs of delay.

It is actually much easier than one might think to determine which delay scenario is appropriate for a particular product. It simply requires understanding some detail about the customer purchase process and buying criteria. Usually you can find evidence to support a particular scenario by looking at the sales ramp-up curves of your own products and competitor products. For example, if someone proposes you have a Case I monopoly scenario, look for evidence that your customers will actually wait for your product introduction. Talk to customers and ask them if they truly have no alternatives and if they will inventory their demand for you. You might find that they cannot carry over their budgeted funds from one year to another and that you lose sales not to competition, but to competing uses for the same capital dollars.

Once we have created the four variations we simply look at the total change in profit from the baseline scenario, and then convert this to a tactical decision rule. The decision rule allows us to make trade-offs between the inputs. For example, we might be able to take 10 percent of the cost out of the product by adding two months to the development process. If schedule was worth $1 million per month and cost was worth $50,000 per percent this means that we would save $0.5 million in cost in return for losing $2 million in cycle time, not a very good deal.

From a practical perspective we notice three key benefits when a team begins to use such economic models. First, they will make better decisions when they use data instead of intuition. We have often tested the quality of a team's intuition on development programs by asking everybody on the team to estimate the cost of delay of the program using their intuition. It is common to find answers on the team that differ by a factor of 100. You can imagine the inconsistency in decisions if people's underlying beliefs about the importance of speed differ by this amount. When we quantify these factors in the form of decision rules we get much better decisions.

The second benefit we normally observe is faster decision making. Quantifying decision rules makes it much easier and faster to reach a consensus on the team. In one case, by using such decision rules a computer product development team was able to resolve a tough decision in one week that had been under debate for the previous two months. Psychologists have found that the absence of factual information actually increases people's attachment to their point of view, rather than decreasing it.

The third benefit of such a model is that we get better buy-in to the team's decision. When everybody operates with the same set of facts, rather than with some hidden beliefs that have not been discussed, we get a stronger consensus. When a decision is made, it stays made, rather than having the same issue resurface over and over in the team for reevaluation.

A more detailed discussion of economic modeling to support development decisions (and cycle-time management), including spreadsheets, is given in Chapter 2 of the book that I co-authored with Preston Smith, *Developing Products in Half the Time.*

APPLICATION MODELS

The second type of economic model used in the development process is a model of application economics. Project models are done from the perspective of the company, whereas application models are done from the perspective of the customer. When we design an application model we are trying to understand how specific product attributes affect the customer economics. As we shall see in Chapter 9 where we discuss the product specification, a model of application economics can be a powerful conceptual frame for designing the product.

For example, consider a company designing a piece of capital equipment for a manufacturing line. The total cost of this equipment from the customer perspective includes more than the purchase price. The machine must be installed and certified. Operators need to be trained and certified. The equipment may use space on the factory floor, consume power, and require some sort of consumable supplies. It must be inspected periodically, cleaned, maintained, and repaired. If the machine breaks it may produce bad parts that have to be scrapped or reworked. And during a breakdown, each hour of downtime may mean lost productive capacity. Each of these factors can be quantified and estimated. We can call them the application economic drivers (AEDs).

There are four basic steps to building an application model. First, we must identify the application economic drivers, which are the key factors that affect the economics of ownership. Second, we must express these factors in terms of dollars. Third, we must combine these factors into a model of the overall economics. Finally, we must translate these factors into decision rules that might be helpful to the design team. Figure 2.6 depicts this process.

The first step of identifying the application economic drivers will usually be done internally by talking with sales, marketing, application engineering, and field service. The combined input from these groups will give us a pretty good starting point in identifying the factors that are important to the customer. We then make an initial attempt to quantify dollar impact. For example, installation may consist of a material cost and a labor cost. The material might be expressed directly in dollars whereas labor costs may be subdivided into hours of installation time and cost per hour. At this stage we have hypotheses about economics.

The second step is to get actual dollar values for these AEDs. To do this we must talk to the customer. This is best done in the customer en-

FIGURE 2.6

Modeling Application Economics

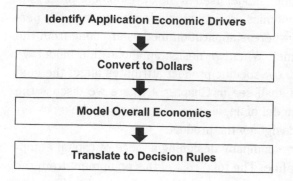

vironment, since we are likely to identify additional costs by observing the equipment in operation. It will become obvious during these interviews that the application economics will differ by customer and that different customers weight different factors differently. Some customers are not even aware of certain costs, so they ignore them. Others are aware of the costs but since other departments pay for them, they attach little significance to them. For example, the selector of a piece of capital equipment may be different than the person that pays for the consumable supplies for the equipment. In such a case, the person who makes the capital decision may not weight consumable costs as a decision criterion.

The third step in the modeling process is to combine this information into a spreadsheet model. The spreadsheet may be structured as shown in Figure 2.7. It is usually important to decompose the AEDs into factors that are invariant between customers and factors that change from customer to customer. For example, the number of hours it takes to inspect the machine may be the same for two customers, but the cost of these hours may vary because labor rates vary geographically.

A refinement that is sometimes useful is to break out cost of ownership into certain time buckets. This approach is useful when different customers think in terms of different time periods. For example, one customer may base his decision on five-year cost of ownership whereas another may consider full life-cycle costs. If we segregate costs by time period we can use the same spreadsheet to evaluate economics for both these customers.

The output of the model is the overall application economics from a cus-

FIGURE 2.7
Application Economic Worksheet

Application Economic Worksheet				
Factor	Assumption	First Year	Five Years	Full Life
Installation Hours	80			
Hourly Cost of Installation	$50			
Installation Labor Costs		$4,000	$4,000	$4,000
Installation Materials	$10,000	$10,000	$10,000	$10,000
Equipment Footprint	200 Square Feet			
Space Cost	$0.50 per SQFT per month	$1,200	$6,000	$24,000
Annual Power Consumption	10,000 KWH			
Cost per KWHR	$0.05	$500	$2,500	$10,000
Etc.				

tomer perspective, which may look like Figure 2.8. Such a chart quickly communicates the key economic drivers for a particular application.

The final step is to convert this model output to information that will be useful to the team on a day-to-day basis. In practice this means providing the team with a way to make trade-off decisions. This can be done

FIGURE 2.8
Application Economics

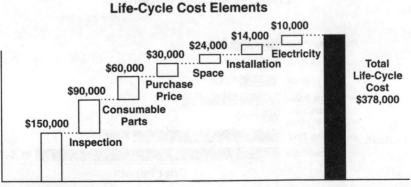

Life-Cycle Cost Elements

by calculating the sensitivity of total application economics to a change in each of the operating parameters. In this area economics are expressed in a form that the product development team can understand, usually in terms of percent changes in a product's parameters. These application tradeoff rules (Figure 2.9) enable us to confront the interaction between different parameters in a deliberate and quantitative manner.

The enormous value in using a model of application economics is that it keeps us focused on the product parameters that are really important to the customer. For example, by quantifying the fact that power consumption is 80 percent of the life-cycle cost of a product we know how much effort to put into the problem of designing a low power consumption unit.

There are a couple of important things to remember about these models. First, the application economic model is likely to change from customer to customer because the impact of particular performance parameters will change. For example, the factory running at high utilization will lose revenue if it experiences downtime. A factory at lower levels of utilization may experience no lost revenue from the same downtime.

Second, it is important to recognize that customers do not necessarily understand their own economics, and often do not base their purchase decision on these economics. People who buy automobiles may be more impressed with the lack of valve adjustments than they are with the low gasoline consumption. One factor may worth $400 over the life of the car, whereas the other may be worth $2,000. You should never assume that all customers either know or care about their application economics.

FIGURE 2.9

Application Tradeoff Rules

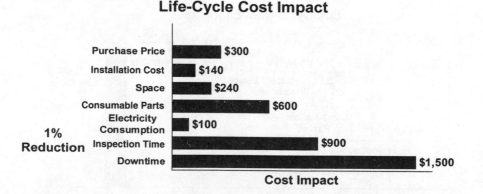

Nonetheless, you will find customers for whom this is a powerful influence. Application economics are most likely to influence the sophisticated industrial purchaser of capital equipment. Such purchasers are more likely to do a thorough economic justification of their multimillion-dollar purchase than a consumer buying toothpaste.

MODELS OF PROCESS ECONOMICS

The final type of model that we use is the model of process economics. Such models go beyond the individual project and concentrate on the enterprise as a whole. We use them to make decisions about changing our business processes. To do so we need to know the economics of the entire process. For example, the CEO may want to know what it would be worth to the company to achieve a 10 percent reduction in production costs or to cut development times in half. We need a model of process economics to assess this.

This process economics model is simply an extension of the project-level model to the enterprise level by recognizing that the process handles many projects. The modeling method is shown in Figure 2.10.

We go through the same steps as we did for the project-level model. First we construct a baseline model using the enterprise-level profit and loss statement. The second step is to calculate the sensitivity of overall profits to changes in development expense, product cost, performance, and schedule. It is fairly easy to do this for changes in development ex-

FIGURE 2.10

Modeling Process Economics

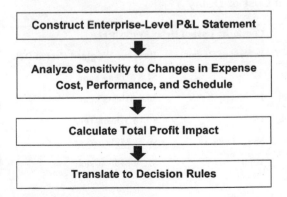

pense, product cost, and product performance, but the schedule delay calculation is a bit more complex.

To get a business-level cost of delay we simply break the portfolio into segments with similar costs of delay and create a composite cost of delay from these segments. The number of segments that we choose depends on the variety of products. For example, a semiconductor company with ten thousand products will not calculate the delay cost of each product. Rather, they will divide the products into categories and calculate a typical delay cost for each category. Such information can be used to create a composite cost of delay for the entire business. An example is shown in Figure 2.11.

Our final step is to convert the results of our sensitivity analysis to enterprise-level decision rules. This is done with the normalization process that we discussed earlier.

We use the enterprise-level decision rules in the same way we use project-level decision rules. They help us to make process design choices. For example, consider the decision to introduce a rapid prototype technology into a company. Let us say the technology is applicable to 20 percent of the enterprise's projects and these projects would be shortened by four weeks on average. If the enterprise-level cost of delay is $10 million per month, then the annual benefit of this technology is $2 million. This benefit can be compared to the cost of investing in this technology to calculate a payback. If the expense impact was $200,000 per year then the payback period would be 1.2 months. Figure 2.12 shows such an analysis.

FIGURE 2.11

Composite Business-Level Cost of Delay

Composite Cost of Delay Worksheet			
Product Category	Cost of Delay	Percent of Revenue	Revenue Weighted Cost of Delay
A	$500,000/Month	30	$1.8 Million/Year
B	$250,000/Month	20	$0.6 Million/Year
C	$100,000/Month	15	$0.18 Million/Year
D	$50,000/Month	35	$0.21 Million/Year
		Total	$2.79 Million/Year

FIGURE 2.12
Rapid Prototyping Tradeoff

Annual Benefit	**Annual Cost**
Schedule Change = 4 Weeks	Annual Expenses = $200,000
Cost of Delay = $2 Million/Month	
Total Benefit =$2.0 Million	Total Expenses = $200,000

Net Benefit $1.8 Million
Payback 1.2 Months

The enterprise-level model is useful for decisions that affect more than one program at a time. It is particularly important when we look at the effect of process queues in the next chapter, because the cost of such queues can only be assessed if we know a cost of delay at the enterprise level.

TACTICAL VS. STRATEGIC DECISIONS

These economic models are nothing new. Business schools have been teaching MBAs to construct profit and loss projections since they were first created. However, we should remember that at business schools the economic models are taught by finance professors. A finance professor will focus on using such a model to make a financing decision. The primary output needed to make such a decision are measures of performance such as return on investment (ROI), internal rate of return (IRR), net present value (NPV), and economic value added (EVA). These are valuable and useful measures that are critical for making the one-time decision to invest in a program or not to invest in it.

The weakness in focusing exclusively on these grand financing decisions is that we create the impression that the only important project decisions are the strategic ones. In fact, there is another class of decision that is far more important to the project manager. It contains the ten thousand little tactical decisions that we confront on a daily basis. It is simply not sufficient for an operating manager to know that the ROI has changed from 24.5 percent to 22.6 percent. Both these figures may still justify continuing work on the project.

The decision rules we have described in this chapter focus on the tactical decisions that managers confront on a daily basis. A project-level decision rule enables the project manager to assess the effect of delaying the program by two weeks to obtain a lower-cost vendor for one of his subsystems. An application decision rule allows him to decide whether it makes more sense to optimize power consumption or installation cost for the product. A process-level decision rule allows him to assess the financial benefit of investing in additional computer-aided design (CAD) capacity. These tactical decision rules are created by taking the same data that we already have and using it to create the new information that will help us make thousands of tactical decisions. The strategic decision rules are useful, but they are simply not enough to meet the needs of the operating manager.

SOME PRACTICAL TIPS

Let us now offer some practical tips regarding the use of these three economic models. The first key to successful modeling is to use a cross-functional team to create economic models. This is important because the data comes from more than one function within the company. We need cost data from manufacturing, expense and schedule data from engineering, and sales volume and price estimates from marketing. Cross-functional participation is also important for psychological reasons because the models will have far more influence when the people using them on a daily basis have participated in their construction. When the ownership of the model is spread broadly the use of that model is likely to be spread broadly. The model should belong to the team, not to the finance or planning department.

A second key to success is the effective involvement of the finance department. Not only are the financial people likely to do the best job at the quantitative analysis, but they are critical to assuring the credibility of the models and the consistency of models between programs. Consider what would happen if the finance department was not involved.

The program manager puts his next slide on the projector and proclaims, "And the cost of delay on this program is $1 million per month, which means—"

"Wait a minute," says the general manager. "Where did that number come from?"

"Well, we developed an economic model for the product and did sensitivity analysis on it," says the program manager.

"Hmm," says the general manager, turning to the controller. "Sam, do you believe these numbers?"

Sam the controller looks up over his bifocals and furrows his brow in deep thought. "You know, it's kind of hard to tell, but let me think . . . they were developed by marketing . . . those are the guys that do sales forecasts. . . ."

But the answer that we really wanted to get from Sam is: "One of my people helped them to create the numbers—if anything, we believe they are conservative."

A third key to successful modeling is to avoid unnecessary complexity. Complexity is a frequent, but misguided, approach of modeling experts, who make models so elaborate that only they understand their models' arcane inner workings, thereby adding to their own personal power and influence. We do not want to create a mysterious black box owned by experts in the finance department. This would backfire in two ways. First, complex models are not likely to be understood by a high percentage of the team, and thus they are less likely to be used. Second, since all models contain assumptions, it is critical to use the models in a domain in which these assumptions are likely to be true. In technical terms, we must respect the model's boundary conditions. We increase the chance that a model will be used correctly when it is simple and transparent.

In practice, we rarely find that complex models are required for this analysis. Complexity will always improve the accuracy of the calculations; however, the accuracy of the model is almost never controlled by the accuracy of the computations. Instead, it is almost always driven by the accuracy of the input data. In particular, there is no input parameter more likely to be in error than the sales forecast. Sales volumes can be off in some cases by a factor of ten. If we ever have an extra few hours to spend on an economic model, we should spend it on cleaning up the input data. This is almost always the best use of our time.

A fourth key to success is to carefully consider the best format to use for the model. My observation after years of doing such models is that a model that is easy to understand is more likely to be used. In practice this means that it should look as much like the income statement of the business as possible. The obvious advantage is that the members of the organization can understand something that they are already using. A more subtle advantage is that management incentive programs are usually based on existing financial measurements, and we are much more likely to get the attention of senior managers if we can show them how their actions relate to the incentive plan.

Finally, the fastest way to improve the accuracy of the model is to begin using it, rather than attempting to make the model perfect before it is implemented. We often have a poor understanding of which input variables are most likely to drive the model until we have done the first model. Once we have done the first model, we can identify the input parameters that have the greatest effect on the answer, and we can focus on improving the accuracy of information in those areas. It is this focus on improving the key drivers of the model that improves its accuracy. In other words, build the model quickly, use it, and fix it. Avoid the common stumbling block for many companies: they never take the first step down the road.

SUMMARY

In this chapter we have discussed three important tools for managing development projects and processes. The first tool is the project economic model which enables us to make tradeoffs between impacts on cost, expenses, performance, and schedule. This model takes a project-level view of economics. By quantifying how each of these inputs affects overall profitability we can make day-to-day decisions that are based on facts. This results in faster decisions and better decisions, with more buy-in from members of the team.

The second tool we discussed is an application economic model, which takes a customer view of economics. Since this customer view is likely to influence the purchase process we need to understand this view to make feature decisions. This model allows us to make tradeoffs between different features from the perspective of the customer. In using an application economic model we must respect the fact that different customers have different economics, and that some customers will ignore certain aspects of their economics.

The third tool assists us in making process design decisions. We use this model of process economics when we are making decisions that affect the entire stream of products emerging from our development process. It would be difficult for us to make good process design decisions without this model. For example, we will see in the next chapter that queues in our development process can only be evaluated with a knowledge of process-level cost of delay.

None of these models is particularly difficult to construct, since all rely on data that already exist in some form. Practical experience has shown them to be exceptionally useful, and I would encourage you to begin using them as quickly as possible. You can then judge the utility for yourself.

3

Entering the Land of Queues

Mr. Big sits in his office puffing on his cigar and thinking about his slow development process. How can he get those clowns down in engineering to develop products faster? Suddenly, he has an idea. He calls up the VP of engineering and tells him, "Our next project, the SuperUltra, is of enormous personal interest to me. We have got to meet the schedule or we will lose all of Megacorp's business, and they're our biggest customer. If we are late, you are out of a job. Anyone who delays that project will have me to answer to—at least for their last five minutes at the company, before they are fired."

The SuperUltra is completed in six months' time—a full twelve months faster than any previous comparable product. In his speech congratulating the team Mr. Big puffs about "how a motivated team can overcome all obstacles" and how "we just need the will to win here in our organization." His audience is unimpressed. What really happened here? Did the team really magically overcome mysterious obstacles? Most likely they did not have to. Consider what really happened when a prototype part from the vendor arrived late Thursday afternoon.

The engineer who ordered the part calls receiving inspection and asks if the part has come in. Receiving tells him, "It just came in."

"Can you inspect it today?" asks the engineer.

"Of course not, young man. Based on our current backlog we can get it to you by next Wednesday," says the inspector.

"But this project is very important," protests the engineer.

"That's what everybody says," says the inspector truthfully.

"Yeah, but Mr. Big wants to know personally whenever this project is delayed!" counters the engineer.

"I was just about to start working on it. It will be done by four o'clock," says the inspector.

What really happened with the SuperUltra is that it got head-of-the-line privileges in a lot of lines. Let us say the average part has a five-day cycle time through receiving inspection. What happens to a part when it gets head-of-the-line privileges? It sails through receiving in four hours. Could this affect cycle time? Yes. In fact, it can affect cycle time more than almost anything else we can do in the development process.

As we shall see in this chapter, these lines, or queues as they are more precisely called, are endemic to our development processes. They arise from the inherent nature of product development which we discussed in Chapter 1. When we combine variability and expanding work we get queues, and often very large ones. Consider for a moment why we would be likely to get queues in receiving inspection.

The manager of receiving inspection is not a stupid man. He knows that people do not like to wait for their parts and he wants to prevent delays. He logically reasons that he must have enough inspectors available to meet the demand for inspections. To plan capacity he must know how many inspections he needs to do and how many each inspector can do. He obtains the daily delivery schedule for all part shipments due in for the next month and calculates how many hours of receiving inspection must be done. If there are 300 hours of work due in, he looks at his two inspectors and sighs with relief. The two normally do 310 hours of inspection during one month, so he clearly has enough capacity.

But, what really happens? Will the queues in receiving go away? Again, we must look at the details. On Wednesday afternoon a batch of parts is due in from the plating shop, and the inspector is ready for them. However, that morning the plating shop calls to say they will be four hours late. This is too bad because Wednesday morning's work was competed early. The inspector spends Wednesday afternoon calibrating his instruments and tidying up his desk. Just before quitting time the lot of parts comes in. "I'll do this tomorrow," says the inspector.

The next day he starts his inspection. It takes a bit longer than expected and he doesn't actually finish until three o'clock. Now he will not be able to finish the Thursday's incoming work that day. Parts will come out of receiving late this week.

What caused this lateness? Was it lack of capacity? No. The inspector had sixteen hours available during this period, and he only did twelve hours of inspecting. He had excess capacity during this interval. *The delays were caused by uncertainty in the arrival times and the task durations.* Whenever task arrivals or durations are unpredictable we have the potential to experience queues.

Since the product development project is normally a one-time activity, it can contain great uncertainty in task arrival times and task durations. We are almost certain to see queues in product development processes.

AN INTRODUCTION TO QUEUEING THEORY

The good news is that smart people have been worried about the mathematics of queues for the last eighty years. A body of mathematics, called queueing theory, models the behavior of queues and it works.

Queueing theory got started back in Bell Labs in about 1920 when a statistician named Agner K. Erlang started worrying about the performance of telephone switches. How big a switch is needed for a town of ten thousand people? They won't all call at the same time, and their calls will vary in duration. In spite of this variance, can we describe the relationship between capacity and service time?

Happily, the answer is yes. And because we can understand these queues mathematically, queueing theory has been successfully applied to problems as diverse as telecommunications switches, computers, manufacturing lines, and grocery stores. Ironically, it has almost never been applied to development processes, despite the fact it is far more powerful than the deterministic approach most companies currently use. In this chapter we will introduce some of the concepts of queueing theory and show how they apply to product development.

Let us begin with some vocabulary. As Figure 3.1 indicates, a queueing system typically consists of a *queue* and a *server.* Consider a bank teller line. When customers arrive in the bank they get in line. When they reach the head of the line they walk to the teller and they do their banking. The time they spend in line is called *queue time.* The time they spend being served is called *service time.* The total time from when they arrive until when they complete their transaction is called *time in the system.*

Another term we use to describe queues is *queueing discipline.* This refers to the sequence with which we handle jobs in the queue. Queues

FIGURE 3.1

Queueing System

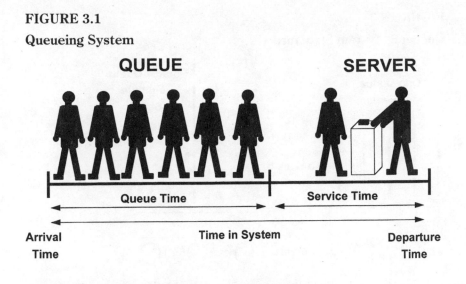

can be served in a variety of ways ranging from first-come, first-served to first-come, last-served. The queueing discipline you choose alters the operating characteristics of the queueing system.

The structure of a queueing system refers to the number of queues and the number of servers. It may be designed with a single queue supplying multiple servers or with a separate queue for each server. We all have experience with queueing systems of various designs. For example, long ago airline ticket lines were structured with one queue per server, as shown in Figure 3.2. If you have ever used such a system you have noticed that things slow down dramatically if someone in front of you decides to pay for his ticket with pennies.

The alternative structure—a single queue with multiple servers—prevents the entire line from grinding to a halt when a single agent gets bogged down with a tough task. This is an important observation in queueing theory, which says that there is less variability in processing time in a system with one queue feeding multiple servers than there is in a system with separate queues for each server.

Two very important properties of all queueing systems will affect us in product development. The first is the tendency of such systems to overload at less than 100 percent utilization. The second is their nonlinear relationship between capacity utilization and delay time. Both these properties can be derived mathematically, but we will illustrate them by reminding you of a queueing system with which almost everyone has experience: traffic.

FIGURE 3.2

Queueing System Structure

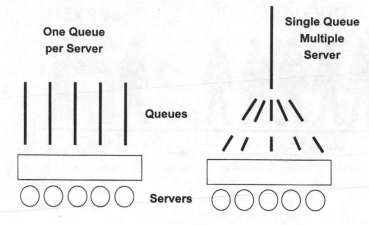

**One Queue
per Server**

**Single Queue
Multiple
Server**

Queues

Servers

The behavior of traffic on the highway illustrates many important properties of a queueing process. Let us consider three of these properties. First, the effect of a change in capacity is determined by the degree of utilization of the system. For example, suppose on a four-lane highway at rush hour one lane becomes blocked because of an accident. Capacity is reduced 25 percent. What happens to cycle time? It may double or triple. Now consider what would happen if the same lane were shut down in the middle of the night, when the system was lightly utilized. There would be almost no change in cycle time. Conclusion: the effect of changes in capacity (and changes in demand) will depend on the degree of capacity utilization when these changes occur.

A second observation that we could make from studying traffic is that cycle time is nonlinear with loading. When utilization moves from 0 to 50 percent the queues increase by a smaller amount than when utilization moves from 50 to 100 percent. This means that queues exhibit non-linear behavior.

Our third observation might be that the system will overload at less than 100 percent utilization. We cannot keep improving output by forcing more things into the system. In fact, on a typical highway maximum throughput is achieved when cars travel at about 40 miles per hour. If we keep putting more cars on the highway, output will decrease until we ultimately end up in gridlock. We can get lots of cars on the road, but they won't be moving.

Such behavior is also predicted by the mathematics of queueing sys-

FIGURE 3.3

Queue Length vs. Capacity Utilization

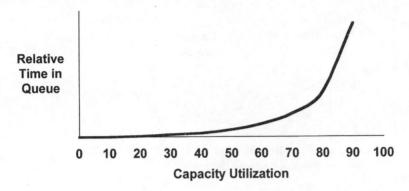

Note: Assumes M/M/1/∞ Queue

tems. Let us look at the characteristics of a classic queueing curve, an M/M/1/∞ queue (Figure 3.3). The label is specialized shorthand terminology for a type of common queue.*

The queueing curve has some interesting properties. The queue time in the system will be quite low until we start reaching levels of utilization of about 60 to 70 percent. At this point the queue gets bigger and bigger as we get closer to full utilization. It doubles as we move from 60 to 80 percent utilization. It doubles again as we move from 80 to 90 percent utilization, and again as we move from 90 to 95 percent utilization.

This curve offers crucial insight, because it differs dramatically from our deterministic view of the world. If the world were deterministic, we would not expect the system to overload until we reach full utilization. We would expect no delays as long as we have excess capacity. In the stochastic world of queueing theory, *we will experience delays even when we have excess capacity in the system.*

THE ECONOMICS OF QUEUES

We can combine this insight regarding queueing behavior with the understanding of process economics that we developed in the last chapter. What is the right capacity for a process? If we have too much capacity we may have expensive resources that are idle. If we have too little ca-

---

*This technical nomenclature refers to a queue with Markovian arrivals, Markovian task durations, a single server, and potential for infinite queue length.

FIGURE 3.4

Total Process Cost vs. Capacity Utilization

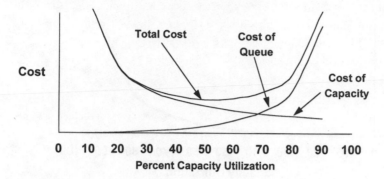

pacity we may have expensive projects gathering dust waiting for resources to become available. The right capacity will balance these two expenses.

We can achieve this balance by optimizing the total process cost. This total process cost is composed of the cost of capacity plus the cost of delay. For example, let us consider a testing process on the critical path of a program. The cost of excess capacity will rise proportional to the amount of this excess capacity. If we operate with little excess capacity we will be plagued with queues that will delay the workflow. We can calculate the size of the queues at different levels of capacity and then calculate the cost of these queues by using cost-of-delay decision rules. The total cost of the process is the sum of these two costs, which is shown in Figure 3.4.

Such an analysis will lead us to conclude that *we will always need excess capacity to optimize the economics of a development process.* This need for excess capacity arises because the inherent variability of development guarantees us queues when we get to high levels of utilization.

It is interesting to note that we apply this type of reasoning unhesitatingly in a manufacturing operation. No rational company would consider loading its manufacturing facility above an 85 to 90 percent utilization because they could never make their delivery commitments. Since development is more variable than manufacturing, common sense would tell us to load a development process to lower levels of utilization. In practice we load the development process to at least 100 percent utilization and then we wonder why things don't come out the door on time.

Before you become too enthusiastic about the need to eliminate queues I must offer one cautionary note. The only expensive queues are queues on the critical path of a project. Such a queue will delay the program, and the resulting cost of delay, as we saw in the last chapter, could be high. If the queue is off the critical path it can be a useful tool to load resources efficiently. Queues are not inherently bad; they are good or bad depending on their relationship to the critical path of a program. This means that you cannot tell which queues to manage unless you know the critical path of a project.*

DEPICTING QUEUES

People have actually been analyzing queues for quite some time and have developed some powerful tools for studying them. One such tool comes out of the world of industrial engineering. Called the cumulative flow diagram, or cumulative arrival and departure diagram, this simple graphical technique for depicting queues can contain a surprising amount of information. Let us start by considering a simple process where work arrives at a queue and the jobs are handled on a first-come, first-served basis.

To construct a cumulative flow diagram we plot cumulative arrivals of work into the queue versus time. We also plot the departures of this work from the queue, which is when the process begins to work on the job. The cumulative flow diagram for a process might look like that in Figure 3.5.

We can make some interesting observations about this diagram. The slopes of the arrival and departure lines tell us about the capacity of the system. The slope of the arrival line is simply the capacity of the upstream process. The slope of the departure line is the capacity of the downstream process which is being fed by the queue.

We can also extract some useful information about the queue from this diagram. Horizontal distances on this chart tell us how much time an individual unit spends in queue. Vertical distances are quantities. At any moment in time, the vertical dimension is a measure of the number of units in queue at that time. For example, if the eightieth unit has arrived and the fortieth unit has left the queue this means that there are forty units in queue at that time.

---

*Critical path is a technical term for the sequence of activities that gets the project done in the shortest possible time. Whenever a critical path activity is delayed the total project is delayed by the same amount of time.

FIGURE 3.5

Cumulative Flow Diagram

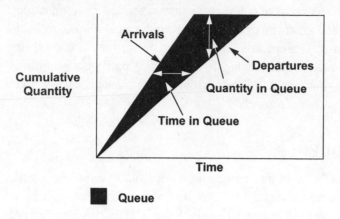

We can also use this diagram to determine the total size of the queue in the process. Since the size of the queue is measured by units times time, the queue is the shaded area on the chart. Thus, the cumulative flow diagram is a powerful tool to visualize what happens in a queueing system and quickly determine how our decisions impact queues in the process.

Let us look at what happens to queues when we change the batch size of the process. Consider the extreme examples of using a large batch process versus a continuous flow process. (See Figure 3.6.) The large batch process will wait for 100 percent of the work to arrive before it starts. A continuous flow process starts work on the first unit of work as

FIGURE 3.6

Batch Size and Queues

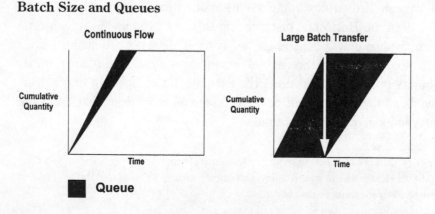

soon as it arrives. Notice what has happened to the size of the queue in the continuous flow process. The size of the shaded area is one-tenth the size of the large-batch chart. This means that we have decreased the size of the queue by a factor of ten.

This is striking because *we reduced the queue without making any change in the capacity of the process or the demand on the process.* The slopes of the arrival process and the slopes of the departure process have remained the same. Thus, there has been no change in process capacity or demand. We achieved a dramatic reduction in queues simply by changing batch size in the process.

In fact, this is exactly what we do when we implement JIT in the factory. We shrink inventory (which is the manufacturing version of a queue) by a factor of ten or more without making any change in capacity. We will return to this diagram later in this chapter to understand more about queues.

IMPLICATIONS OF QUEUEING THEORY

The queueing behavior of systems has some very interesting implications. As we mentioned earlier, queues depend on two factors: the level of capacity utilization and the variability of the system. Both of these factors could be used to reduce queues in a process. Let us examine each of these factors in a bit more detail.

Capacity utilization, or system loading, is a function of the relationship between capacity and demand. A small change in loading can lead to a large change in cycle time. For example, if we add 5 percent more work at 90 percent utilization we double the length of the development cycle. This means that our projects take twice as long to finish. This is exactly the opposite of what management intuition might indicate. Our management intuition tells us that everybody will stay busy if there is a surplus of work stacked up in engineering. In reality, such high levels of loading in development processes are a prescription for disaster.

Variability is the second factor that affects the size of the queues. This variability can show up as uncertainty either in the arrival rate of the tasks or in the duration of the tasks. Such variability can come from a variety of sources. For example, consider the work stacked up in front of the CAD area in a typical company. Some drawings arrive at unpredictable times. This is arrival rate variability. However, even if we could totally eliminate this type of variability, we would still have queues because task durations are also unpredictable. Some drawings take more time to complete than others, due to differences in content and differences in the productivity of our CAD operators.

If we could eliminate all variability in the development process we would eliminate queues, but experience shows this is impossible. Here we might return to our analogy with the factory. A factory loaded to 95 percent utilization will miss delivery commitments. Yet in the factory we might perform the same tasks 100,000 times in a row. Despite masses of statistical data and years of effort to reduce variability, we are still unable to load this relatively stable process to 100 percent utilization. This does not bode well for our prospects to eliminate variability in engineering, which is inherently a more variable process.

What is worse, as we shall see in the next chapter, the total elimination of variability is a futile quest, because value-added in the development process comes from variability. A totally predictable process will generate no information. This will be discussed in the next chapter, after we have looked at some concepts from information theory.

For most organizations the biggest opportunity to reduce queues lies in managing the level of capacity loading, not the level of variability. Unfortunately, we must educate management on the danger of trying to achieve 100 percent utilization. This is a difficult concept for most managers to grasp. They are bombarded with slogans exhorting them to eliminate all waste in their processes. And idle time certainly looks like waste. How can we explain to the CEOs that some "waste" is good? They must understand that this "waste" is the vital margin that prevents the development process from being in a constant state of gridlock. It is incorrect to assume that excess capacity in a development process is wasteful. Yet this goes against our management instincts.

Our basic management instinct leads us astray every time. Whenever we see any idle capacity in engineering we instinctively start more projects. We would not start turning on machine tools in our factory just because they became idle. In manufacturing we understand the need for excess capacity. Yet in engineering we charge down the slippery slope leading to project overload.

Overloads in development are especially likely because development is a one-time process. In a repetitive process like manufacturing we know how much work remains in a particular job. A one-time process may offer no clue as to what lies on the path ahead. Our capacity to start a job can easily exceed our ability to finish it. Queueing theory suggests we need to be good at capacity management to manage product development well. An overemphasis on efficiency can prevent us from seeing the queues that we create by overloading our development process.

DEALING WITH QUEUES

Just as queueing theory gives us some insights into the behavior of the development process it can provide us with some tools to control it. Queueing theory would suggest four general strategies for dealing with process queues. They are shown in Figure 3.7.

First, we can increase capacity. Many of our options fall in this category. Since it usually costs money to increase capacity, this path requires good salesmanship. Second, we can manage demand. This is another rich area of opportunity. In fact, if we fail to manage demand we can totally neutralize any success achieved in adding capacity. Third, we can reduce variability. As mentioned earlier, there are modest options available in this area. Finally, we can focus on control systems. This is a very powerful area, too often ignored in development processes. We will look at each of the options in turn.

Increasing Capacity

The classic way to address a queueing problem is to add capacity. If the lines begin to get too long at the ticket window then we open up another window. This is straightforward and easy to implement but can be a tough sell in most companies. We are reluctant to open another window because we risk having attendants idle later in the day if demand slackens. This would be wasteful.

FIGURE 3.7

Strategies to Control Queues

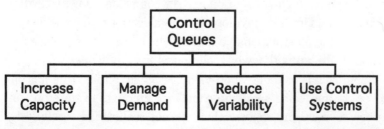

What other options do we have beside operating with a permanent excess of people in all areas of the process? Fortunately, there are a number of other choices. For example, one pharmaceutical company uses SWAT teams of highly trained and talented specialists that go to the site of the problem. This is useful because it is difficult to anticipate exactly where in the development the problem will occur. Another solution is to use part-time workers and overtime. These help us deal with heavy peaks in demand, but allow us to shed capacity when the workload lightens. At one computer peripheral company much of the testing load is handled by temporary contract workers. Another common way to create excess capacity is to use external resources and business partners.

One word of caution if you decide to use external resources: such resources do not become productive immediately. They often require a learning period which can place an added burden on the project team. The trick to managing external resources is to feed them an uninterrupted stream of work. This ensures that the contractor is always working to your latest standards, making it possible to increase their workload quickly without added training. A common mistake is to use external resources only to handle peaks of workload. The danger of this approach is that there is little continuity.

Thus far, we have talked about adding people in various forms. The other general method to increase capacity is to raise productivity per person. In most companies you can sell productivity increases much more easily than you can sell increases in headcount. Since this is an attractive way to add capacity, let us review five key ways to improve productivity.

First, we can bring in better tools. If we bring in a better CAD system we can cut the number of hours it takes to do a drawing by 50 percent. The equipment upgrade almost never costs as much as the people it replaces. We will discuss the use of different types of tools in more detail in Chapter 10.

A second approach to improving productivity is to increase support. It is increasingly common to see product development organizations with inadequate levels of technician support. As companies downsize they set headcount limits in their development organizations. Since the organizations retain the most expensive heads, which are the engineers and scientists, they are left with fewer technicians than they need.

A third approach is to reduce non-value-added activities. It is not unusual to see design teams spending excessive amounts of time preparing progress reviews and reports that are not really read carefully by anyone. For example, at one company I observed a program with a $3 million dollar a month cost of delay. The CEO was visiting once a month and the team had to stop all work for a week to prepare for the review. In effect, 25 percent of available capacity was being used for management reviews. Anything that can ensure the team will spend a higher portion of its time doing useful work will improve productivity.

A fourth approach to improving productivity is to invest in training. Experienced employees are more productive than new employees because they have come down the learning curve. Such learning curves can be accelerated by systematically transferring knowledge from the experienced employees to the new ones. In general, the only organizations that are effective in doing this have allocated specific resources to doing this. For example, Motorola has an internal university that conducts training all around the world. And even small companies can do training. In one small mechanical equipment company, the design engineers provide monthly lectures on the design of their products. These lectures are optional, but are well attended not only by other engineers, but also by people from manufacturing and marketing.

Finally, we can improve effective capacity by cross-training our workers. Since critical bottlenecks are likely to occur in specialized areas, we should create backups for these workers. For example, test specialists can be supplemented by cross-training some of the engineering technicians to assist in this area during heavy periods. You might think that this is inefficient, because cross-trained people can never be as efficient as the specialist. This is true, but irrelevant. We do not cross-train to create an efficient resource, we cross-train to create a resource that can deal with bottlenecks. Remember, when the system is heavily loaded a small change of capacity can lead to a large change in cycle time. Even if an engineering technician is half as productive as a tester it can lead to a big improvement in cycle time. At one company a single tester was assigned to provide two days of testing for a development team. On the second day of testing he was sick with the flu. There was no backup for the tester, so the tests were not done even though the equipment was available. The team had to go to the end of the line to wait for the next available test slot, which was four weeks later. One day of missed testing led to a four weeks' delay in the program. The problem would have never occurred if a technician had been cross-trained to work in the test area. Even if the technician was not as efficient, the four weeks of delay saved would overwhelm any inefficiency added.

Earlier in this chapter we talked about the importance of having more than one server per queue to avoid the queue grinding to a halt due to one difficult job. This problem also occurs when we have no backup for specialists in our process. If we train people to do more than one thing, even if they cannot do the second task efficiently, we will shrink our queues.

The need to cross-train resources has interesting implications for how we compensate our people. In most organizations the compensation system sends a strong signal that we value specialists more than we value people who can do more than one thing. One company gives engineers who earn more than ten patents a special gold-colored ID badge. This sends a clear signal that intense specialization is highly prized. In contrast, it is rare to find companies that compensate their technical people on the *breadth* of their skills rather than the *depth* of their skills. Yet it is breadth that we vitally need to deal with queues in our process.

Interestingly, this is an area in which manufacturing managers are far more sophisticated. It is routine in modern plants to develop cross-trained workers and to compensate them for the breadth of their skills. This adds enormous flexibility to manufacturing processes. Unfortunately, it is the rare company that has transferred this lesson to product development.

Managing Demand

The second broad set of techniques that can be used to deal with queues attacks the demand side of capacity management. There are four key tools for managing demand.

First, we can control the number of projects in the system. This is done by screening them at the front end of the process. When we have a good understanding of our process capacity we can avoid starting too many projects. The key indicator of process overload is the presence of queues in the process. This suggests that we should monitor these queues, which we will discuss later in this chapter.

A second useful tool for managing demand is controlling the feature content per product. This can be done by reducing the number of features and the difficulty of individual features. Unfortunately, most companies do a far better job of managing the number of projects than they do at managing the number of features in their projects. Feature overload is far more dangerous than product overload because complexity increases dramatically as the number of features increases.

Project overload does less damage because projects are usually loosely coupled to each other through shared subsystems, shared development resources, and the like. In contrast, feature overloads are very dangerous because features tend to be tightly coupled. Such tight coupling produces dramatic increases in complexity by adding small numbers of features. We will discuss ways to limit and control feature growth in Chapter 9 which treats the problem of creating and using product specifications.

A third useful tool for demand management is the creation of a relief valve as a means for demand relief during the design process. We must be able to drop requirements when we discover ourselves stuck at a bottleneck. The decision to drop a requirement should be structured as a business tradeoff between the cost of waiting in queue and the value of meeting the requirement. Furthermore, the tradeoff must be made quickly. For example, if a feature adds two weeks to the critical path on a program whose critical path is worth $500,000 per month, the cost of the delay is $250,000. If this feature adds 5 percent more sales on a program where one percent of sales is worth $300,000, the value of the feature is $1.5 million. In such a case the queue is less expensive than the feature and we should not grant requirements relief. It should be clear that the decision rules from Chapter 2 are essential for making these decisions.

Unfortunately, to some people the idea of changing a requirement is heresy. After all, if it is called a requirement it must be required. For example, ISO 9000, a popular quality standard, requires us to "identify all design inputs" as the first step in the design process. It strongly implies that requirements are not to be taken lightly. In fact, the whole quality movement is focused on the notion of conforming to requirements rather than ignoring them.

Some readers might be more comfortable with the term "resegmenting the market" rather than "relaxing the requirement." For example, if our original requirement was to design a car seat for 100 percent of the market it might be difficult to make it comfortable for basketball players as well as jockeys. By respecifying the product we could serve people with heights in the middle 90 percent of the population perfectly. The key point is that changing the requirement does not imply a lack of commitment to quality. We are still committed to delivering a product that meets 100 percent of its performance claims—we are just changing these claims.

This dynamic modulation of requirements is an increasing trend in design activities for software. The "relief valve" for a development process is no longer schedule, it is increasingly becoming the product requirements. We discuss this concept in more detail in Chapter 11 in connection with metrics and process control.

The fourth tool for managing demand is the reuse of the design content from previous products. This can have an enormous impact on the magnitude of the design effort. It can often eliminate 80 percent of the actual effort in the design with very little effect on design quality. Let us look at an interesting example of reuse discussed in Ben Rich's book *Skunk Works*. The first version of the F-117 stealth fighter was designed by reusing the flight control actuators and servomechanisms from the F-111, the flight control computer and the pilot's seat from the F-16, the inertial navigation system from the B-52, and the heads-up display of the F-18. Two prototype planes were built and tested for $30 million. Ben Rich, manager of the Lockheed Skunk Works after the legendary Kelly Johnson, reported that a typical advanced technology prototype would cost three or four times as much. This represents a reduction of workload by 66 to 75 percent, which would obviously have a huge impact on queues.

Instead of redesigning a large number of subsystems that had little effect on performance, Lockheed concentrated its design effort on the critical factors: radar cross-section, aerodynamics, and flight control systems. By focusing on the 20 percent of the design that controlled 80 percent of the performance they were able to do a rapid design with extraordinarily limited resources. Such reuse is a powerful tool to reduce the overall demand on design resources. It requires careful architectural choices, as we shall see in Chapter 8.

Reducing Variability

A third way to reduce queues is to reduce process variability. This is a standard technique in repetitive processes like manufacturing. As we mentioned earlier, variability reduction is much harder in nonrepetitive operations like product development, but it is still available.

If we wish to reduce variability in the design process we can tackle the problem a number of ways. First, it is useful to begin by measuring variation, because we will not be able to assess any improvement if we do not know where we are starting from. As obvious as this point is, it is surprising how many engineering organizations collect no data on task duration.

Second, we can increase the reuse of design solutions. Earlier we mentioned how reuse reduces demand. There is a second important benefit of reuse: it reduces variability. The beauty of a reused subsystem is that we know exactly when it will be available. There is no uncertainty in the completion date of something that has already been designed.

A third powerful tool to reduce variability is process standardization. If we can get people to do things in similar ways there will be less variation in task duration. Ideally, we would want to find the more efficient ways of accomplishing tasks and standardize these.

An effective way to achieve this standardization is to introduce computerized tools. These tools help reduce variability because they turn "art" into science. They embed certain skills in the tool rather than leaving them dependent on the designer. This has the potential to reduce the number of iterations in the design process. For example, consider what happens with application specific integrated circuit (ASIC) development. Professor Thomke at Harvard Business School contrasted the number of iterations done in ASIC development, one type of integrated circuit, with those done in FPGAs, another type of integrated circuit. ASIC designers do their design slowly and get it right the first time (or sometimes the second). FPGA designers do their design quickly and go through multiple iterations. Anytime we go through multiple iterations there is potentially more variability in the outcomes of the design process.

A final technique that will reduce variation in the design process is the use of smaller batch sizes. We will discuss this approach in the next section.

Using Control Systems

The fourth way to reduce queues is to use control systems. This is perhaps the most intriguing approach for reducing queues. The five important techniques in this area consist of removing queues from the critical path, using capacity planning, using reservation systems, controlling batch sizes, and monitoring queues. We will talk about each of these in turn.

The first and most attractive tool is removing the queue from the critical path. Once the queue is off the critical path it does not delay the program, so we do not incur the cost of delay. In fact, a queue off the critical path is free, and even valuable, because it helps load a resource and keep it efficient.

A second approach is to use reservation systems. These systems allow us to get into the queue before we have finished the prior activity. With a reservation we can overlap the upstream and downstream activities, thereby taking the queue off the critical path. Let us look at an example of this. A development team needs to use scarce resources in the prototype shop. There is a four-week queue to access these resources. The team makes a reservation three weeks before they need the prototype parts made. This shrinks the queue for the team to one week, which is a 75 percent reduction, with no change in process capacity.

A third approach is to do capacity planning to prevent the formation of what are called "predictable queues." Predictable queues are self-inflicted wounds because they can be avoided with a bit of planning. For example, one consumer products company noticed that their product introductions were seasonal and that massive queues occurred in testing about the same time every year. These queues could be dramatically reduced by planning to have excess capacity available during these periods.

In development organizations we tend to ignore capacity planning because we are distracted by the nonrepetitive nature of development. We assume that every project is different and that the inherent variability makes planning useless. This is a dangerous oversimplification. Upon careful examination we normally find that the number of hours it takes to do a particular design task can be roughly predicted by looking at other similar design tasks. Some companies have found very simple predictors, such as the number of components in the design, that will roughly predict the number of hours of design work. Even crude measures of demand allow useful planning, because predictable queues can be reduced even with imperfect estimates.

The same principle is true for predicting the workload at individual work centers. Some people think that it is useless to look at figures like the number of drawings that must be done by the drafting center, or the number of bugs that must be corrected during testing. They would say that each drawing takes a different amount of time and a complex drawing might take one hundred times the effort of a simple one. They would assert that a gross count of drawings would be useless. In practice, we find a simple drawing count is extraordinarily useful. The fact that drawings differ in complexity is not vital, because the basic mix of hard vs. easy drawings stays about the same from project to project. Hard drawings such as layout and assembly drawings represent a relatively constant percent of the overall drawing load. Likewise, hard software bugs represent a relatively constant percent of the overall bug population. Aggregate measures of workload turn out to be very valuable.

The careful reader probably recognizes that capacity planning depends on measurement of demand and capacity within processes. Most companies do not have such measures in place. We will talk more about this issue of measurement in Chapter 11.

A fourth approach is managing batch size. This is an area that is dramatically mismanaged in most development processes. As we mentioned earlier in this chapter the length of queues is directly influenced by batch size. When we move to a small process batch size we achieve a dramatic reduction in the queues without changing either capacity or demand.

Fifth, and finally, we can monitor queues in our process. This is a powerful metric that alerts us very quickly to potential cycle time problems. Unfortunately, most companies do not measure the sizes of queues in their processes. We will discuss the value of doing this a bit later in this chapter and we will describe how to do it in Chapter 11, which covers metrics and control systems.

THE LOCATION OF BATCH QUEUES

At times we find large batch transfers in our processes. As we mentioned earlier, we must try to do everything we can to eliminate these large transfers, because they can cause queues in our process. Once we have done our best to eliminate these queues we must carefully evaluate their position within our process, because it is very dangerous to intermingle large batch sizes with small batch sizes in the same process.

We can illustrate this by giving an example that most readers have encountered. Consider what happens in processing an international airline flight. The flight itself is an inherently large batch transfer. We cannot change this easily, because all passengers must take off and land at the same time. The customs process is a small batch transfer process because we cannot handle four hundred people at once. Instead we handle them one or two at a time.

We have two options as to how we might sequence these queues.

FIGURE 3.8
Location of Batch Queues

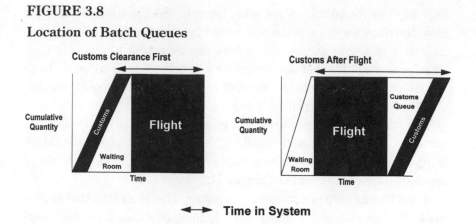

We could process people through customs after the plane arrives which will create an instant queue of four hundred people. A smarter alternative is to process people for customs before they board the plane. This will result in shorter wait times because the arrival rate at a preflight customs queue is much lower than at the end of the flight. People will arrive for the plane over a one-hour period prior to the flight. In contrast, people will exit the plane over a five-to-ten-minute period at the end of the flight. By placing the small batch size process before the large batch size process we will decrease overall cycle time. As Figure 3.8 shows, we can roughly double the size of the queue if we follow a large batch queue with a small one, compared with the reverse sequence.

It is interesting to look at the typical phased development process in this context. Whenever we insert phase checkpoints into the process we are creating large batch transfers. We interpose these large batch transfers between low-batch-size design processes. This almost automatically doubles the size of the queues. This means that if we are trying to optimize the development process for cycle time we should not intermingle large batch transfers with small ones.

Many companies are beginning to understand this, at least unconsciously. For example, consider how a program manager at a workstation company handled their phased development process. Recognizing that it would slow down the development process, he made a special request to the CEO to eliminate three of the phases from the seven-phase process. He agreed to keep management informed by submitting monthly written letters, which increased his personal workload. However, the cycle time benefits were enormous. You can see how the simple step of eliminating these checkpoints would remove weeks from the development process.

It is also interesting to look at the typical R&D budgeting and planning process from the perspective of batch size. We usually do strategic planning once each year and use this plan to create an annual R&D budget. In effect, this is a large batch transfer that hits engineering once per year. Since engineering is a small batch transfer process we have sequenced the large batch size ahead of the small batch size processes, exactly the opposite of what we should do. We will discuss these two problems in more depth in Chapter 7 when we consider the problem of development process design. The important thing to remember is that we must try to avoid large batch transfers in our process. If we have to have them, we should put them near the end of the process. This will minimize the queues that will be caused in the rest of the process.

LITTLE'S LAW

Earlier in this chapter I mentioned that it was valuable to measure queues. This is actually much more beneficial than most managers realize. To understand this we must introduce one of the more famous observations of queueing theory: Little's Law. Little observed that we can calculate the size of a queue two ways, and that the two are equivalent. We can show this using the cumulative flow diagram in Figure 3.9.

As we saw earlier, vertical distances on a cumulative flow diagram represent the number of units in queue at a given time. Horizontal

FIGURE 3.9
Little's Law

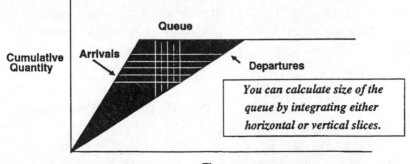

distances represent the time that a given unit spends in queue. The size of the shaded area in the diagram is the size of the queue. What Little observed is that we can compute the average size of the queue by integrating this area using either horizontal slices, which are cycle times, or vertical slices, which are queues. Both will give the same answer.

This appears obvious on a cumulative flow diagram but was not quite so obvious before Little demonstrated it. It has a rather important implication for managers. It suggests that there are two ways to monitor the health of a development process. One method is to monitor cycle times through the process. This is what most companies focus on. Everybody wants to reduce cycle times. The other method is to monitor the queues. Very few companies are measuring and managing queues. The striking thing is that Little's Law says both approaches will give an identical answer. We can find out the same thing by monitoring queues as we can by monitoring cycle times.

There is, however, one very important advantage in monitoring process queues. *Process queues give us instant information about the health of our process.* We do not have to wait for work to arrive late out the other end. A simple analogy will illustrate this advantage. Assume you are approaching the toll plaza on a highway. There are four booths with lines in front of them. We want to predict how long it will take us to get through the toll plaza. One way to do this is to stop cars leaving the toll booths and ask them how long they waited in line. This will give us some idea of how long the wait might be. An alternative way to assess our cycle time is to monitor what is happening to the queue of cars stacked up in front of each toll booth. This system is depicted in Figure 3.10.

What would happen if two of the four toll booth operators went on lunch break at the same time? If we were monitoring cycle times we would note that the first few cars through the system would be reporting normal cycle times. But the cars that were stuck in line at booths 3 and 4 would not even be exiting the system, so we would not know their cycle time. We would wait a long time before we learned about our cycle time problem.

Contrast this with what would happen if we were monitoring the size of the queue. The instant that the two toll booth operators stopped working our queue would begin to grow. The queues for booths 3 and 4 would get larger very quickly. Thus, queues are a leading indicator of future cycle time problems. For this reason, they are a very valuable mea-

FIGURE 3.10

Toll Booth Analogy

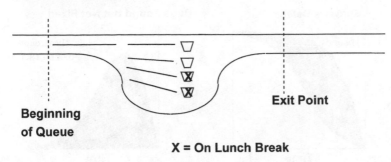

**Beginning
of Queue**

Exit Point

X = On Lunch Break

surement to track in development processes. Curiously very few companies consciously monitor their development queues. We will discuss the value of monitoring them more in Chapter 11.

TYPICAL QUEUES

Let us look a some examples of product development queues that we could start monitoring today. We commonly find queues at resources that are shared between programs such as testing, prototype shops, and engineering services.

We can almost guarantee that most organizations will have queues in their test area. This is a great place to start because test queues are almost always on the critical path of the program. Testing meets the key requirements for getting queues: variability and high-capacity utilization. Test duration is hard to predict and test processes are usually loaded to full utilization. Furthermore, because testing is near the end of the development process the benefits of reducing test queues show up almost immediately.

Another attractive place to look for queues is in front of any expensive piece of capital equipment. For example, the CAD system is often sized based on average workload. If the work does not come in precisely as planned we are guaranteed to have queues in this area. Some managers are proud that they bought five seats of CAD and that they keep them all busy. This makes it almost certain that design work is sitting in an in-box waiting for a CAD station to become available. As we shall see in Chapter 10, the economics of the CAD area are not optimized when all terminals are being used.

FIGURE 3.11

Software Bug Detection and Fix

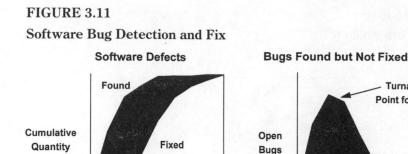

We can also find queues in software debug. In fact, this is one of the few areas in which companies are monitoring queues, except they usually don't realize that they are doing it. They collect bug detection and fix statistics like those shown in Figure 3.11.

The upper curve represents the detection of bugs in the software test process. The lower curve represents the correction of these bugs. You will notice that this looks exactly like a cumulative flow diagram. This is no accident, because this is exactly what it is. If we monitor the number of bugs that are found but not fixed we have a clear indicator of the current health of our software. If we monitor the balance between the find rate and the fix rate we get an indicator of whether our resources are properly balanced between testing and debug. As we do more programs using this metric we can use it as a tool to predict future bug levels on a program.

This metric illustrates a point we made earlier about the usefulness of monitoring queue sizes even when items in the queue differ in size. Some people think that it would only be useful to monitor the queue of bugs if we could precisely measure the difficulty level of each new bug. They would argue that bugs can differ by orders of magnitude in difficulty; therefore they cannot be compared to each other. In practice, people who use this metric observe that it is very useful simply to monitor the total number of bugs in the process. It turns out that the mix of hard and easy bugs stays about the same from product to product. We do not need to know the workload associated with each bug to make aggregate bugs a useful measure.

Another typical place to find queues is in prototyping shops. Teams typically wait to get prototype parts from either internal or external sources. By measuring the size of these queues we can tell when these sources are getting overloaded. This may alert us to add another source or to use overtime. One medical products company that did not monitor these queues accumulated a significant backlog in their prototype shop. By the time they added overtime in this shop the queue was already weeks long and they had to deal with both a backlog and the new arrivals into the queue. If they had been monitoring the queue they would have found the problem weeks earlier.

SUMMARY

In this chapter we have talked about the concepts of queueing theory and how they apply to the design process. We have seen that for many processes the waiting time in queues can be much more expensive than the cost of the process itself. We have also discussed approaches for dealing with queues, which fall in four main categories. First, we can increase capacity. Second, we can manage demand. Third, we can reduce variability. Finally, we can use control systems.

We learned the importance of controlling batch size in the development process and the importance of placing large batch queues near the end of the development process. We have also learned how monitoring queues can be a very valuable metric for the health of the development process.

Finally we discussed some typical places where queues show up in the development process. These included testing, prototyping, CAD, and software debug. We will use the ideas of this chapter more when we get to Part Three of this book.

Now we must take a deeper look at another key area that affects the way we design our development process. It is the way we create information within the process. To look more deeply at this we must use some technical concepts from another area which is called information theory.

4

It's All About Information

In Chapter 1 we said that the only purpose of the design process was to produce economically useful information. In Chapter 2 we talked about economics. Now, let's talk about information.

The optimum design process must generate valuable information cost-effectively. We can break this problem into two subproblems as shown in Figure 4.1. First, we must determine how to generate information efficiently. Second, we must generate the information that is of greatest value. When we understand how to do both of these we can generate high-value information cheaply. In this chapter we will discuss both these issues and explore their specific implications for managing the development process.

INFORMATION THEORY

The early work on information theory was done at Bell Labs, the same place that did the early work on queueing theory. The application of information theory to development process design is really just a minor application of some very advanced concepts.

The study of information theory began when engineers were struggling with formal ways of measuring the amount of information that was being transferred on communications circuits. This was important because they wanted to compare different ways of communicating to see which is most cost effective. It was easy to calculate cost, but harder to measure effectiveness. Eventually, they developed a consistent, useful way to measure information, which is shown in Figure 4.2.

FIGURE 4.1

Generating Information

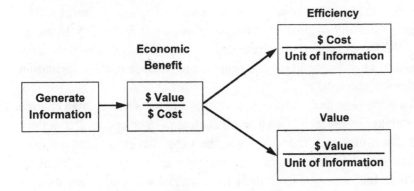

This equation says that the information contained in an event is proportional to the base 2 logarithm of the inverse of the probability of the event. In plain English it says that events that are less probable contain more information. It also says that the increase in information is not linear but rather logarithmic, which is less than linear.

This equation fits our intuition. It says that the more probable the event, the less information is contained in discovering that the event has occurred. If you receive a message that you expect, it contains very little information. Furthermore, the equation suggests that the information required to communicate something is not linearly proportional to the probability of the event. For example, you need one bit to communicate a binary choice. With two bits of information you can communicate four choices. With three bits you can communicate eight choices. With four bits you can communicate sixteen choices. Thus, as I move from one to four bits I raise the information content of the message by sixteen times rather than four times.

An obvious implication of this equation is that risk and information

FIGURE 4.2

Defining Information

$$I = \log_2 \frac{1}{P_e}$$

I = Information in bits

P_e = Probability of an event

are directly related. If there is a reduction in risk, then information has been generated. Conversely, to generate information we must have a change in probability or risk. Imagine that we want to try a new material that has a 50/50 chance of working. We do a test to see if it works. The test generates information because we change the probability to a certainty. We have changed our expectation of the probability of the material failing. This change in expectation occurs because of the information contained in the test.

As we shall see later in this chapter, this suggests that a small change in probability or risk produces a small change in information. If it is very likely that a new material will work, then the success of this material contains very little information, whereas the failure contains a lot of information. Likewise, if it is unlikely the material will work, then its success contains lots of information and its failure contains very little. This has important implications for how we should think about success and failure in the design process.

EFFICIENT GENERATION OF INFORMATION

First we must look at how to generate information efficiently. To do this we must maximize the information that we generate and minimize the cost of resources consumed in creating this information.

We can view any design activity in terms of the four economic factors described in Chapter 2. In general, our costs in a design activity are the expenses of the activity and its delay cost. For example, consider a test in the design process that costs $10,000 to perform. The test takes two weeks on the critical path of a program with a cost of delay of $300,000 per month. Ninety-four percent of the total cost is the delay.

This has interesting implications if we are trying to optimize the efficiency of this test process. We could do this either by decreasing the test cost or by raising output. Cost could be reduced by minimizing the time and expense of the test. We will discuss techniques for doing this in Chapter 12. In this chapter we will discuss how to maximize test output.

MAXIMIZING INFORMATION:
THE MAGIC NUMBER 50 PERCENT

Let us view the problem of maximizing the output of the test through the perspective of information theory. When we test a product we get

FIGURE 4.3

Information and Testing

Information = $\log_2 (1/p_{\text{event}})$

$I_{\text{TEST}} = p_{\text{FAILURE}} (I_{\text{FAILURE}}) + p_{\text{PASSING}} (I_{\text{PASSING}})$

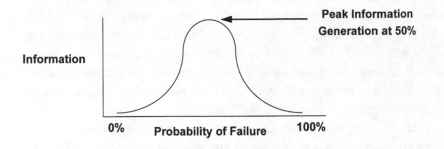

"messages" back from the test regarding the success or failure of the test. Each of these messages contains measurable information that, as we saw earlier, is mathematically related to the probability of receiving this message. When success is likely, the message of success contains little information, whereas when success is unlikely, the message of success contains a lot of information. Likewise, a message of failure contains more information if the failure is highly improbable.

We can actually look at the total information provided by a test as being composed of two messages, success or failure, each of which has a certain probability. When we weight the information content of the message by its probability we can calculate the total information contained in a test, as shown in Figure 4.3.

This curve has some very interesting implications. It shows that the information content of a test is maximum when the probability of failure is 50 percent and that it approaches zero at two points: when we have a very high chance of success or when we have a very low chance of success. This suggests that *we cannot maximize information generation by maximizing the success rate of a test*. We maximize information content of the test by approaching a 50 percent failure rate. *Our testing processes need to have an adequate failure rate to generate sufficient information.*

This principle of structuring tests so that they have equal chances of success and failure is applied every day by people have never heard of information theory. Smart electronic technicians will typically test a broken system by starting in the middle of the system, finding the bad half, and then subdividing the bad half until the problem is found. This will always find a problem faster than a sequential search from input to output. In a system with thirty-two subsystems the smart technician will be three times as productive as an average one, simply by using this approach.

This principle is also applied in the field of software in what is called the binary search algorithm for searching files. When you use this algorithm you make probes into the file which separate the file into two parts with equally likely chances of containing the information. Such a search approach dramatically reduces the time it takes to search a file. You can find a record in a file with one million records in roughly twenty probes instead of an average of 500,000.

This 50 percent number has some interesting implications for how we must manage testing processes. For example, it is common for low-level testing processes to generate insufficient failures. This makes them inefficient because we have to do a lot of testing to find a few failures. One way to improve efficiency is the approach used in statistical process control (SPC), which tries to reduce the cost of testing by using a sampling approach. But information theory suggests another way to attack this problem. We can maximize the information generation rate by achieving a higher failure rate. By testing at a higher level of system integration with system-level tests we raise the failure rate. In effect, this means that we should shift our testing strategy as the product improves in quality from the testing of individual components to testing at a system level.

This optimization of information output at a 50 percent failure rate is a surprise to those who are seeking to "do things right the first time." It suggests that driving the design process to extremely high success rates means that the information being generated by the entire process is being driven to low levels. We need a high enough failure rate to be efficient in our design process.

INFORMATION DIFFERS IN VALUE

Once we understand how to be efficient, we should consider the problem of generating information of highest possible value. The primary determinants of the value of information are its economic impact, which depends on when it arrives during the design process, and its potential profit impact. Let us look at these two factors separately.

Timing: Earlier Is Better

As we saw in Chapter 1, early detection of errors is very important in the design process. Early design decisions form the foundation upon which the remaining structure of the design is built. When early decisions are incorrect, the entire structure based upon them may have to change. This means that the cost of change rises dramatically the later we get into the design process. If the cost of change is rising, then receiving failure information early in the design process is much more valuable than receiving it late in the process.

The key implication for management is that we must be concerned with both the efficiency with which we generate information and the timing of that information. These two factors are frequently in conflict. The pressure to control testing costs often encourages us to use a few big "killer" tests, but such tests will delay the arrival of information. Is there is a better way to trade off the efficiency of testing against the value of early information?

Batch Size Affects Timing

The central element of such a tradeoff is the batch size used in the testing process. A conventional view of this problem would suggest that since each test has a fixed cost, we should try to minimize the number of test cycles in our development process. The fewer testing cycles, the fewer times we pay this fixed cost. This perspective leads us to using large batch sizes in our test process to minimize both the expense and the time it takes to do testing.

In reality the problem of testing batch size is more complex. There is another cost that we have been ignoring when we do large batch testing, which is the cost of receiving test results late. We need to find a way to balance the economies of large batch testing against the value of getting test results early.

To analyze this problem let us define the batch size of our testing process to be the amount of design work that we complete before we start testing. The largest batch size would be waiting for the entire design to be complete before we start the test. This will minimize the number of tests, but we will discover our defects very late in the design process, when it is expensive to react to them. In contrast, if we test a partially complete design we deliver the information associated with the

FIGURE 4.4

Optimum Test Batch Size

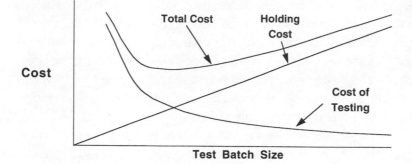

test earlier. Our problem is to balance the cost of extra test cycles against the cost of making expensive changes late in the design cycle.

The solution to this problem is well known, if we recognize that this is just an economic order quantity (EOQ) problem is disguise. The fixed cost per test is equivalent to the fixed cost per order in the EOQ model. The holding cost in our test process—the cost of making changes late in our design process—is equivalent to the holding cost in our EOQ model. The profitability of our test process will be maximized when the total of these two costs are minimized which occurs when we do our tests in the optimum batch size, as shown in Figure 4.4.

We can visually illustrate the advantage of smaller batch sizes in testing by thinking of the design process as producing potential errors at a certain rate. When we test early, we choose to receive these errors when the cost of reacting to them is low. The later we perform our tests, the more expensive it will be to react to these errors. Figure 4.5 shows how the population of potential errors varies using different batch size strategies.

There are two striking advantages to the small batch size strategy. First, the information arrives earlier. Second, our total population of errors never gets very large because it arrives in more manageable small chunks. Such small chunks are much easier for us to process.

An example of such a strategy can be found in the evolution of testing processes at Microsoft which has been described in Cusumano and Selby's book *Microsoft Secrets*. "Big-bang" testing at the end of the process has been replaced by very short build-test cycles. Microsoft has discovered enormous advantages in controlling the size of the total

FIGURE 4.5

Error Population and Batch Size

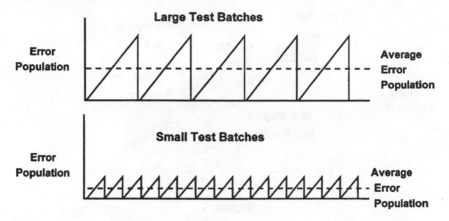

error population of the product. Whenever the average error population is small and bounded, it is much easier to predict the completion date of the product. It is also much easier to fix these defects, because the time between when the software module was written and when it is fixed is short.

Iterations Generate Early Information

This insight on batch size also affects the way we think about iteration in testing processes. A conventional view of testing cycles holds that iterations waste design resources. Each iteration incurs a cost in cycle time and expenses. Extra iterations incur extra costs, and extra costs are bad, so iterations should be reduced to improve efficiency.

Now that we understand the economics of testing batch size we can see the problem of iterations a bit more clearly. We iterate on our design to correct errors and eventually get a good design. There are two schools of thought as to how we might get to this good design. One school holds that we should strive as developers to reduce the error rates. If we keep analyzing the design to minimize the number of errors we will get a better design on the first try. When our analysis shows us a potential defect we can use a conservative design approach to prevent the defect. Such an approach will lengthen the time it takes us to do an iteration, but it will ensure that each iteration is of the highest possible quality. Proponents of this school usually campaign under the banner of quality.

FIGURE 4.6

Defect Rate vs. Iterations

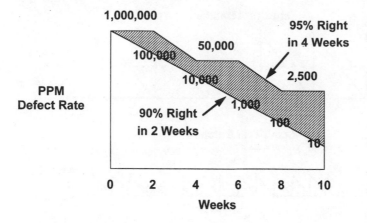

The other school of thought says: do it, try it, fix it. This school lacks the moral high ground of the other group, but is well-grounded in the practical observation of what works for successful companies in the real world. This school argues that prototyping early will inevitably lead to success. They would argue that it would be impossible to have too many prototypes or to do the prototyping too early.

There may be a common logic hidden under these superficially different approaches. Our final quality in a multipass design process is a result of the cumulative effect of each testing iteration. Each iteration starts on a base of the quality of the previous pass. As we can see from Figure 4.6, if we double the defect rate per pass in return for cutting the cycle time per pass by a factor of two we get a substantial improvement in overall quality in the same time. In fact, in just three passes, taking six weeks, we will be at 1,000 ppm defect rate, compared to 2,500 ppm defect rate in eight weeks using our higher quality process. On the surface, this seems too good to be true. The try-it-fix-it approach is faster and higher quality.

On closer inspection we would recognize that the testing costs differ between these two approaches. They could be twice as high if we do four iterations instead of two. This means that when testing costs dominate the economics we should concentrate on quality per iteration. We do not want to incur extra, expensive trials when the cost of a trial is high. In contrast, when testing costs are lower, we will get to higher quality faster by using multiple iterations.

The studies of integrated circuit design practices by Professor Stefan Thomke at Harvard, reported in his 1995 Ph.D. thesis, bear out these findings. When the cost of doing an iteration is high, such as in ASIC development, companies drive for high quality per pass and low iterations, averaging 1.5 iterations. In contrast, when iteration cost is low, in terms of dollars and time, such as they are with FPGAs, companies will gravitate to the multipass approach, averaging 13.9 iterations. On ICs of equivalent complexity the FPGA designers took an average of 8.45 man-months while the ASIC designers took an average of 19.24 man-months.

There may be less difference between these two schools than might appear on the surface. Both approaches are trying to maximize overall economics, they are simply responding to different economic drivers: when the cost of iteration is high we should concentrate on first-pass yields; when it is low, we should concentrate on how quickly we can get through an iteration. Both paths can lead to improved economics but they will differ in their utility for specific businesses. In particular, when the cost of delay is high the cycle time advantages of multiple iteration processes may become much more important than the added testing cost.

Thus, we have discovered some useful tools for maximizing the value of information. We need to plan to do our testing early in the design process. We should be very careful about the batch size of our testing process, since it drives us to late information generation. Finally, we must be very careful about how we treat the problem of design iterations. Frequent cheap iterations can actually be much more valuable than people suspect.

The Potential Profit Impact

Let us now look at the other determinant of value, which is the potential profit impact of the information. We can assess the potential profit impact by asking the question: what is the maximum price that we should rationally pay for the information?

Let us consider a situation where we are choosing between technology A, a new material that might work on our product, and technology B, the old material, which is more expensive, but well understood. Technology A might save us $10 million over the shipping life of the product. What is the maximum amount of money that we should spend for a test to assess technology A?

FIGURE 4.7

Decision Tree

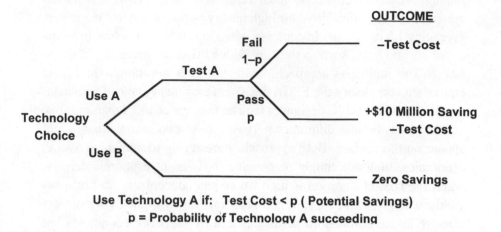

Use Technology A if: Test Cost < p (Potential Savings)
p = Probability of Technology A succeeding

This is a simple problem of decision analysis. We can depict it with the decision tree shown in Figure 4.7. We either use technology B and save nothing, or we test technology A and save $10 million if it works. The value of the information in the test is the probability-weighted savings less the cost of the test.

We will measure test cost in terms of the time and resources required to produce it. As we showed in Chapter 2, time can be converted directly to dollars. We will measure profit in terms of cumulative profit impact.

Let us consider a practical example. If the results of a test allow us to reduce the cumulative cost of the product by $1 million, then profit will increase by $1 million. The cost of obtaining this information may be one month on the critical path and $200,000. If time on the critical path is worth $200,000 per month, then the cost of this test would be $400,000. If we have a 50 percent chance of success then the value of doing the test is $100,000 (the expected payoff less the cost of the test).

What is important about this is that the economic value of information can differ substantially depending on what the information is about. To maximize value we need to go beyond early generation of information, we need to generate high-value information early. This means that we should carefully consider the sequence in which we try to generate information about possible failures. Not only should we focus on high-risk areas first, but we should focus particularly on those areas where the information has highest economic significance.

When we put together the two concepts of efficient information generation and the generation of information with high profit impact, then we can maximize the economic value of information-generating processes during product development.

DO IT RIGHT THE FIRST TIME?

Let us now look at the concept of doing things right the first time in the context of what we know about information theory. As we saw earlier in this chapter, the closer our first-pass success rate is to 100 percent, the lower the information generation rate. This means that if we succeed at doing things right the first time we will have driven all information generation out of our design process.

The fallacy in thinking that high first-pass success optimizes the design process lies in underestimating the important information generation that occurs with failure. This tendency to treat failure as the enemy is relatively new; people have not always considered failures to be negative. For example, consider the statement of Robert Stephenson, one of the great engineers of the early industrial revolution. As Henry Petroski points out in his book *Design Paradigms,* Stephenson strongly advocated discussing failure in engineering literature. In 1856 he wrote: "A faithful account of those accidents, and of the means by which the consequences were met, was really more valuable than a description of the most successful work."

Why is it that so many great engineers consider it so important to remember failures? I would argue that this is because they intuitively grasp the extraordinary information contained in a failure.

Before we get too excited about failure we must make a distinction between two types of failures: those that generate information and those that do not. When the design fails because we try something *new* that does not work, we generate useful information. When the design fails because we neglect something that we already know we should do, then it is not generating information. Thus, when we rediscover that we have to connect two wires together to get current to flow, we have not generated any information in the design process.

When we try to drive failures out of our design process we must focus on those failures that generate no information, since they simply consume time and resources without producing benefit. In contrast, we need to be very careful about how we manage the second class of failures, those that generate information. Astute companies guard their failures as well as their successes, because both contain information. For example, a company in the appliance industry observed a major recall of appliances by one of their key competitors. The competitor had used a new technology which turned out to be unreliable. The recall cost hundreds of millions of dollars. The company already knew that the new technology did not work, because they had experimented with it years earlier. They had treated the results of those experiments as proprietary, since they believed that knowledge of design failures was as important as knowledge of design solutions.

COMMUNICATING FAILURES

Let us now consider an important management implication of these observations. We need to be very careful about how we handle information concerning failures in our design process. This is difficult for us to do well because we have strong human bias to value successes more than we value failures. In most organizations failure is stigmatized and nobody wants to be associated with it.

Unfortunately this produces some dangerous side effects. Since improbable failures have high information content it is important to communicate information about failure quickly and widely throughout the organization. To the extent that we hinder the flow of this information, we will force people to reinvent failures that we have already experienced, and that generates no useful new information.

Cognitive scientists have discovered that the key to expert performance in many fields is domain knowledge rather than intelligence. It takes about ten years to achieve an expert level of domain knowledge. Information theory suggests that events of low probability contain the most information and thus are the foundation of domain knowledge. Expert knowledge comes from being exposed to and remembering low-probability events. The most important of these events are low-probability failures because we are unlikely to conceal low-probability successes. Since these low-probability failures occur infrequently, it takes a long time to acquire knowledge about them. This implies that one of the most important mechanisms for building expertise rapidly is the rapid and wide dissemination of information about failures.

PROTECTING AGAINST FAILURE

Another useful strategy for managing information about failures is to embed protection against these unusual failures in our development process. This is typically done by using checklists to ensure that the same lesson does not have to be learned more than once. By structuring a deliberate verification step we make people consciously check for unlikely failure modes. At one software company a development team was warned about the bugs most likely to occur in their code based on an analysis of similar programs. The error rate on this program was half the rate of similar programs.

A variant of this verification step is the design review by experts who are not members of the team. This is extremely valuable because external experts have little ownership in the specific project, which protects them from certain self-serving biases that the team is victim to. This means that an outsider can process certain information more accurately than a team member can.

TASK SEQUENCING

With this new perspective towards information comes a different view of task sequencing within the design process. If our objective is to generate information of high utility we must ask ourselves which design activities will generate such information. It should be clear that the design activities with the greatest risk generate the most information, and that this information is most useful when it has the greatest impact on profits.

For example, we know that design activities generate new information proportional to the risk that they contain. Let us say we wish to try a design alternative, like using a new material for the product. To the extent that the alternative is highly likely to succeed, the total information contained in trying it will be low. However, what would happen if the chance of success was 50 percent? When in the design process should we consider this option?

Information theory would suggest that the information content of such an option is high. Furthermore, there is an advantage to testing this option early, because as we saw in Chapter 1 there is substantial value in generating information early in the design process. Thus, if we resolve risk early we generate maximum information at the time when this information is most valuable. Clearly, we should try to test this option as early as possible in the design process.

This sheds new light on the age-old debate whether design should proceed from the top down or from the bottom up. Most academics argue for top-down design, pointing out the traps one can fall into with bottom-up design. In contrast, experienced designers argue that it is foolish to view the world as a choice between the two alternatives of top-down and bottom-up. They would argue that one should switch at logical points between these two alternatives. For example, the design of an electronic circuit will start with a top-down approach but must shift to bottom-up when it comes time for component selection.

Information theory provides powerful support for this perspective. It would suggest that we should always perform the step that generates the maximum amount of information first. For example, early in the design process we may have no idea where the greatest risk is. In that case, we should do top-down design. In the course of this top-down process, we may discover that a single subsystem will govern the performance of the system. For example, in a test instrument like a voltmeter the input circuitry is usually the critical subsystem. Once we identify this high-risk subsystem we want to concentrate our effort at reducing its risk, or, expressed a different way, at generating information. We might, for example, prototype the input circuitry to determine whether our concept will work, and then revert to top-down design to identify the next area of high risk. The point is that it is neither top-down nor bottom-up that drives the design process, but rather the path of maximum information generation, or in other words, the path that reduces risk fastest. At times this path may travel from the top down, at others from the bottom up.

MONITORING

Our perspective on information theory also affects the way we might choose to monitor our program. We have concluded that the most important objective of the design process is to generate information. We also know that the events with the greatest change in risk generate the most information. If we are trying to monitor the success of the design process we should therefore be monitoring the events that mark a significant change in the risk of the program. The greater the change in risk, the higher the information content. How should we identify such events?

A common method is to perform a risk assessment at the beginning of the program, which we will discuss in Chapter 12. This assessment should be followed by some action. Since the high-risk events contain high information content, we want them to occur early in the design process. Therefore, we sequence the highest risk events first, put our best people on them, and monitor them carefully. Such events are ideal choices for milestones for our control and tracking systems.

SUMMARY

Information theory can increase our insight on the management of the design process. We have observed that the design process is primarily concerned with the efficient generation of valuable information, and that this information can only be generated efficiently if the failure rate is high enough.

The need for a high failure rate is in direct contradiction to many popular management approaches, like that of trying to do everything right the first time. Rather than trying to drive failures out of the process we must be very careful to communicate them widely, because they contain large amounts of information.

It is always important to distinguish between the failures that generate useful information, which are new failures, and those that generate information that we already have, which are the old failures.

We have also explored some of the management implications of this focus on information generation. For example, task sequence in the design process is more logically driven by the need for risk reduction, and thus information generation, than it is by pure top-down, or bottom-up approaches. Finally, our monitoring approach for programs should be heavily influenced by where the maximum information is likely to be generated, that is, the events of maximum risk. In the next chapter we will discuss the final thinking tool—systems and feedback theory.

5

Just Add Feedback

In 1927 a scientist at Bell Labs by the name of Harold S. Black designed the first amplifier that used negative feedback. This was a dramatic breakthrough because it resulted in massive improvements in stability, frequency response, and reduced sensitivity to noise and component variation.

In this chapter we will explore the behavior of systems, which is different from the behavior of individual components. We will focus on a particular type of system, which is one with feedback, because such a system has desirable properties for a product development process. Let us begin by describing what we mean by a system.

SYSTEMS THEORY

A system is a group of coupled components. The value of a system exceeds the value of its component parts. For example, when you combine two hydrogen atoms with one oxygen atom you get water. Water is a system. By creating this system you have created properties that did not exist in the original components. At room temperature oxygen and hydrogen are gases, whereas water is a liquid. When the new properties are desirable, they create new value. What caused this change in value? The cause lies in the relationships between the elements of the system, in this case the bonds between the atoms.

Because a system has properties that are different than any of its components, it follows that we cannot predict the behavior of a system simply by understanding the behavior of its components. This is an important general principle for product developers. It implies that we will only be able to verify system-level behavior by testing at the system level, not by simply testing individual components.

The value of a system lies in its interfaces, not in the individual components. These interfaces also determine the complexity of the system, because the number of interfaces and interactions between elements grows exponentially with the number of components in the system. This means that the complexity of the interfaces will rise much faster than the complexity of the components, which rises linearly with the number of components. In fact, a scientist once observed that there are more possible interactions in a system with 150 components than there are atoms in the universe.

The implication of this complexity is that we must concentrate our time and attention on interfaces, not on components. This fact has been consistently observed by system architects, and is constantly rediscovered by every company that makes the transition from component to system design.

A careful reader will recognize that the properties that we attribute to systems appear in many forms within our development processes. This makes any insight about the behavior of systems useful in many places. For example, the products we design are systems. The teams we use to design them are systems. The process that we use to design the product is a system. Since systems appear so frequently it is worth understanding a bit about them.

Whenever a system is being designed we go through a certain sequence of steps. As Eberhardt Rechtin points out in his book *Systems Architecting,* the process of architecting a system will first attempt to aggregate similar functions, then to partition them, and then to attend to the interfaces between the components. The act of partitioning the system is extremely important, because it creates interfaces. As we saw earlier, these interfaces are both the primary source of value within a system and the primary source of complexity.

A basic property of the system is the degree of coupling that we have between its elements. We cannot create a high-value system unless we have coupling; however, higher coupling raises system complexity. A common heuristic for controlling the complexity of a system is to partition it in such a way to reduce the communications between components. Such a reduction in communications reduces the coupling within the system.

Let us look at an example at the product level. An electronic product can be designed with a common bus or backplane into which many components can be plugged. An alternative design would be to have a cable running from each component to every other component within the system. A system with five components would require ten cables. If it had ten components it would require forty-five cables. For fifteen components it would need 120 cables. The single backplane starts looking more and more desirable because it reduces the complexity of the design task.

At the team level, consider a team where work is distributed to everyone independent of skill or ability. Since everyone is working on everything, they need to communicate constantly. The team spends most of its time in meetings. In fact, as we will see in Chapter 6, this is a common characteristic of organizations that have poor role definition. They never know who is authorized to make a decision, so they gather everyone into the room and make most of their decisions in meetings.

Whenever we see an intense need for communications it is typically a sign that the system has been incorrectly partitioned. We can tackle this problem either by improving communications or by fixing the partitioning. In practice, we would observe that there is no communication tool that is as powerful as correct partitioning of the system.

There is another practical issue when we try to implement systems in the real world. We discover that the optimum final structure for the system may not be the optimum structure for building a system. For example, you can create many interesting bridge designs that are not buildable because the structure must be capable of remaining erect during the building process. Likewise, a complex system can often be built faster when there are stable steps along the way. This is what the Nobel laureate Herbert Simon called "stable intermediate forms" in his book *The Sciences of the Artificial.*

This issue will show up as we build teams and as we build systems. A product development team should be capable of functioning before all of its members are in place. It should be capable of functioning with one of its members missing. If we create an organization that is so sensitive that it will only function with all members present, we will constantly find our work disrupted. This is also true for products. For example, it is usually smart to design product modules with enough intelligence to self-test rather than saving all testing for the system level. This avoids finding all problems in a system test, which would create a long unpredictable activity on the critical path of the program. We will discuss these architectural issues in more detail in Chapter 8. Let us now move from general systems to a specific type of systems, those with feedback.

SYSTEMS WITH FEEDBACK

Let us look at two types of systems for controlling room temperature. Engineers make a basic distinction between them, calling one an open loop system and the other a closed loop system. A closed loop system is another term for a system with feedback. Let us look at an example of how we could use each of these systems to control the temperature in a room.

Figure 5.1 shows an open loop control system. An open loop system for heating a room might consist of a heater on a timer. The timer would run the heater a certain number of minutes per hour. The timer might be calibrated with settings to achieve different room temperatures. We might set the heater to be on for ten minutes per hour if we wanted the room to be 75 degrees, and five minutes per hour if we wanted the room to be 65 degrees. We would set the control knob to the desired temperature and the heater would cycle according to a predetermined plan.

We would discover some interesting properties of this open loop system. Our room would probably be too cool on cold days, and too warm on hot days because the system cannot respond to changes in the environment very well. And what would happen if the control knob on the timer became loose? We would have a terrible time controlling the temperature.

This suggests two important negative properties of open loop systems. First, they do not respond to changes in their environment very well. Second, they are dependent on the stability of their components. If an individual component changes, then the performance will change.

FIGURE 5.1

Open Loop Control System

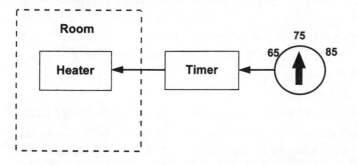

FIGURE 5.2
Closed Loop Control System

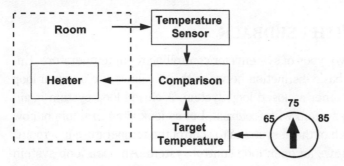

Now, let us look at the design of a closed loop heating system, shown in Figure 5.2. This system uses a thermostat to sense the temperature and then run the heater when the temperature falls below the target temperature. The system has a goal. It monitors actual performance versus this goal. It generates a control signal to the heater to turn the heater on and off.

A closed loop system has some positive properties compared to an open loop system. On a very cold day the heater would run more often to keep the room at 75 degrees. On a very warm day the heater may not come on at all. The system would automatically compensate for this need to run at different rates. Furthermore, the system would still do its job even when some of its components were substandard. What would happen if some of the gas jets in the heater became clogged and it produced less heat? The room would still be regulated at 75 degrees, the system would just run the heater more.

This suggests two important properties of closed loop systems. They can tolerate changes in the external environment well and they continue to perform well even when some of their elements are not performing well. These properties turn out to be important to us, as we shall see later.

You might also note that the closed loop figure has more boxes than the open loop figure. This is a third important characteristic of a closed loop system. It always has more parts because it must sense output and generate a control signal.

What type of system should we use for product development? In the world of product development our environment is constantly changing. Furthermore, the elements of the system can be quite variable. The people on our team may be new, or may change during the program. This suggests that product development might be a good place for closed loop systems. Let us look a bit more deeply at some of the interesting properties of such systems.

PROPERTIES OF SYSTEMS WITH FEEDBACK

When we introduce feedback in a system we get certain dynamic properties that are different from those of systems without feedback. Systems with feedback are difficult to troubleshoot and they are prone to instability. In return for this we get greater system accuracy and reductions in variability.

Difficulty in Troubleshooting

Feedback makes systems difficult to troubleshoot because the output of the system is being fed back to the input. This breaks the linear sequence of cause and effect which we see in an open loop system. If we get the wrong output in an open loop system we can work our way back through the system until we find the problem. For example, in our timer-controlled heater system if we discovered the room was too cold we would check for two problems. The heater could be producing too little heat or the timer might not be on long enough. If the timer was not on long enough, we would check the settings and the timer. The troubleshooting process is quite simple.

In the closed loop system problems are more difficult to troubleshoot. Because the output is being fed back into the input it is very hard to find root causes of problems. The system tends to compensate automatically for problems, often masking the problem itself. For example, in the thermostat-controlled system we might observe that the temperature of the room is too low. This might be caused because the setpoint is incorrectly set, or because the actual temperature is being reported incorrectly, or because the comparison process is defective. Thus, the troubleshooting is a bit more complex.

In fact, for certain problems a system with feedback can totally mask the problem and fool you into thinking you have a correctly functioning system. For example, if the heater output was low the closed loop system would still maintain temperature until it got so cold that running the heater continuously would not produce enough heat. Thus, you would discover you had a problem on the coldest day of the year. The very robustness of closed-loop systems works to our disadvantage when we are trying to fix them.

Instability and Chaos

Another interesting quirk of closed loop systems is that they can become unstable. When electronic engineers first began building amplifiers with feedback they discovered such systems would become unstable and turn into oscillators. As electronic theory developed, they discovered that subtle interactions between noise, gain, and frequency response caused instability at certain levels of feedback.

Now, many years later, this observed phenomenon is used as an example of chaos theory. The nonlinearity of the system causes chaotic behavior and the frequency at which it naturally oscillates is a "strange attractor." Interestingly, the nonlinearities that lead to chaotic behavior are all over the place in development processes. If you think back to Chapter 3, you may remember the queueing curve that we showed. It is nonlinear. This means that whenever we load our development process to high levels of utilization we will get chaotic behavior (a fact that has been observed by developers for many years).

Let us look at a simple example of the oscillation that occurs with instability. Imagine we are trying to regulate the temperature of a room, but our thermostat only takes a reading every hour. If the reading at the beginning of the hour is low the heater stays on until the next reading. If it is high, the heater stays off for the next hour. How would the system behave? The room temperature cycles from too hot to too cold continuously. It has become unstable because of time lags in the feedback system.

Accuracy and Feedback

Another important difference between open loop and closed loop systems is how they achieve accuracy. In an open loop system we try to make the process as accurate as possible. We must do this because there is no feedback. In a closed loop system we focus on the feedback loop.

This distinction has quite far-reaching implications, because it dictates where we will spend our time as managers. If we are dealing with an open loop system everything must do what it is told, because it is the only way to achieve the desired objectives. In a closed loop system what is most important is the feedback loop. The quality of our output will depend on the quality of the feedback loop.

Let us illustrate this with an example. Consider two approaches to steering a ship between Los Angeles and Toyko. One approach would be to use an open loop system. We could accurately calculate the course that we needed to follow, point the ship perfectly in that direction, and sail off to the destination. Success in this situation requires a ship that goes exactly in the direction that it is pointed. Unfortunately, this is not very practical because we cannot set and maintain direction accurately to a thousandth of a degree.

A more practical solution would be to lay out a course and buy a global positioning system (GPS). The GPS will tell us where we are in relation to our planned course. If we find ourselves straying from our intended course we will steer back towards the baseline. This is a closed loop system. Feedback on actual position causes us to modify our behavior to come closer to our goal.

Notice where the key control point is in each of these solutions. For the closed loop system we need to accurately assess our current position. If the feedback system which tells us whether we are on track is accurate, then we will achieve our goal. If the GPS breaks then we will fail. If it works, the feedback system will compensate for changes in the environment. If wind or tides blow us off course feedback will allow us to compensate for these changes and reach our goal. The feedback system even compensates for changes in system performance. The ship could drift back and forth from its course and we would still achieve our goal. The key to system performance lies in the feedback loop. In contrast, an open loop system depends on the system to function. The ship must stay perfectly on course to reach its destination.

These general observations contain another subtle implication. We often discover that the key to controlling the feedback loop lies in the accuracy of a single component, such as the GPS. It is usually much easier to assure the accuracy of one component than the accuracy of the entire system. For example, the course of a ship would be affected by the speed of the engines as well as the position of the rudder. The speed of the engines might be affected by the temperature of the ocean, the density of the fuel, the settings of the throttle, and so on. Thus, we get entangled in very complex control problems when we try to control the entire system, as we do for open loop systems, instead of just controlling the feedback loop, as we do for closed loop systems.

This means it is important for managers who are used to operating with open loop systems to change their focus when they shift to using closed loop systems. For example, with an open loop approach, if you were asking a designer to design a circuit board you would try to constrain all the things that he might do incorrectly. You would give him very detailed instructions and rules to ensure that he would reach his goal. If you were trying to manage the same designer using a closed loop approach, you would request that he work on the design a bit and then come back to see you. Based on what had been accomplished you would provide additional instructions.

Variability Within a System

Another characteristic that we must understand about systems is the peculiar way that variability compounds within a system. It does not follow the math we learned in grade school. Such math, called scalar arithmetic, works for things that have a single dimension, like counting money. Once we start dealing with things that have more than one dimension we use a form of mathematics called vector arithmetic. A vector is simply a way of depicting something that has more than one dimension. For example, velocity is measured as a vector because it has both a magnitude and a direction (which may be measured in three dimensions).

This vector arithmetic is what we use to measure variability in a system. We do this because the variation of one activity is not aligned to the variation of another activity. As a result we cannot use the scalar arithmetic that you may be used to.

Two interesting properties of this sort of arithmetic are important to us. First, when we add vectors that are not aligned the resultant sum grows slower than the scalar sum that we are used to. This means that as we combine variable activities the sum becomes less variable than the individual activities. For example, if we have ten variable activities that take one month each, the percent variability of the sum of these activities is lower than the percent variability of each individual activity. As shown in Figure 5.3, this means that we can reduce the overall variability of a project by combining things that are variable. This is a pretty neat trick. We combine a bunch of things that are hard to predict and get something that is easier to predict.

FIGURE 5.3

Reducing System Variability

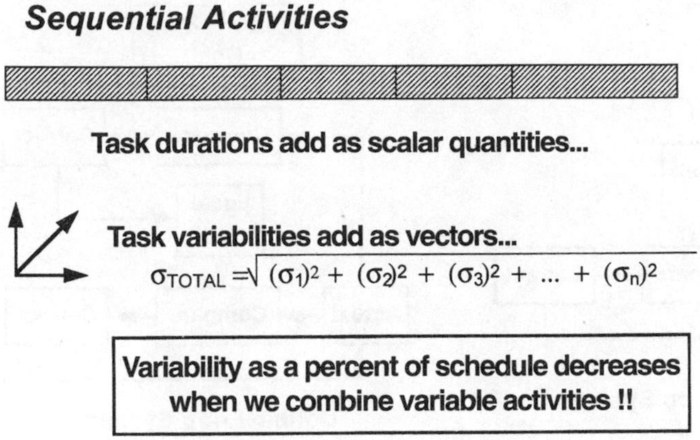

Sequential Activities

Task durations add as scalar quantities...

Task variabilities add as vectors...

$$\sigma_{TOTAL} = \sqrt{(\sigma_1)^2 + (\sigma_2)^2 + (\sigma_3)^2 + ... + (\sigma_n)^2}$$

Variability as a percent of schedule decreases when we combine variable activities !!

This has an important managerial implication. It means that we can predict the overall duration or expense of the project with more accuracy than we can predict any individual component activity. This points the way to creating good estimates of overall project duration and expense. By estimating tasks at low levels of detail and combining these estimates we can arrive at an answer that is more accurate than any of the individual estimates going into it.

The second thing we need to realize is that the variability of the system will approach the variability of its most variable component. If one activity has high variability the variability of the overall project will approach that of this activity. In fact, the only way to deal with this problem is to remove the variability from the system by decoupling this variability from the system. We exploit this principle when we undertake technology development as a separate activity from product development. This decouples a variable activity from the more predictable activity of product development. If we do not do this, then the variability of the overall process will become as variable as the technology development process itself. This variability can be a variation in cost, schedule, or performance. We will discuss this issue in more detail in Chapter 7.

Finally, we should observe that the nonlinear behavior of queueing systems will amplify variability within the system. Anyone who has ever missed a plane flight has noticed that a five-minute difference in arrival at the gate can mean a six-hour difference in the arrival at the destination. In effect this means that the variability in departure time has been

FIGURE 5.4

Single and Double Loop Control Systems

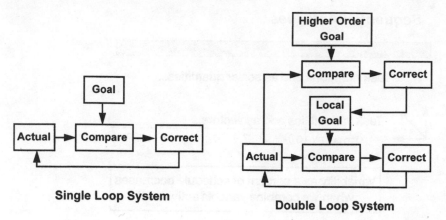

Single Loop System

Double Loop System

amplified. We get into an interesting death spiral when we overload our development processes. Overloads cause queues; queues, being nonlinear, raise the variability of our process, and variability raises the size of queues. If you want to make your development process more predictable you should attack queues in the system.

MORE COMPLEX CONTROL SYSTEMS

Control systems can be made even more complex. For example, we can make a distinction among different types of closed loop control systems. Some closed loop control systems are designed to maintain the status quo, whereas others are inherently adaptive. These are sometimes labeled single and double loop systems. A single loop system has a local control goal. A double loop system has a local control goal which can be altered by the system to achieve some higher order goal. These systems are shown in Figure 5.4.

For example, consider our thermostat system. If it simply turns the heat on and off to maintain the temperature of the room it is a single loop system. If it alters the target temperature based on other factors then it is a double loop system. For example, the system might be designed to provide a climate profile for a particular type of tropical plant. It could assess the number of hours of daylight per day and change its temperature control program accordingly. This would provide a more accurate replication of natural growing conditions than a simple single loop system.

This terminology is used in management literature by Chris Argyris and Donald Schön who discuss single loop and double loop learning in organizations in their book, *Organizational Learning II.* Double loop systems are generally of greatest interest to us, despite their higher complexity. They are valuable to us because they can deal with a level of environmental change that would break a single loop system.

SUMMARY

In this chapter we discussed some of the things that engineers have learned about the design of systems that have feedback. We discussed the difference between closed and open loop systems and the disadvantages and advantages of both.

We explained the importance of closed loop systems and the unique properties that such systems have. Such systems can be difficult to troubleshoot and prone to instability and chaotic behavior. They derive their accuracy from the quality of their feedback loop, unlike open loop systems, which derive their accuracy from the components in the primary system.

We also explained why managers are likely to have trouble adjusting to closed loop systems if they are used to open loop systems. The success of a closed loop system depends on the quality of the feedback loop not the accuracy of system components.

Finally, we discussed double loop control systems. We will see applications of many of the principles discussed in this chapter when we begin to look at the design of the development process, which is covered in Chapter 7.

We are now at the end of Part Two of our book. We have discussed four important tools for analyzing and understanding development processes. Equipped with the concepts of economic modeling, queueing theory, information theory, and system theory we can now tackle the problem of designing a development process. Without these tools we might be condemned to blindly imitate the "best practices" of other companies. With these tools we can make conscious decisions to optimize what we should.

In Part Three we will explore the practical issues of designing a development process. In Chapter 6 we will look at the problem of organization design. This is typically a major constraint on our process choices. In Chapter 7 we will tackle the problem of process design. This is probably the longest chapter in the book. In Chapter 8 we will discuss product architecture. This issue is invisible to most managers, but it can have a major impact on the outcome of development programs.

We will then begin to discuss several key process building blocks. In Chapter 9 we will talk about the critical subprocess of developing a product specification. We will follow this in Chapter 10 with a discussion of the role that technology can play in the process, when implemented properly.

We will then talk about the key problems of execution. In Chapter 11 we will discuss process control and the important role that metrics can play. Chapter 12 follows up with a discussion of managing uncertainty and risk. Finally in Chapter 13 we will discuss what you might do to implement changes in development processes.

Part Three

ACTION TOOLS

6

Choose the Right Organization

The design of an organization is intimately linked with the design of its development process. Theoretically we could treat organization form as a response to process design; in practice it is more useful to think of organization as a context for the product development effort. For this reason I will preface the discussion of process design with a look at the question of organization. Our organization is a key element of the context in which we design our process.

As we saw in the last chapter, an organization is a system. We should therefore expect that many of our observations about systems would apply to organizations. Let us start by looking at how system-level properties might show up when we look at the problem of organizational design.

THE ORGANIZATION AS A SYSTEM

Like any system, the organization is composed of parts that have relationships to each other, and these relationships or interfaces determine the value of the organization. Without them the efforts of a group of people could never exceed the sum of their individual abilities. In fact, we create relationships between elements of the organization because we believe that we will create some value that is not present in the individual parts. If we create this value then we created a useful organization. If we do not we have failed in designing the organization.

It follows that the primary value of the organization is contained in the interfaces between its elements, not in the elements themselves. It has been popular to think of core competencies such as low-cost manufacturing or excellence in marketing as being the key assets of an organization. Such thinking falls into the trap of seeing the obvious components of the system, rather than the more intangible interfaces. If we recognize the lessons of system theory, we will look for the value of the organization in its interfaces, not in its component parts.

If the primary determiner of an organization's value is its interfaces, it follows that this is where we should spend our design efforts. Our attempts to influence organization performance should focus on the interfaces rather than the functional blocks themselves. We do this in an obvious way when we draw organization charts. The simple lines that we lay down, and the white space that we choose to leave, have enormous impact on the organization.

System theory would also suggest that the coupling, or level of feedback, between the elements of an organization will have a strong impact on the properties of the organization. In a simple sense, this coupling can be more intense along an internal or an external dimension. When internal coupling is strongest we will create an organization that is robust with respect to environmental changes. It continues in its planned direction despite environmental change. Put another way, it fails to adapt to changes in its environment. Many organizations that would be characterized as having strong cultures have this strong internal coupling which can hinder adaptation. For example, IBM appears to have responded very slowly to the emergence of decentralized data processing structures such as client-server architectures. Its strong internal culture made it less sensitive to the dramatic shift that took place in the data processing environment in the 1980s.

In contrast, stronger external coupling results in more responsiveness to the external environment. In the extreme this can lead to reactive behavior, being blown hither and yon by every shift in the market. Such organizations are often seen to lack constancy of purpose. It is only when external and internal coupling are properly balanced that we get an organization that responds well to changes in its environment.

ASSESSING ORGANIZATIONAL FORMS

As we saw in Chapter 2, a development project can be modeled to determine the importance of four key parameters: expense, cost, performance, and delay. The relative importance of each of these parameters will vary from project to project. Different organizational forms are optimized for different economic parameters. Let us now look at some classic organization forms and see how they are likely to differ in their development process economics.

EFFICIENCY: THE FUNCTIONAL ORGANIZATION

The most common organization for product development is the functional organization. People are grouped together by functional specialty: the engineers are in engineering, the finance people are in the finance department, and so on. This organization is under attack by the recent drive for "reengineering"; however, it remains a good choice for certain situations (see Figure 6.1).

Why might we want to group people by professional discipline? Why create an engineering department? When we concentrate the engineering task in a single department we can hire specialized people, we can manage them as a group, and they can exchange information more easily among themselves. We will get more output from such a group than we could get from the same number of individuals scattered about the company.

In essence, the functional organization exploits economies of scale inside the function, which can be exactly the right thing to optimize in certain situations. For example, consider a company making telecommunication switches containing circuits that operate at very high speeds. Only an expert can design printed circuit boards that operate at

FIGURE 6.1

Functional Organization

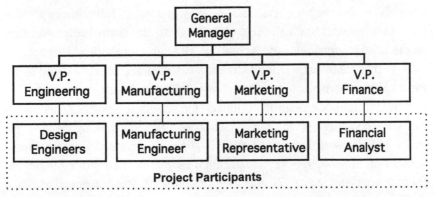

ultrahigh speed. By having one centralized expert the company can avoid duplicating this skill on multiple projects. Thus, it spends less money per design.

The essential benefit of functional organizations is that they generate, choose, and test design options efficiently. The result is more output per dollar of input than any other organizational form. When the economic objective is to maximize efficiency, then this is the preferred form.

Unfortunately, this efficiency does not come for free. It affects the other economic objectives that we defined in Chapter 2. Our functional organization is not optimized for speed, because every centralized expert involved in the design is likely to add a bit more delay to the project. Furthermore, it will not always lead to the lowest cost designs, because such designs require intense communications between the design engineers and the experts on cost, who are in manufacturing. It is also unlikely to maximize either sell price or market share, because such issues require intense communications with marketing and the customer. In essence, the weak cross-functional communication of the functional form sacrifices our other economic objectives.

SPEED: THE AUTONOMOUS TEAM

When people get dissatisfied with the functional organization they typically try another form, known in its extreme form as the autonomous team. Their logic is that if the functional organization, with its vertical silos, does not work, perhaps its opposite will. By breaking the links between the project and the function and creating a "horizontal" organizations, the autonomous team places cross-functional resources completely under the control of a team leader. This leader has full authority and responsibility for the program. Take note of the term "full authority." In a truly autonomous team the budget belongs to the team leader and that leader does performance evaluations on all team members. (Most organizations that claim to be using autonomous teams are actually using some form of hybrid organization, which we will discuss later.)

The autonomous team is optimized for speed. It achieves this speed in two ways. First, it seldom experiences decision-making delays, because the locus of decision making is at the team level. Second, members of an autonomous team are much more likely to work outside of their primary specialty. This is a more subtle effect, but one that has a

FIGURE 6.2

Autonomous Team Organization

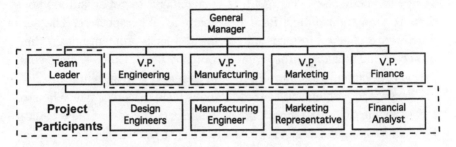

big impact on cycle time. As we saw in Chapter 3, one of the big enemies of cycle time is the queues that form in the development process. These queues are inevitable because of the inherent variability of development tasks. When a queue forms on the critical path of a program a small change in capacity can lead to a large change in cycle time. In autonomous teams, this small change in capacity comes from the willingness of team members to work outside of their primary specialty. This happens automatically in a cohesive team because the team goals become very important to team members (see Figure 6.2).

In one audio equipment company, I observed the accounts receivable clerks assembling prototypes on the production line. It turned out that the prototypes were needed for a trade show the following week, and the cost of using accountants to operate screwdrivers was far lower than the cost of missing the show.

This ability of autonomous teams to align resources to bottlenecks is extremely important because it minimizes queues in the development process. Since these bottlenecks can shift rapidly and unpredictably during a program, the flexibility of team members to work outside of specialty is a critical tool for dealing with such bottlenecks. It is not unusual for an autonomous team to have a speed advantage of a factor of two over a similar functionally organized team.

However, this advantage in speed does not come for free. The essential problem with autonomous teams is that they believe what we tell them about being autonomous. This leads to a variety of problems. First, it is difficult to achieve compatibility between projects. The field service department looks at the design one such team has developed and says: "We already use seven thousand types of screws in this company, yet your design uses ten types of screws that we have never used before.

Why did you do that?" The team replies, "Hey, we're just autonomous kinds of guys. We choose the right fastener for the job. We don't care what everybody else is doing." It is very difficult to get an autonomous team to view their project from a company-level perspective. They are much more inclined to focus on solving the local problem within their project than the global problem at a company level. Cross-project compatibility becomes a significant problem as teams gain autonomy.

The second problem with an autonomous team is inefficiency. When we create an autonomous team we break the links to the rest of the organization. This can limit access to the experience and knowledge which will affect our product cost, product performance, and development efficiency. Instead of tapping into the existing knowledge of the organization the autonomous team is prone to reinvent the wheel, and the wheel that they reinvent will not always be superior to the one we are currently using.

The third problem with autonomous teams is the inability to build expertise in specialized areas. The centers of technical excellence that are so common in functional organizations disappear. We are much less likely to excel technically with autonomous teams. For example, autonomous teams often do their own product testing or market research. Their work is likely to be less effective than that done by a professional market research group because they cannot afford to have expert skills on the team. The team has no budget to automate product testing on their program, and they are disinclined to take the risk on their program. Thus, product testing takes ten times as much time and money as it really could take. Autonomous teams weaken functional expertise.

These three problems can affect the economics of the development process. While autonomous teams are fast, they are not efficient. One computer peripheral manufacturer tried to implement such teams and found that engineering costs mushroomed with no change in the number of projects being worked on. Autonomous teams will rarely optimize unit costs, because they optimize the design for their individual project needs instead of looking at cross-project standardization opportunities. A manufacturer of presentation systems discovered that every team was choosing a power supply based on the need of its individual project. This created excess variety in manufacturing and eliminated any chance to get purchasing scale economies. The inability to build expertise can also affect sell price and market share. Since we cannot bring our best marketing skills to bear on each project we often find ourselves making the same mistakes over and over again. If one team finally understands what the customer wants, it is very difficult to inject that knowledge into another team without triggering an "immune response."

Thus, while we get speed of execution with autonomous teams we sacrifice our other economic objectives. When speed is truly crucial, then this is a good choice. When other economic objectives become important we should look for a better answer. Companies that experiment with autonomous teams learn their lessons, and conclude that the disadvantages are significant. Then they try to combine the advantages of the functional form with those of the autonomous team. They start experimenting with hybrid organizations.

PERFORMANCE AND COST: HYBRID ORGANIZATIONS

The third structure, the hybrid organization shown in Figure 6.3, lies somewhere between the functional organization and the autonomous team. Such organizations, which have more than one reporting relationship, are sometimes labeled matrix organizations. I try to avoid this label because people have preconceived notions about what it means.

We will use the term hybrid organization to stress the fact that the label is less important than the operational characteristics of the organization.

We commonly use hybrid forms of organizations for two reasons. First, they help us avoid some of the inherent disadvantages of the functional and autonomous team forms. Second, they will typically optimize our two other important objectives, product performance and product cost.

Let us examine how a hybrid organization achieves low product costs. As we mentioned earlier, to minimize product cost we must achieve

FIGURE 6.3

Hybrid Organization

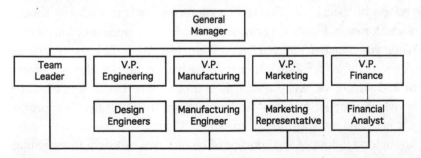

close links between the people making design decisions and the people who are most expert on the manufacturing cost implications of these design decisions, the manufacturing department. Every analysis of design for manufacturing (DFM) shows that the greatest potential to influence product cost exists during the design phase of the product, not during the manufacturing phase. To achieve the lowest product cost we must bring the expertise of manufacturing to bear upon the very early stages of design—the first 10 percent of the development process.

A hybrid organization will also optimize product performance.We need to distinguish between two paths to maximizing product performance: adding new functionality to a product and improving performance by doing old functions better. In the first case we need very close coupling to the marketplace, since the customer is the expert on what new functionality will add the most value in the product. In the second case we may need very close coupling to our technology experts, so that we can push the performance to the limits of the best technology available. In both cases, you will observe a common theme: we need to effectively engage people from outside the team in the team activities. In both cases, the hybrid team is an effective solution.

The hybrid organization appears to be the most effective way to both combine the benefits and avoid the extremes of the functional and autonomous organizations. Skillfully applied we can use it to tune the specific attributes that we want the organization to have.

To implement a hybrid organization, we must go far beyond simply drawing an organization chart. We must make careful definitions of specific authorities to be placed along the functional and team axes of the organization.

DIVIDING RESPONSIBILITIES

The most useful tool we have found for making these choices is the systematic review of specific decision areas to determine where authority should be placed for each. Figure 6.4 provides a sample list of such decision areas.

When you construct such a list on your own you want to be careful to focus on specific decisions rather than abstract concepts like empowerment and strong vs. weak teams. It is much more useful for teams to know which product features they can change without outside approval than it is to find out they are "empowered."

An understanding of the concept of boundaries can help in assigning

FIGURE 6.4

Key Decision Areas

- ☐ Select product features
- ☐ Modify product features
- ☐ Prepare project budget
- ☐ Modify project budget
- ☐ Prepare project schedule
- ☐ Modify project schedule
- ☐ Prepare manning plan
- ☐ Modify manning plan
- ☐ Select team members
- ☐ Hire team members
- ☐ Remove team members
- ☐ Evaluate team member performance
- ☐ Determine team member compensation
- ☐ Determine team member bonuses
- ☐ Authorize travel

- ☐ Cancel project
- ☐ Select development location
- ☐ Set layout of team work area
- ☐ Select key business partners
- ☐ Manage key business partners
- ☐ Select key technology partners
- ☐ Manage key technology partners
- ☐ Select outside contractors
- ☐ Manage outside contractors
- ☐ Select vendors
- ☐ Manage vendor contracts
- ☐ Select manufacturing site
- ☐ Determine required level of quality for introduction

- ☐ Pay for manufacturing variances
- ☐ Select product processes
- ☐ Select engineering tools
- ☐ Select development methods
- ☐ Modify development methods
- ☐ Determine test procedures
- ☐ Determine test criteria
- ☐ Set reuse objectives
- ☐ Determine reporting requirements
- ☐ Set manufacturing yield targets
- ☐ Set documentation standards

such authorities. A boundary defines the limit of the team's authority, which is the point at which they must go outside the team for approval. A boundary is a formal way of dividing authority in an organization. Boundaries can be defined many ways. For example, budgets are a typical boundary device. A team that stays within its tooling, capital, manpower, or expense budget can make decisions with autonomy. Once it exceeds these limits it needs to get approval from someone outside the team. Delegations of authority are another way to set a boundary. For example, the team may have authority to buy software that costs less than $500 without external approval. Approved choice lists are another tool. The team may be given an approved parts list, approved vendor list, or standard test list. Figure 6.5 summarizes the boundary devices that might be used to deal with certain decisions.

It is extremely important to define these boundaries early in the program and to communicate them effectively, so that the team has clear expectations regarding what they have authority to do and what they cannot do. These expectations will affect how team members perceive events.

There are two ways of communicating boundaries inside the organization. Unfortunately, the most common approach is trial and error. Some people refer to this as discovering the location of the invisible electric fences. Consider for a moment the big difference in your own organization between experienced and inexperienced team leaders.

FIGURE 6.5

Boundary Devices

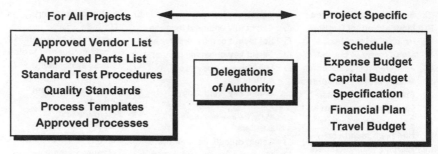

For All Projects ◀————————▶ Project Specific

Approved Vendor List Approved Parts List Standard Test Procedures Quality Standards Process Templates Approved Processes	Schedule Expense Budget Capital Budget Specification Financial Plan Travel Budget

Delegations
of Authority

The experienced leader knows where the invisible electric fences are. He knows that even though the organization says he is empowered to make all feature decisions, this does not give him permission to change the corporate color scheme. The inexperienced leader has to discover the unwritten rules by trial and error.

There are two practical problems with using trial and error as the primary way of communicating boundaries. First, from a technical perspective, it is too slow. The information regarding rules becomes available too late in the process, which wastes time and resources. The design team designs the product to run in the California plant. The VP of manufacturing expected the product to run in the Puerto Rican plant. Now we have a frustrated team and a potentially costly redesign. Hidden expectations can easily erode project performance and team morale.

The second problem with trial and error is a human problem. Touching electric fences does not encourage the team to use initiative in making decisions. In fact, it will reduce the initiative exercised by the team. Trial and error tends to create the perception that the company is full of invisible electrified fences. This causes teams to adapt by pretesting their decisions with management, an approach that slows decision making.

There is a better approach for setting boundaries. It consists of clarifying expectations for the entire team regarding their authority to make decisions. This is done by making a list of specific decisions and discussing them with the functional managers and the team. A two-hour meeting early in the program can have enormous impact on clarifying intended operating practices to the team.

COMMUNICATIONS

Almost every company would like to improve communications on their development teams. Too often they think this requires getting more information to flow faster inside the organization. More people are invited to meetings. More decisions are documented. More memos are sent to more people. Do communications improve? No. Ironically, the difference between companies that claim to have good communications and companies that have bad communications is never the quantity of information that is exchanged. Companies that have bad communications can still be buried in information. The key driver of good communications is the amount of usable information communicated compared to what is needed to make good decisions.

What most companies miss is that the first attack on communications problems should always be to reduce the need for communications, not to increase the information flow. These communications needs can be reduced with a well-partitioned architecture, well-defined responsibilities on the team, and dedicated team members. Let us examine each of these factors in turn.

Architecture has a big impact on communications because it affects what information is needed to complete a given design task. Consider what happens when we decide to use a standard interface to connect subsystems A and B of a larger overall system. Because the standard interface is already characterized and defined, the teams working on both sides of this interface have a stable target. They have very little need for communicating with each other. On the other hand, if we chose to implement a new interface design we would have a moving target necessitating a great deal of communication between the two groups to work out the interface issues. The fewer interfaces we create in the architecture, and the more standard and stable these interfaces are, the easier our communications problem becomes. We will discuss other implications of product architecture choices in Chapter 8.

In a similar manner, well-defined responsibilities within teams reduce the need for communications. If everybody knows their roles, we do not have to be talking all the time about who will do each task. Contrast this with the team that has not defined roles clearly. Its members don't know who has authority to make each decision. What do they do? They gather everybody in the room who has the power to veto the decision and then try to get approval. If everybody assents then they can proceed. On such a team most important decisions are made during the team meetings. Since there are a lot of important decisions, these teams complain about spending too much time in meetings.

Another important tool to reduce the need for communications is to increase the percent dedication of team members to the project. This automatically reduces the number of people needed on the team and the overhead associated with these people. The communications overhead goes down because in any communications system the number of nodes in the system will affect the number of communications links that have to be maintained, and this number rises roughly with the square of the number of nodes. The more full-time people you have the less communications overhead you will observe.

Once we have reduced the need for communications we can start improving the quality, speed, and quantity of communications. Of these three factors speed and quality are far more critical than quantity. Let us start by looking at some traditional communications tools, and then move to some of the newer technologies.

Old Communications Tools

The problem of human communications has been around for a long time. We know that we get higher quality communications when people share a language and a vocabulary. Without this common ground we are likely to have communications problems.

For example, we can have communications problems between teams from two different locations. In such cases it is wise to bring these teams together on some common ground for one or two weeks to work jointly on some project activities. This joint work enables people to know each other at a personal level, which pays enormous dividends later in the program. The key reason for this is that we perceive "strangers" very differently and much more simplistically than people that we have worked with. This distortion in perception will affect our decision-making processes and relationships.

We can also create common ground by doing training on the project and development process early in the program. Such training ensures that the team will have a common vocabulary. Furthermore, if the training is related to the objective of the project we will provide the team with relevant skills immediately before they need them.

We also know that we get better communications when people share common experiences. In the military we use this technique in "boot camp." People from vastly different backgrounds are put through a common, and memorable, experience. This enables soldiers to meet one another for the first time and be guaranteed that they have a shared experience to talk about. This type of shared experience is a valuable tool for building bonds between team members. It can be provided by having the team work jointly on activities early in the life of the project.

Yet another way to improve communications is to compose teams of people who have already worked together on projects in the past. This sort of continuity makes it much easier to establish good communications. On teams that come up to productivity quickly it is not unusual to discover that 80 percent of the members have worked previously with other team members.

Thus, between creating common ground and using sound psychology we can improve the way that people communicate with each other. We should not assume that people are automatically endowed with these skills, but they can be developed and are certainly worthy of attention.

New Communications Technologies

Whole sets of new communications technologies are now available. Good teams use them because they help solve one of the most vexing management problems: getting good communications. Figure 6.6 summarizes the characteristics of team communications systems focusing on four key dimensions:

1. Real-time
2. Self-documenting
3. Leverage
4. Bandwidth

Let us look at each of these dimensions in more detail. First, consider the time dimension. Tools like meetings, phone calls, and videoconferences are inherently real-time. This is very important in dealing with problems that have a complex structure because such problems require a lot of interaction. Memos and E-mail make interaction much clumsier.

Second, we can consider the degree of documentation that we achieve. Written communications excel here. Memos and E-mail leave a paper trail. They are inherently self-documenting. Sometimes this paper is a disadvantage, but normally it is critical to efficient functioning.

FIGURE 6.6

Team Communications Systems

Systems	Real Time	Self-Documenting	Leveraged	High Bandwidth
Meetings	✓			✓
Telephone	✓			
Voice Mail		✓	✓	
E-Mail		✓	✓	
Paper Documents		✓	✓	
Web Sites		✓	✓	
Videotapes		✓	✓	✓
Videoconferencing	✓			✓
Chance Encounters	✓			✓

Third, we can look at leverage. We use this term to quantify the relative time spent by the sender vs. the receiver of communications. Leverage is good for the sender but bad for the receiver because it can easily lead to information overload. Any communication that can be stored and reproduced has this unfavorable leverage. For example, it takes only thirty seconds to send a one-hundred-page E-mail to one hundred people. Voice mail can be equally bad. The president of one medical products company sent a special voice mail to all of his employees. It overloaded the entire voicemail system and shut it down for twenty-four hours.

The danger in leverage is that it causes the volume of received communications to grow very rapidly. This is currently occurring with E-mail. Some team leaders get two to three hundred E-mail messages per day. They complain that they cannot both read their E-mail and do their job in the same day. They flatly acknowledge that they only check the name of the sender and read the subject line on most messages. Leveraged communications tools must be used with care because of the overhead they create.

The final characteristic, bandwidth, is a technical term for the amount of information that can be conveyed in a particular time. The highest bandwidth methods are those that rely on visual communications, since human brains have the highest bandwidth in this area. This means that graphics, videoconferences, and face-to-face meetings will transmit a lot of information in a small time. Written communications and E-mail are inherently lower bandwidth and take longer to disseminate. Furthermore, they require more time for preparation.

Face-to-face contact is an unusually valuable tool because it is real-time, unleveraged, and has high bandwidth. Its key disadvantage is that it is not self-documenting. Teams frequently exploit the value of such face-to-face contact by colocating members. This is an extraordinarily powerful tool.

COLOCATION

Colocation is the closest thing to fairy dust that we have to improve communications on the development team. By clustering people together we get a dramatic improvement in communications on teams. We have been in contact with thousands of people who have worked on development teams. Without exception, those that have worked on colocated teams insist that this is the most effective way to do development. It is amazing that this simple technique is not used more frequently.

The Lockheed Skunk Works is legendary for its rapid development of complex advanced technology aircraft. As Ben Rich describes in his book *Skunk Works,* colocation was a key element of its management approach.

"Our designers spent at least a third of their day right on the shop floor; at the same time, there were usually two of three shop workers up in the design room conferring on a particular problem. That was how we kept everybody involved and integrated on a project. My weights man talked to my structures man, and my structures man talked to my designer, and my designer talked with my flight test guy, and they all sat *two feet apart* (emphasis added), conferring and kibitzing every step of the way."

The classic work on communications within technical organizations has been done by Tom Allen from MIT. Figure 6.7 shows the results of his classic study published in 1977. You will notice how steeply communications fall off with distance.

When we carefully observe teams that are colocated we notice that one of the great benefits of colocation is that it increases "unimportant" communications. When people work together closely they discover things about each other like how old their children are, and what their hobbies and outside interests are. While these things would seem to have no impact on the project, in reality they have enormous effect on the quality of communications. As we mentioned earlier, shared characteristics improve communications. The less simplistic people's perceptions are, the better their communications.

FIGURE 6.7

Distance Effects on Communications

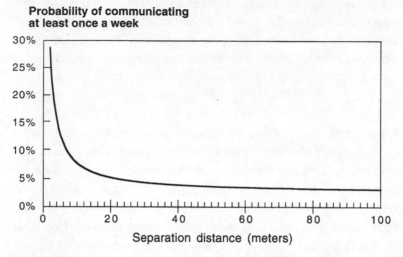

Source: Thomas J. Allen, *Managing the Flow of Technology* (Cambridge, MA: MIT Press).

Many people perceive colocation as an all or nothing choice—either we colocate the entire team for the full duration of the program or we don't. There is in fact a far richer range of options. We can vary the number of people we colocate and the duration of time they spend together as shown in Figure 6.8.

Let us look at some real-world examples. At one car company they

FIGURE 6.8

Partial Colocation

Portion of Team Colocated

Some	*All*	
Liaison	Ideal	*All*
Core Team Meetings	Off-Site Meetings	*Amount of Time Colocated*
		Some

bring the radiator team on site for a certain portion of the program. A radiator is a pretty mature technology; however, when you are styling the front end of the car there is a need for quick responses from the radiator team. Once front-end styling is completed, the radiator interface is stabilized, and you can send that team back to the radiator factory. In contrast, the radio team is never on site during the design program. They don't need to be on site because the interface between the radio and the car is standardized. When an interface is standardized, the need for communications is limited.

This illustrates a very important interaction between the architecture of the product and the logical and geographic organization of the team. The product architecture will create needs for more intense communications around the undefined interfaces within the design. The less well-characterized the interface, the more likely we are to have questions about it. Thus, an architectural interface will act as a region of the design which requires heightened and accurate communications. This heightened communication cannot be achieved if we place such an interface at either an organizational boundary or a geographic boundary. Communications will be worst if we compound the problem by placing an undefined interface on top of both an organization boundary and a geographic boundary. This suggests a powerful rule of thumb: *Never place an organization or a geographic boundary on top of a poorly characterized architectural interface.*

Astute companies have learned this lesson already. At Boeing, during the design of the Boeing 777, subcontractors were brought on site during the early stage of the program. They remained until the interface control documents (ICDs) were defined. While these documents were being defined there was an intense need for communications, so geographic distance was minimized. Once these ICDs were completed there was no longer a need to keep the subcontractors on site continuously. Thus, colocation can be used very effectively for key portions of the program even when it is not available for the full duration of the program.

At one U.S. laser printer company the representative of the Japanese print mechanism vendor is located in a trailer behind the facility. By having this representative on site instead of in Japan they gain important improvements in communications. Because the Japanese representative is acting as a liaison to his business's largest customer, he is an influential member of his parent organization. If he says that there is a problem with the print mechanism, then the people in Japan pay attention. His personal network back in the parent company has created a distortion-free high-bandwidth communications channel back into the Japanese company. This could never have been achieved if there was a geographic boundary between the two locations.

One semiconductor company debugs its capital equipment at the vendor's facility instead of at their own fabrication facility. It might appear that it would be more efficient to do this at their own fabrication facility; however, experience has shown that having a representative at the equipment vendor is a better approach. The debug goes much faster because whenever there is a problem with the equipment the engineers that designed it are only a few seconds away from the test area. If they tried to debug the equipment at their own semiconductor facility it might take days to resolve a problem.

At a medical product company a team wanted to be colocated but they could not convince the organization to do so. They finally found a small conference room back in the factory that they took over as their war room. They had telephones put in and obtained hook-ups for computer terminals. Aware of the virtue of frequent meetings, they decided to meet daily. After about a month they concluded that it was a waste of time to hold a meeting every day. Instead, they decided simply to work in the same room together from eight o'clock to nine every morning. They discovered that working in the same room produced all the benefits of a colocation. Whenever they needed to resolve an issue that cut across functional boundaries they would resolve it in the daily meeting. They were resolving issues within a day that were taking weeks for the typical team to resolve.

SUMMARY

In this chapter we have discussed the problem of designing organizations. This is a critical element of infrastructure for most development processes. We observed that many of the observations that we made about the behavior of systems apply to organizations, which are a form of system.

We examined a number of organizational forms from the perspective of their likely economics, and noted that the functional form with its vertical silos was not obsolete but likely to be optimum when development efficiency was critical. Though the autonomous team can often be optimum for speed, it has important disadvantages that arise from its autonomous nature.

We then discussed hybrid organizational forms which place power along both the functional and team axes. These forms usually optimize performance and cost. Because power is along two axes it is important to achieve clear division of responsibilities. If clear expectations of functional and team authority are not established a hybrid organization will produce little advantage.

Finally, we discussed the problem of communications, starting with the critical first step of structuring the project so that the demand for high quality communications is minimized. We also discussed both old and new technologies for communications, and the critical role that colocation can play in improving communications.

Our basic organization structure is now in place. Now we need to examine the design of our development process, which is the topic of the next chapter.

7

Design the Design Process

Once the organization context is determined we can tackle the problem of process design. In contrast to the relatively simple organizational choices in the previous chapter, development process design is much more complex. In this chapter we will try to examine this problem systematically, highlighting the key decisions underlying development process design.

To begin, we will talk about the unique and fundamental problem of designing processes for one-time activities. Then we will discuss the specific design of certain key stages of the development process. We will follow this with identification of some general design principles, and discuss the implementation of these principles to optimize certain economic objectives. Finally, we will discuss the problem of continuous improvement.

The approach outlined in this chapter is likely to be new for many product developers. Most companies' development processes are more a result of random evolution than conscious design. Such random process evolution can produce well-adapted solutions, but it is increasingly dangerous. Evolution is simply too slow when the external environment changes rapidly. Instead, we must shift to an approach of deliberate evolution, in which we analyze the process and make conscious choices.

Before we dive into the problem of process design I should be clear about how I intend to use this term. It is useful to think of design activities as recipes that contain ingredients and methods. For design the ingredients are the budget dollars, manpower, and technologies to be used. The method of using those ingredients is the process. This process defines which activities should take place, the sequence of these activities, and who should do them. Thus, our process constrains what will be done, when it will be done, and who will do it.

COMBINING STRUCTURE AND FREEDOM

The problem of designing processes is inherently different from most of the other process design problems that we confront. In life, we design most processes for repetitive activities because a process is a way of preserving learning that occurs when doing an activity. In contrast, we typically muddle through one-time activities. We unconsciously recognize that the extra effort in designing a process for a one-time activity may not improve it enough to justify this effort. Product development is one area where the extra effort of process design is rewarded handsomely. It is one of the few nonrepetitive processes that warrants careful process design.

One-Time Processes

Most manufacturing processes are inherently repetitive in nature. In contrast, as we saw in Chapter 4, when our development process becomes repetitive, it stops generating new information, and when it stops generating new information it stops being useful. This means product developers must live in a world of one-time processes. Things must constantly change, because change is the key to information generation.

Yet this constant change must be controlled. While we want to generate new information by making new mistakes, we must protect ourselves against making the old mistakes again and again. We need to find some way to preserve what we have learned without discouraging people from doing new things. I believe that the secret to doing this is to concentrate at the right level of the process architecture.

Let us start with a familiar example. Consider the design architecture of the English language. At the letter level we have rigidly standardized on twenty-six letters. Users of English cannot invent new letters, and if they did other users could not recognize them. If we move up to the word level we have about 450,000 words, of which a high school graduate might commonly recognize 40,000. We have almost complete standardization at this level. It is possible to introduce a new word into the language, but we cause some confusion when we do this. If we move up to the sentence level, there is little standardization. We have a small set of syntactic rules, such as the subject-verb-object word order, and enormous freedom everywhere else. We can produce an infinite number of well-formed, recognizable sentences in English. This infinite flexibility at the highest level of the architecture has been achieved by the standardization at the lower two levels.

This contains an important lesson for us when we design any process that needs to be flexible. Flexibility does not come from allowing all levels of the architecture to vary. This will only produce chaos. Flexibility at high levels in the architecture comes from standardization at low levels in the architecture. Paradoxically, structure is the key to freedom.

If we try to standardize product development at a high level of the process architecture we will be endlessly frustrated. We will send teams off to cover conference room walls with process maps only to discover that those maps only tell us how we chose to develop one product at one time. We might not even choose to do that product the same way a second time, because we learned something by doing it the first time.

The key is to standardize the lower levels of the process architecture. Let us now look at the two basic approaches to doing this: using a modular structure and superimposing a sequence of patterns.

Modular Processes

The simplest approach to combining structure and flexibility is to build the development process out of modules. By altering the use and sequence of these modules we can produce millions of possible process configurations without losing control.

How can we develop such modular building blocks? One answer may be in the methods that are emerging in software development in the discipline of object-oriented design. This term is a label for a number of techniques, of which one is enormously interesting to us. This is the concept of information hiding. Information hiding refers to the ability to define externally visible properties of an object at the same time as we hide certain details of internal operation. Objects can present a well-structured external interface to the world, while still preserving design freedom in their internal structure. A well-planned external interface gives us a great deal of flexibility and is the key to reusing objects.

When we design a development process we want to exploit the same properties. We want to create standardized building blocks that are defined primarily at their interfaces rather than by their internal procedures. If we standardize the interfaces we can evolve the internal structure as necessary to meet changing requirements. Because the external properties are controlled, we can change internal methods and data without unraveling our entire development process.

What might this mean in practice? Consider the problem of reliability assurance, shown in Figure 7.1. In product development we want to assure the reliability of the product. We use such things as design rules, component testing, testing of prototypes, life testing of final production versions, and field testing to do this. We might label this process module reliability assurance. The owner and designer of this module would be reliability engineering. The inputs to the module are specific objectives, constraints, and data. An objective might be attaining a 100,000-hour mean time between failures (MTBF) with a 99 percent confidence level. A constraint might be the time and budget available for testing. The data may consist of design data or physical implementations of the design, such as prototypes. The output of this module would be specific reliability data at specific times in the project. Once the inputs and outputs are defined the module owner can worry about the internal methods for doing reliability assurance.

What is powerful about this approach is that the choice of method to assure reliability is now hidden within the module. This means that the

FIGURE 7.1

Reliability Module

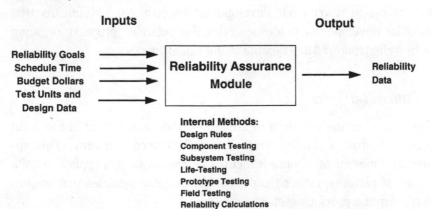

method may be flexibly tailored to fit the needs of an individual program. For example, if we were designing a consumer product like a toaster, which would be used a few minutes per day, we could dramatically accelerate testing. By running the toaster continuously, we may be able to put as much wear on it in one day as a normal consumer would create in a much longer period. If the toaster were designed for a twenty-year life with ten minutes of use per day we could test at a rate one hundred times faster than normal consumer use. In two months we could simulate an operational life of twenty years. Thus, an accelerated life test would be an appropriate tool for such a program.

In contrast, let us consider what would happen if we were designing a disk drive that would operate twenty-four hours a day with a requirement to achieve a 1,000,000-hour MTBF. It would be impractical to test the product for one hundred years before releasing it. Instead, we must find another approach to assure reliability. In this case, we could use subsystems of proven and tested reliability, and calculate the overall system-level reliability. Calculating reliability is more practical in this case than testing.

In both these cases the inputs to the reliability assurance module are objectives, constraints, and data. The module has to produce certain output information. What will be radically different between these two products is the timing of the reliability assurance activities and the specific methods used by reliability engineering. Because we have standardized the external interface instead of the internal activities, we have created a module that can be reused by many projects.

We have also created an architecture that is tolerant of change, because most changes will only affect the internal structure of the module. Thus, we can easily introduce new testing equipment and methods without having to rewrite our development procedures. This means that modular development processes offer the desirable property of being both well-structured and flexible at the same time.

A Pattern Language

There is a second approach to creating a wide assortment of top-level processes from a smaller number of well-defined elements. This approach is more subtle, since it focuses on the sequential application of a series of patterns, rather than the more tangible modules that we described in the previous section.

The use of such an approach in architectural design is described in the book *A Pattern Language,* by Christopher Alexander and colleagues. Professor Alexander provides a profound insight into the design of complex systems. He observes that the design of a complex structure, like a building, can be viewed as the sequential application of a series of patterns. For example, one architectural pattern is that rooms should have light coming in from two different sides to prevent harsh shadows. Another pattern is that there should be a transition area between the street and the inside of the house. By applying these patterns to a design problem you can create highly complex solutions to completely unique problems in a disciplined and organized way.

This search for underlying patterns is in strong contrast to the standard approach of trying to understand the world by classifying things into categories based on observable traits. We could classify houses into categories by the number of stories, the number of rooms, the architectural style, and the like. While this creates extremely complex taxonomies, it does not help us design good houses. To design good houses we must understand the underlying patterns that were applied to generate solutions for the specific design problems.

In much the same way, we could approach the development process by coming up with many ways to classify it. We could count the number of process stages, identify specific activities that occur in different phases, or compare what we do to what is done in other companies. However, unless we penetrate to the level of the underlying patterns we will not truly understand the design process. When we do penetrate down to these patterns, we break through to a level of breathtaking simplicity and clarity.

This means that we must resist our natural tendency to focus on the solutions, which are concrete, visible, and complex. Instead, we must focus on the underlying patterns which are abstract, less visible, but much simpler. A small set of powerful patterns can provide an extraordinary degree of complexity and adaptiveness without creating an extraordinarily complex process. Later in this chapter we will identify some of these underlying patterns of process design.

DESIGNING PROCESS STAGES

Let us now examine a few of the key stages of the development process, and how they might be designed. We can divide the overall process into input subprocesses, processing, and output subprocesses. Let us examine each of these in turn.

Input Subprocesses

The development process begins with some sort of input subprocess. This consists of an arrival process for the work that must be done, and a second arrival process for the resources that will do this work. Let us first look at the arrival process for the work. Do our projects arrive in clusters or one at a time? How big is the average project? How uncertain is the work associated with an individual project?

Work Arrival Processes. Our arrival process has enormous impact on the potential to generate queues in our process. As we discussed in Chapter 3, large batch sizes in our arrival process will lead to queues. Projects that arrive in clusters will increase these queues. Uncertainty in project work will further aggravate these queues. This means that we must take a careful look at the arrival processes.

The first batch size issue that we face in the development process is whether to do a large project or a small one. We can call this the choice between a megaproject or an incremental one. This is the batch size that feeds the development process, and it is important because we feel its consequences throughout the entire process. For example, imagine you are a restaurant manager and a crowd of thirty people walk in the door at the same time. All of your subsequent activities for the next two hours will be affected by initial batch size. The waiter, chef, and busboys now have a very different problem than if the people had arrived at different times in small groups. Unfortunately, most companies have a bias towards large batch sizes, or megaprojects. Since they rarely understand the full consequences of this choice, we should examine its impact.

From a purely financial perspective the megaproject extends the time between our first cash outflow and our first cash inflow. As Figure 7.2 illustrates, we not only lengthen the time until break-even but we increase the financial exposure by increasing the level of design-in-process inventory.

From a marketing perspective, we have an exponentially more difficult problem with the megaproject. The difficulty in forecasting depends on the degrees of freedom in the problem and the rate of change of the parameters. If we apply this to product development, the uncertainty in

FIGURE 7.2

Financing Megaprojects

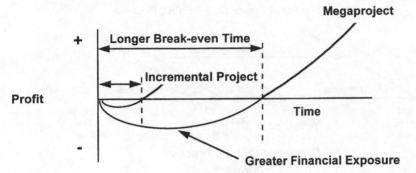

the product specification depends on degrees of freedom in the specification—usually more than two—and the rate of change in the marketplace, which can at times be significant. This means that forecasting difficulty goes up exponentially with the distance to the planning horizon. The more incremental we make our programs the easier it becomes to create a solid product specification. In most markets looking one year ahead is easy, whereas forecasting requirements five years in advance can be a fool's mission.

There are also advantages in a more incremental approach from an engineering perspective. It is much easier to motivate a development team with a short deadline than a long one. For example, the B-1 bomber took more than twenty years from when the development began until the plane flew. You could have joined the Air Force after the program started and retired twenty years later and the plane still would not have flown. It is hard to convince yourself to work late on a Friday night when you know the project you are working on won't fly until after you retire from the Air Force. Another advantage from an engineering perspective is that the complexity of the design task increases nonlinearly with the number of elements in the system. This occurs because the number of interactions between system elements rises much faster than the number of system elements, as Preston Smith and I discussed in the book *Developing Products in Half the Time*.

If we wish to be more incremental we need a front-end process that will permit this. Unfortunately, the classic annual strategic planning process is not well suited for fast cycle time, because it releases a large batch of ideas into the development process at one time. For example, the strategy planning process might collect ideas all year long and sub-

FIGURE 7.3
Alternative Arrival Processes

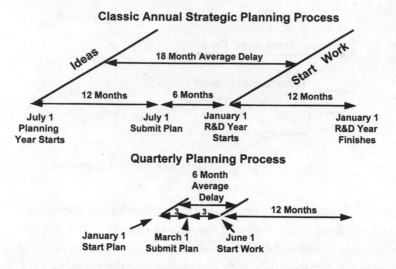

mit them in July for the next year's product development plan. Work for the next year would begin in January and last until December. This means that the average idea has waited eighteen months between the time it was conceived until when it got worked on. An idea that appears in August will wait until January two years later for the earliest time work could begin. This is a minimum delay of sixteen months and a maximum delay of twenty-eight months. What causes this delay? Quite simply it is the faulty design of the input process, which is releasing large batches to our design process.

We might contrast that with a quarterly planning process. When new ideas are planned one quarter in advance the average delay drops to six months. This is a three-to-one improvement in front-end cycle time with no change in development capacity or demand. It is a dramatic compression in front-end cycle time for a relatively simple change in the structure of our planning process, as shown in Figure 7.3.

Optimum Batch Size. In addition to smoothing the arrival of work coming out of our strategic planning process, we are interested in controlling the magnitude of work in individual projects. The magnitude of the development task that we undertake on an individual project is equivalent to the batch size of our development process. Let us borrow some concepts developed for evaluating batch size in manufacturing processes.

FIGURE 7.4

Optimum Product Increments

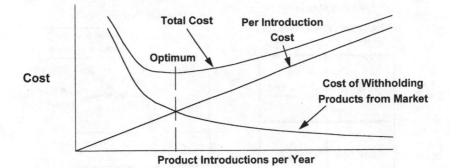

To calculate the optimum batch size in an engineering process we must make a tradeoff between the holding cost of the design-in-process inventory and the fixed cost of doing each product introduction. If our batch size is very small—that is, our steps are very incremental—we will incur the cost of doing an introduction many times. If our batch size is very large we will withhold economically useful ideas from the marketplace. When we withhold such ideas we incur a cost which is proportional to the value of the ideas and the time that we withhold them. Fortunately, we can calculate this using the cost of delay analysis that we presented in Chapter 2. We can arrive at an optimum batch size by minimizing the sum of these two costs.

Figure 7.4 shows the results of one such calculation. You will note that the optimum batch size is neither very small nor very large. Furthermore, the optimum point is a shallow-bottomed U-curve which means that you don't have to get a perfect answer.

Is incremental innovation automatically a best practice? No. Let us illustrate this with the example of the locomotive industry in the United States which went from 95 percent steam to 95 percent diesel in about ten years. During those ten years there were tremendous incremental improvements in steam engines, yet every steam engine manufacturer went bankrupt. The problem was that there is no incremental path between steam and diesel.

But consider what would have happened it we had bet on diesel ten years too early. We would have lost all our money. Likewise, if we had bet on diesel ten years too late we would have missed the opportunity. Using a tool from game theory we can construct a payoff matrix like that

FIGURE 7.5

Game Theory and Incremental Innovation

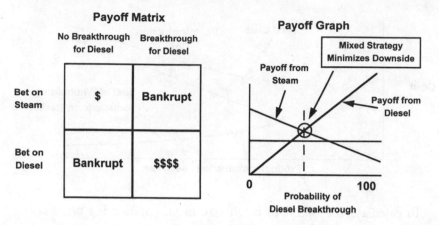

shown in Figure 7.5. The classic solution to this problem is to use a mixed strategy betting a certain portion of your resources on incremental innovation and a certain portion on the breakthrough. In an uncertain world this will give us the best overall outcome. In the uncertain world of product development the best product portfolios will have a mix of large and small batch size projects.

Technology vs. Product Development

We have discussed the arrival process of the development tasks, or problems. There is however, another important arrival process: the timing of when technological solutions to these problems become available. We can wait for the technology to be developed before we start product development, or we can develop it while we do product development. If we wait to develop technology first, we lose the opportunity to overlap technology and product development. If we embed technology development in our product programs we run the risk that our product programs will be held hostage by delays in this technology. Let us take a careful look at these issues.

Our key design decision is how closely to couple our technology development and our product development. Technology development is inherently different from product development because it is more uncertain in its costs, performance, and schedule. Tight coupling of technology and the program has some advantages. In general we should get better performance, lower cost, and cheaper development if we build our technology on the critical path of the program. In theory, by working on the critical path we get very tight coupling to the needs of the program. We will only develop the technology necessary to meet the needs of the program. Furthermore, technology transfer becomes very easy. Thus, tight coupling fulfills the economic objective of low development expense. Unfortunately, tight coupling can lead to project delays. To understand why, we must look more carefully at what will happen to variability of the product program.

If we couple technology too closely to the product program, its variability will taint the variability of the product. This technology variability raises the uncertainty of product cost, schedule, and performance. As we mentioned in Chapter 5, this occurs because a system will have at least the variability of its most variable component. If we insert highly variable technology development onto the critical path of the program, then the product schedule will become as unpredictable as the technology development is.

Achieving the objective of low unit cost or high product performance requires solutions lying between these two extremes. When we find a single candidate technology, it is appropriate to tightly couple technology and product development. This ensures the product is designed to fully exploit the technology, and the technology is optimized for the intended product design. In contrast, when there are multiple competing technologies to sort out, it is usually better to pull technology development outside of the program. This prevents premature polarization around one particular solution, which will naturally occur in cohesive work groups.

Let us look at an example of what can happen when we incorrectly put technology development on the critical path. Consider what happened at an industrial component manufacturer that waited until it needed to develop technology. They did not want to risk investing $50,000 of R&D into an area that might not be useful. Instead, technology development took place on the critical path. Ironically, they saved no money, and delayed the program by three months, incurring a cost of delay of $500,000. They paid $500,000 for the chance of saving $50,000 of technology development—a bad bargain.

An alternative that many companies are beginning to use is to develop technology off the critical path. This is quite common in Japanese companies where it is sometimes referred to as creating a technology shelf. While this approach brings many benefits it requires skillful management in its execution. We face a new set of problems when we do technology development off the critical path. We now need a technology planning system, a way of preserving resource allocation, and a technology transfer mechanism.

First, a technology planning system is necessary because we no longer have the program to force development of the technology. Instead, we are trying to anticipate the needs of the program, which requires us to forecast technology. Second, we need a way to preserve resource allocation for technology development. It is quite common for companies to steal resources away from technology development to use for other product programs. This is common because product programs have near-term profits associated with them and technology programs do not. Third, we must have a technology transfer mechanism. For all that has been written about technology transfer, the solution for this problem is extraordinarily simple. Transfer some of the people when you transfer the technology. Doing so will dramatically increase the chance of a successful transplant.

In summary, we will lean to tightly coupled technology when we are trying to maximize the efficiency of our development process. We will loosen this coupling when we are concerned with development speed. The objectives of performance and unit cost lie between these two extremes, depending on the number of candidate technologies that are available to solve the design problem.

Controlling Queues

Thus far we have talked about input processes for product development. Now we must consider what goes on inside of the development process. As we saw in Chapter 3 a critical question in process design is the batch size of the process. We get large queues whenever we have large batch transfers in the process.

Interestingly, most of the current dogma on product development is based on the use of large batch transfers. Consider for a moment what are called phase-gate development processes. These processes require that a project stay in a given phase until all criteria to pass into the next phase are met. No product can be in more than one phase at time. The basic batch size in such a process is 100 percent of the work product. This is maximum theoretical batch size—we cannot make batch size larger than this.

Such large batch sizes are likely to have some scale economies. For example, transferring three thousand engineering drawings to purchasing the day after the final design review will be more efficient than transferring these drawings one at a time. However, we pay a very high price for these scale economies. In practice such large batch transfers are likely to maximize unit cost, minimize performance, and increase development cycle time. Let us look at each of these issues in turn.

Cost and performance suffer because large batch transfer processes typically suffer from a rigidly sequential mindset. The manufacturing people get involved late in the development process when it is difficult and expensive to change the product. A slight change in dimensions, one that could have easily been accommodated early in the design cycle, is identified too late to make the change. As a result the design is not quite tuned to the production process, sacrificing quality and cost. In fact, the whole movement to concurrent engineering has been motivated by this recognition that quality, schedule, and cost are optimized when we overlap development process stages. To overlap stages is simply another way of saying that we have moved to smaller process batch sizes.

Furthermore, there is another very serious conceptual flaw in embedding large batch transfers in development processes. Remember what we observed in Chapter 3 about combining large batch size activities with small batch size activities. We said that the small batches should be grouped and placed in front of the large batches. This ensures that the large batch activities will not create queues for the downstream processes.

But what does a phase-gate system do? It alternates design activities which are small batch processes with phase gates that are large batch processes. This is almost the worst possible process design from a queueing perspective. It guarantees repeated and massive queues. It will almost automatically double the cycle time of the process, as is shown in the cumulative flow diagram in Figure 7.6. Such phase-gate systems are poorly suited for fast development, but they can be useful for risk management and can be used effectively in markets with low costs of delay.

Subprocess Design

Just the way we can design the overall process we can design the individual activities that make up the development process. For example, let us pick the person who does finite element modeling in the design. This finite element modeling has the same four economic objectives that we

FIGURE 7.6

Phase Gate vs. Overlapping Process

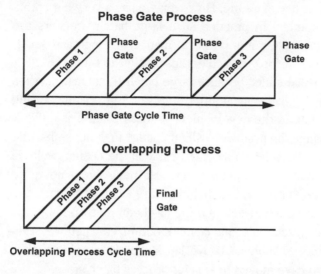

discussed in Chapter 2. Mirroring the way we think about overall process design, we need to optimize our subprocesses based on economics.

For example, the finite element modeler may have eight hours of work to do on the average product, costing $50 per hour. The queue in the finite element modeling area may be one week on the critical path of the program, having a cost of delay of $500,000 per month. A good finite element model may remove 5 percent of the material cost on a subassembly of which $5 million worth will be purchased during the life of the product. The finite element model may have no effect on performance, in the sense of impacting sell price and market share. What do the total economics of this subprocess look like? As we can see from Figure 7.7, the process economics are dominated by the cost of delay and the unit cost impact. The actual expenses are worth $400. The delay cost is worth $125,000. The unit cost impact is $250,000.

This suggests priorities for designing this subprocess. First, we should be critically concerned with how much it reduces product cost. Second, we should try to reduce the delay cost, either by taking it off the critical path of the program or by minimizing the size of the queue. Our lowest priority should be optimizing the efficiency of the modeling activity. Yet ironically, optimizing the efficiency of subprocesses is the primary focus of many development processes. Most of the control effort is focused on efficiency. For example, Wheelright and Clark's excellent

FIGURE 7.7

Finite Element Modeling Subprocess Economics

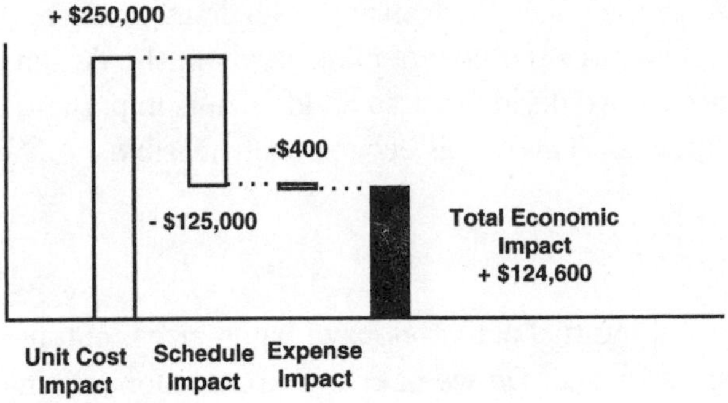

+ $250,000

-$400

- $125,000

Total Economic
Impact
+ $124,600

Unit Cost Schedule Expense
Impact   Impact   Impact

book *Managing New Product and Process Development* depicts an efficiency curve which peaks when two projects are assigned to each engineer. Such a curve is only important when development process efficiency is the key objective. For example, for high-cost-of-delay settings the cycle time savings of one project per engineer are likely to be much more important than the efficiency penalty of having fewer than two projects. In contrast, in situations where technical performance is paramount a shared expert is likely to have such performance impact that the inefficiency of sharing the expert across more than two products will be trivial.

A second consideration for subprocess design is the batch size of the subprocess. The EOQ model applies at the subprocess level. There are optimum batch sizes for individual subprocesses. For example, if a life test on a product took eight weeks to complete, we could do the test and prepare a report at the end of the eight weeks. In this case our batch size would be 100 percent, which maximizes the efficiency of the person writing the report. An alternative would be to write four reports during the life test, with equal intervals between them. Multiple reports take more effort but they make key test findings available to the design team much earlier.

A final lesson to remember when we do subprocess design is that what we call "fixed cost" in the EOQ model is not always as fixed as it appears. For example, in the test process above we might assume that writing the test report takes four hours each time we do it. In reality, four smaller reports should take much less time apiece. We might be able to lower preparation time to ten or fifteen minutes by designing some preformatted spreadsheets to analyze the data, and word processing templates to report it. In the extreme, we might put the data on-line so that every life test failure is available to the design team on-line immediately after the failure is logged by the tester. Such an approach dramatically reduces the lot size, and accelerates the flow of information in the design process. The key is that once we decide that small lot size is important, then we can design our process to make this economically feasible.

Output Processes

Just as input processes and internal activities have batch sizes, output processes have batch sizes as well. Do we offer our product for sale in one large batch or do we offer it in smaller increments? For example, one computer peripheral company had a standard doctrine that they must have 100,000 units available for sale in the warehouse before they could offer the product for sale. The time it took to build these first 100,000 units was an important portion of the overall development process. When they reevaluated this decision they realized that it was better to start selling smaller quantities early.

The issue of output batch size also applies to product features. For some products it is very realistic to offer a version for sale that has not been completely optimized. For example, we may desire to offer the product for heavy duty applications. However, if the test to validate the product in this application will take three months to complete, we can begin selling the product for light duty applications and then revise the product ratings when the new test data become available. This allows us to generate sales, develop distribution, and get market position before we complete the final testing.

KEY DESIGN PRINCIPLES

Let us now try to distill some general principles or patterns for development process design. Four key patterns begin to emerge when we look at the above issues of process design. First, we must choose the degree of overlap to use in the process. Such a choice increases the concurrency of activities in the process and decreases the process batch size. Second, we must decide how to manage information profiles within the process. Early generation of information can be expensive, but in certain cases it is very valuable. Third, we must decide how centralized to make our control processes. This decision will usually affect our ability to respond to change. Finally, we must decide on the location of our large batch queues. Large batch queues can affect cycle time, particularly when they are incorrectly sequenced.

Sequential vs. Concurrent Processes

The critical design choice to overlap process activities can be described in different ways. It can be labeled as an increase in concurrency. Alternatively it can be viewed as a decrease in process batch size. Viewing it from the perspective of concurrency highlights the impact on cycle time. Viewing from the perspective of batch size highlights other benefits such as faster feedback cycles and lower design-in-process inventory.

As we have seen earlier we emphasize the pattern of overlapping processes when we wish to minimize time, minimize product cost, or maximize performance. Such goals come up very frequently. We choose the opposite approach of using a very sequential process when we wish to minimize development spending, and to carefully control risk. The vast majority of academic literature on product development is skewed towards the sequential approach. This is in striking contrast to the enormous shift that is taking place in managerial practice towards a more concurrent approach. The academic bias towards sequential functional processes may be due to the fact that most business schools are still functionally organized, as business was forty years ago, and they have had trouble reacting to the shift to cross-functional activity.

The importance of overlapping processes for speed is universally recognized. As Preston Smith and I described in detail in our book, *Developing Products in Half the Time,* there are many sound reasons for improving the speed of the development process. There are also many exciting and unexpected benefits to improving cycle time. This does not, however, mean that cycle time will always be the process parameter of greatest value or that concurrent processes are universally preferred. Sequential processes will remain very common in organizations that are resource-constrained. Since many organizations fall in this category, the need for sequential processes is likely to persist.

For example, consider a company that makes hardware components for electrical contractors. Such components may have a sales life of thirty years. Having a larger number of components in its catalogue is important because many customers would like to use fewer suppliers.

The margins in this business are low, so they cannot afford to spend much on product development. Therefore, it becomes very important to do a cost-effective design and get it right the first time. Delay in product introduction is not likely to be a big issue since the adoption process of customers is slow and switching costs for customers are low. Thus, a late market entrant with a full product line and a good cost position can still get lots of market share. What would the best process be for such a company? Clearly, a sequential development process would optimize the parameters that are of greatest economic value.

I should however caution that many organizations do not achieve the potential efficiency of sequential processes. Problems occur because downstream groups are involved too late in the design process. Since most of the performance, cost, and expense is controlled by activities early in the design process it is essential to get inputs from the experts in these areas early, before the cost of reacting to these inputs becomes too high. The experts on cost are in manufacturing. They may include material vendors, assembly workers, and manufacturing engineers. Getting their input early is critical to achieving low costs. The experts on value are the customers; they too must react to the product early to maximize value. This leads us to our second design pattern.

Managing Information Profiles

The second design choice is the way we generate information during the development process. We call this the information profile of the process. As discussed in Chapter 4 we generate information early when we reduce risk early in the design process. This early information generation is valuable because the cost of change rises very rapidly near the end of the development process. In other words, information has less economic value when it is generated late in the development process. It follows that a key attribute of the development process will be how it accomplishes risk reduction. If this risk reduction takes place late in the process, the economics will suffer.

In Chapter 12 we will segment risk more precisely into market and technical risk. Of these two, the larger risk is typically market risk—the risk that the product specification will not meet the customer's true need. We can accelerate the reduction of market risk with testing in the early and middle stages of the development process.

Likewise, the technical risk—the risk that the design will not meet its specification—can be proactively managed. For most products, this risk will come from two sources: high-risk modules and system integration risk. Of these two system integration risk is usually the highest. This means that technical risk can be substantially reduced by pulling system integration to an earlier phase of the process.

Thus, the critical issue for managing risk profiles is the timing of our risk reduction activities. To force early risk reduction we normally have to spend more money. For example, a test market is an extra expense for a program. Whether this expense is justified or not depends on the value of the information that is generated and the expense of obtaining this information. We would not spend $1 million to assess the sales forecast of a product that will generate $4 million of revenue over its life. Instead, we will rely on actual sales data. We need to buy information for the right price, at the right time, in our process. We will discuss techniques for doing this in Chapter 12.

Decentralizing Control and Feedback

Another critical process design choice is whether to centralize or decentralize control. Centralized control is usually more economical in terms of expenses, whereas decentralized control typically results in better responsiveness. It is usually preferable to decentralize control when we are trying to make a process adaptive to external forces. Thus, a decentralized control strategy is usually best in rapidly moving market segments.

Thinking back to the systems theory of Chapter 5, such decentralization is typically achieved by defining specialized roles within the system and assigning these roles to different modules. A risk in doing this is that the individual modules may try to optimize locally to meet their own needs, rather than respecting the need for system-level optimization. For example, someone who does technical documentation may be given a budget, a schedule, and a definition of the work project. If we measure this person primarily on budget adherence she may resist spending extra money on outside contractors. Yet at a program level outside contractors may reduce the cost of delay by more than they add expense.

Perhaps the most powerful way to maintain control while forcing actual decisions down to low levels of the organization is to provide control rules for the organization. This causes decisions to be made within predetermined parameters without delaying these decisions. For example, we might tell a design team that every square millimeter of an integrated circuit design is worth $100,000 and every month late on the design is worth $2 million. This would establish clear tradeoff rules between these two parameters. With such rules, we do not have to participate in every decision. Such a rule-based control system gives excellent control without delaying decision making, as we will discuss in Chapter 11.

Location of Batch Queues

The fourth key decision in our process design is the location of our large batch queues. As we discussed earlier in this chapter large batch queues damage cycle time. Nonetheless, a development process with a few massive go/no-go checkpoints has one important advantage. It permits management control of program risk with a relatively small effort. By having a few centralized decision points we can control the entire program's financial exposure in just a few hours of meetings. This is clearly economical in terms of management time, which permits management to control more programs to a greater level of detail.

The price we pay for these checkpoints is that they can delay the program substantially. As we discussed earlier, if we intersperse phase checkpoints with small batch size design activities we lengthen cycle time. This illustrates a key principle: keep small batch processes together. This clustering of large and small batch transfers into separate process stages will minimize total queues.

If you must have large batch sizes, they should be placed at the end of the process. As you may recall from the customs processing example that we discussed in Chapter 3, any time we follow a large batch process with a small batch process we will lengthen the cycle time of the process. The key thing to remember is that we have to make a choice on both the size of our queues and the sequence in which they appear in our process. The worst place to place large batch transfers is near the beginning of the design process, which is unfortunately where many development processes put them.

SPECIFIC PROCESS IMPLEMENTATIONS

Let us now summarize how we might use these techniques in real development processes which have to be optimized for the four key economic objectives that we discussed in Chapter 2.

A process designed for speed will emphasize high levels of overlap and small batch sizes. The best strategy for speed is to minimize the magnitude of market and technical risk. We do this by targeting known customers and developing the technology off the critical path of the program. Our subprocesses will be designed to have low fixed costs and small batch sizes. We will be trying to optimize the entire design process for minimum queue sizes, which, as we saw in Chapter 3, can be directly translated into faster cycle times.

A process optimized for low development expense will make almost opposite choices. We will use little overlap and large batch sizes. We must keep technology development off the critical path to avoid any wasted spending on technology development. We can do annual strategic planning and have large batch sizes in our output processes. We should optimize our subprocesses for minimum expenses. We will be unconcerned about queues in our process, because these queues ensure efficient loading of our resources.

A process design for low unit cost will lie somewhere between these two extremes. To achieve low unit cost we must obtain heavy input from manufacturing early in the design process. This will drive us to use a more concurrent approach to the process, but this concurrency will be specifically focused on activities related to unit cost. We will often use smaller batch size with regard to manufacturing-related tasks. For example, on the Boeing 777 the release process for engineering drawings provided for different levels of manufacturing release. A traditional approach treats a drawing as having two states: released and not released. Boeing established up to seven levels of release which gave the manufacturing planners a clear indication of the confidence level and expected stability of information contained in a particular drawing.

A process design focused on maximizing performance will take a different approach, since we are trying to push the technology of the product to its limits. This means that there may be significant technical risk in the design which we need to resolve as early in the design process as possible. To do so we will structure the process to do technical testing early. Such tests will include feasibility tests for key concepts, subsystem tests, accelerated reliability testing, and the like. These tests may increase costs, but they provide a solid technical foundation for the design. We also want to get lots of market feedback early in the process. Early market testing gives us feedback on whether the changes in technical performance will translate into a change in the revenue stream, which is our measure of business performance.

It should be clear that there are no general "best practices" for process design. There are only "best" ways to achieve certain objectives. These best methods are really patterns that are useful in a particular context. Since this context will vary for each company it is very likely that each company's development process will be unique.

EVOLVING THE PROCESS

The task of creating a development process is never completed. Once we have designed the process we need to change it to keep up with changes in the environment. This process improvement will only occur if we attempt to learn from new information generated by the development process itself. Importantly, this is not information about the product, but rather information about the process. Everything we learn in development has potential implications to change our process. For example, we may discover in beta testing (our first user tests of the completed product) that the user thinks our new oscilloscope design is too complicated to use. We could react to this defect by simplifying the design of the instrument. However, we must not stop here. We also learned about the defect in our process. The process did not cause us to either avoid this problem or detect it early enough. The process must be changed to safeguard against this problem. In an evolving process each failure generates information that results in a change in the process.

One way to look at this is in terms of the number of cycles of learning that we go through in a particular period of time. When we reduce the length of a learning cycle, which in our case is the length of our development cycle, we decrease the time it takes to incorporate new information into our development process. The development process always generates new information about itself, but we cannot capture this value until we incorporate it into our process. The faster we do this the sooner our development process begins earning money for us.

How do companies actually make such process changes? It usually requires some kind of formal review of the lessons that are learned in the course of development. For example, Michael Cusumano, in his book *Microsoft Secrets,* describes the post-mortems that are routinely done on software projects at Microsoft. Process-oriented reviews go under many names, of which we prefer a term which focuses on learning, like "lessons-learned session." Whatever you choose to call it, there a couple of things to remember when you do it.

First, it should be done as soon after the end of the program as possible. Often, much of the key learning is very perishable. Product developers, particularly the good ones, are quickly shifted to other activities as soon as a project is over. The last project rapidly fades into the background as the new one becomes the focus of attention. Since most of the thinking during a project is focused on product, it is quite easy for process-oriented insight to vanish like the morning fog. You must move fast to capture this learning. In theory, it could be extracted continuously throughout the development process. In practice, we rarely find companies are capable of doing this. The pressure to work on product invariably shifts the focus away from process. Most organizations are more effective when they try to learn at the end of their development process. An added benefit of end-of-project reviews is that the true impact of a process choice may not be visible part way in the process. For example, we may consider ourselves clever for having done our market research very quickly, only to discover at product introduction that we missed critical customer needs.

Second, the review should take a balanced approach. There are natural perceptual errors that humans fall victim to. We are prone to exaggerating both the good aspects of a good project and the bad aspects of a bad one. We will identify a handful of obvious factors and deemphasize many other useful aspects of the project. We will also tend to treat a project as being much more homogeneous than it really is. People will talk about good projects as if everything done was good, and about bad projects as if everything done was bad. Both of these mindsets will prevent us from learning as much as we could. The best projects always do some things poorly and the worst do some things well. One way to protect yourself from this imbalance is to structure the review to identify strong and weak points for all projects.

Third, it is very valuable to get people who were not members of the team involved in the review process. For a variety of reasons the opinions of those involved in the process are likely to be influenced by the program itself. They are unlikely to be as aware of certain strengths and weaknesses. For example, one company used a competitor product as the target to beat in their design. This concrete, stable target acted as an anchor for the program. The result was a superb new product with almost no feature creep. Interestingly, none of the members of the team recognized the power of using a competitor product as the stable, concrete target or their weakness in generating their own specification. It required an outsider to the team to identify these issues.

Fourth, the review session should be solution-oriented. The best post-mortem reviews discuss both the problems and the potential solutions for these problems. They must focus more on preventing the problems in the future than they do on assigning blame to the guilty.

Once we have generated a healthy set of opportunities we must weed them down to a limited set of high-impact actions. It is dangerous to dilute the attention of the organization over too many issues. A good approach is to capture many opportunities but to plan action on only a handful of them. The obvious reason for this is that the true payoff of the post-mortem is the action that results from it. In organizations with limited resources you cannot do everything immediately. If you try to take action on too many things you are unlikely to get rapid progress on any of them. Then, because you fail to get rapid progress, people who are committing time and attention to post-mortems lose interest. The best way to maintain organizational energy is to take quick action on a subset of opportunities identified in the post-mortem reviews.

This, of course, implies that such reviews require the support of top management. A common way to do this is to have top management introduce the review process, explain to reviewers its importance, listen to its findings, and announce the action that will be taken as a result of the review. By taking action quickly, or even identifying action plans quickly, you energize the process and signal its importance.

You may wonder how long it takes to do such a review. Usually, there is little correlation between the value of the review and its duration. Very lengthy reviews are often based on generating piles of data. Such reviews may create an aura of objectivity because of that, but in practice, the data is rarely as useful as insightful discussion among project members and outsiders. It is not unusual to do a post-mortem review and discover that the most important issues for the team did not appear on any of the data collection forms.

Finally, if we practice what we preach, we should treat the post-mortem as another process. It too, can be improved. This means that the last question that we ask during a postmortem is always, "How can we make the postmortem process itself more effective?"

SUMMARY

In this chapter we have tackled the complex problem of process design. Our key message is that there is not one "best" process design but rather that there is a logical way to approach the problem. When we systematically look at issues like the design of input and output processes using some of the concepts of queueing theory and information theory, we identify different design solutions for different contexts.

We began by discussing some powerful concepts for designing one-time processes which were modular process structures and pattern languages. We then studied the design of particular process stages and subprocesses. Following this we reviewed some general principles that can be extracted from specific solutions, and we looked at how these principles could be applied to design processes optimized for speed, expense, unit cost, or performance. Finally, we discussed the problem of evolving the process to deal with changes in technology and changes in the external environment.

Again we must stress that the design of process should be driven by the economic objectives that we are trying to achieve and the relative importance of these economic objectives. There are no best processes, there are only processes that are designed to attain certain objectives.

Two key contextual factors have influenced our product development discussion in the last two chapters: the design of our organization and the design of our process. There is a another factor that is almost invisible to most managers, yet it has extraordinary impact. It is the architecture of the product. In the next chapter we will examine this issue.

8

Product Architecture:
The Invisible Design

The architecture of the product is a third key context for our product development process. In many ways the importance of product architecture is a well-kept secret. It is a topic that rarely gets management attention. At best it is left to the system architect, at worst it is managed by nobody. In some companies it gets so little attention that you cannot even find the person who is in charge of product architecture. Yet, architecture is what determines the fundamental economics of the product.

Let us illustrate this with a fairly well-known example, the Japanese attack on the low-priced copier market. The Japanese companies faced a formidable challenge. Xerox, with a dominant technological advantage, owned the copier market in the United States. It had a sales and service organization that was larger than all other companies combined. How could the Japanese meet the needs of the marketplace without a huge investment to duplicate Xerox's sales and service organization? The solution was a striking example of the astute use of product architecture.

The Japanese recognized that Xerox's huge sales and service organization was only an asset for certain market segments. In other market segments, such as the market for low-priced copiers for small businesses, this huge organization was simply a cost burden. Selling low-cost copiers through a low-markup channel such as an office products distributor would eliminate the cost of direct selling. However, since these office product dealers could not match the service organization of

144

Xerox, they would need a product that was highly reliable. This is where architecture came in.

The primary reliability problem on a copier was the handling of the document that was being copied. This document might be bent, folded, or deformed with staple holes. When this original moved through the paper path, it often jammed. How could this reliability weakness be avoided? By not moving the original document. The Japanese redesigned the architecture of the copier to use a moving platen that handled the original document. Now the only paper that had to be handled was the copy, which was a sheet of brand-new, high-quality paper. The paper-handling problems disappeared. This highly reliable architecture did not need a service organization. It could be sold through a low-overhead channel like an office products dealer. Overnight, Xerox's great strengths in sales and service were turned into a millstone around their neck. This example illustrates not only the extraordinary value of good architecture, but also how it must be tightly integrated into the business strategy.

Like the development process, the architecture of the product can be optimized to achieve certain objectives. In this chapter, we will discuss some underlying principles of architecture management and then look at how we can apply these principles to optimize the architecture for the four key economic objectives from Chapter 2, expense, cost, performance, and schedule.

UNDERLYING PRINCIPLES

There are three key underlying factors that we exploit when we try to use architecture to achieve our economic objectives. First, we must make decisions with regard to how modular to make the product. Second, we must partition the design to control the impact of variability. Third, we need to manage the internal interfaces of the design. We will discuss each of these factors in turn.

Modularity

Our first key decision is whether to make the product modular. The decision to use a modular structure is a complex one. It impacts economics and interacts with organization structure and development process design. Let us begin by considering the economic dimensions of the problem.

As a general rule, the two economic objectives most favored by modularity are development expense and cycle time. The advantages that we gain in these areas will typically come at the expense of gross margin, either in the form of higher unit costs or performance weaknesses that will hurt our revenue stream.

First, let us look at how modularity affects development expenses. It can reduce the communications overhead on a team, allowing designers to concentrate more time on value-added tasks. This lower overhead arises because modularity inherently hides details about the internal implementation within a module from the other modules that it interfaces with. By hiding these implementation details other module designers only need to know how the interfaces work. This means that each module team needs to know less total information about other parts of the system, which in turn means more time spent doing design work and less time talking about it.

We should note that the benefit of reduced expenses will only come when a system is partitioned properly and the interfaces are properly defined. This is the secret art of product architecture. If we partition the product poorly then everything will interact with everything else and we will need more communications, not less. If we fail to provide adequate margin in the interfaces then they will change during the design, which will cause rework. We will talk more about these critical issues later in this chapter.

The second broad impact that modularity has on development expense is that it permits reuse of modules from other designs. This can save enormous amounts of design time on projects. It is not unusual to see more than half of the required design hours of a project eliminated by a carefully designed reuse plan.

While modularity reduces development expenses, this is not its only impact. It also has a dramatic impact on development cycle time because it permits us to do concurrent development of subsystems rather than having to develop them sequentially. Figure 8.1 shows two ways of designing a system. In the first, we do the modules in a logical sequence. We wait until we have all the information required for the next module before we start it. This is the traditional approach to engineering design, and the one most engineers are trained at in college. It is efficient, but very sequential.

There is another approach to design, which emphasizes parallel design activities. In this approach we define a modular structure and work

FIGURE 8.1

Sequential and Parallel Design

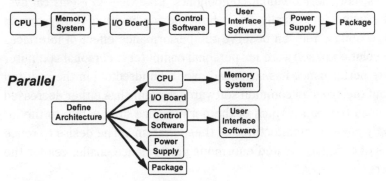

on these modules in parallel. Such parallel effort requires that we define interfaces between subsystems early in the design process. When managed correctly, the parallel approach to design will result in much shorter development cycles.

The potential dark side of modularity is its cost and performance consequences. The interfaces that we create within our systems do not come for free. They can either add cost to the system or act as a performance bottleneck. The cost impact of modularity can be complex, because there are two counterbalancing factors, one at the interfaces and one in the modules. At the interface level cost usually increases because we add parts such as connectors, cables, couplings, flanges, or lines of code. At the module level costs can either rise or fall. They will often rise because the module is designed to meet the needs of many products instead of just one. For example, one software company discovered its general-purpose, reusable modules had three times as many lines of code as equivalent specialized modules in similar products. On the other hand, module costs can also fall when the scale economies of larger production volumes outweigh the cost of added functionality. For example, a multipurpose power supply can often be purchased at lower cost than a dozen specialized power supplies, even though no individual application requires all of its capability. We need to be careful analyzing the cost impact of modularity because it depends on cross-program economics and cannot be assessed on the basis of a single development project.

Modularity will also affect performance. Interfaces typically act as bottlenecks within the system, which means that we cannot achieve the same level of performance as a tightly coupled nonmodular system. For example, the weak spot in most mechanical structures is likely to be the interfaces, not the individual components. Likewise, in electrical systems the connectors usually either limit the bandwidth of the system or reduce reliability. You can observe the performance effect of interfaces in the evolution of software for personal computers. Personal computer hardware performance has advanced over a hundredfold in the past ten years, but the speed of common software programs has either decreased or remained the same. Much of the performance drag is due to the increasingly modular architectures of these systems. The desire to reuse modules of code has created enormous performance challenges for the designers.

An interesting example of the effect of economics occurs in oscilloscope design. Early oscilloscopes by Tektronix had strong modular structures. Such structures offered significant advantages to both the purchaser and Tektronix. However, low-priced oscilloscopes cannot bear the cost of much modularity. Interfaces add expensive parts such as connectors, and add extra labor cost to the design. As a result, virtually all low-priced oscilloscopes use nonmodular designs. They simply cannot afford the cost penalty of modularity.

Finally, we should emphasize that there is a strong interaction between the design of our organization structure, our architecture, and our development process. The modules in the architecture represent natural groupings for the team members. Teams will usually be most effective if they are organized around the modular structure of the product. For example, if a piece of heavy machinery is divided into power train and auxiliary systems, the team should be organized around these modules. This will be much more effective than grouping all the structural engineers in one section and the hydraulic engineers in another. Product architecture and organization structure should fit one another.

Furthermore, there must be a fit between architecture and process. If we have partitioned the design into relatively independent modules we have the ability to run these modules on decoupled paths. For example, we can begin reliability testing on the drive train before we have completed detailed design of the auxiliary systems. This allows us to break away from a traditional approach that insists that all detailed design must be complete before we do any testing. Such a paradigm shift can be worth amazing amounts of cycle time.

In summary, the choice to be modular is in its essence an economic decision, not a philosophical one. We must look carefully at how the modular structure might affect schedule, development expense, unit cost, and performance. We must know how much it is worth to change each of these parameters on a particular program. Fortunately, if you have performed the project-level analysis described in Chapter 2, you already know this.

Segregating Variability

A second key architectural decision is how we handle variability within the system. In Chapter 5, we discussed how the variability of the entire system was driven by the variability of its most variable element. This was an oversimplification. In reality, not every system has to be as variable as its most variable element. Instead, we can segregate the variability into a limited area of the system. This principle applies to variability in cost, expense, performance, or schedule. This is actually a rather striking departure from the traditional way of partitioning a system. Most classical architectural doctrine advocates grouping related functions and minimizing communications within the system. It is argued that this will produce simpler interfaces and less complexity in the program. I would argue that one should also consider partitioning the system to concentrate key economic risks.

For example, consider the design of an electronic musical synthesizer. There may be great uncertainty regarding the button configuration on the front panel. Users may express preferences before purchase that change once they get experience using the system. This means that the button layout is very risky. A traditional approach would use a single-piece plastic enclosure with holes for the individual buttons. This exposes the program to both schedule and cost risk if field testing forces a change in the button layout. How can we segregate risk within the system? We could make the enclosure from two pieces of plastic. The first would be the main body of the enclosure, the second a small flat plastic insert with the holes for the buttons which could be attached to the main body. All of the potential change would thus be contained in a small inexpensive part. Changing this part would cost less, and take less time, than modifying the much larger enclosure.

Once we have segregated variability we can use other management techniques to control its impact. For example, we can buffer these subsystems from our schedule by taking them off the critical path. We can buffer these subsystems from our development budget and unit costs by creating back-up design solutions, or using vendors to assume some of this risk. First, we partition the system on the basis of risk, and then we develop methods of protecting ourselves from this more concentrated risk.

Interface Management

As you may suspect by now, interfaces are where the action is in the problem of architecture. It is almost universal that experienced system architects recognize interfaces as the most important control point in the system. Unfortunately, it is easy to be distracted by system components because they absorb most of the design work and determine the cost of the system. Despite this, as we discussed in Chapter 5, it is the interfaces that determine performance, riskiness, and ultimately, the value of the system.

The importance of interfaces is often overlooked because we are constantly lured away by the concrete nature of module design. For example, Pahl and Beitz, in their book *Engineering Design,* conclude that most design problems originate in component design. It is easy to reach this conclusion. When you have a design problem, and ask what needs to be changed to fix it, the answer is always a component, so you conclude that the component was the cause of the problem. In reality, for many systems the root cause of component redesign is really poor interface design. The solution to your problem may be to modify the component design, but the cause was that the component design was done either with an inadequate interface definition or with one that unrealistically constrained the component designer.

This focus on the tangible problem of component design can easily distract us from the problem of managing interfaces. Most companies devote too little attention to interface management. For example, it is quite common to encounter design teams that have established clear responsibility for each subsystem. Yet, when you ask them, "Who is responsible for the interfaces?" they struggle just to name the interfaces in the system, let alone identifying accountable individuals. Such negligence of interfaces is unusual in organizations experienced with system design. On the Boeing 777 one of the first steps in the design process was to define the interface control documents (ICDs) and to put them under configuration control. The program was too important to tolerate drifting interface definitions.

Let us now look at some of the practical steps that we can take to control architectural interfaces. First, we want to be sure that all interfaces are defined. The new question we wish to ask is, "What is the worst thing that subsystem A could do to subsystem B?" If the answer is nothing, then there is no interface issue between these subsystems. If there is an interaction, then we have an interface to be managed. A simple way to create a list of interfaces is to prepare a matrix listing each of the system elements and identifying which other elements each interacts with.

We should recognize that two elements can interact even though they are not physically connected. For example, in software if two modules share the same data they can interact through the changes they make to this data. It is a bit like two accountants who never see each other interacting because they keep making entries into the same ledger. The same thing can happen with hardware. Two electrical modules can interact through a shared power supply. The surges produced by one module can cause problems in another module even though the two modules are not directly connected. Remember, a direct physical connection is not necessary to produce an interaction.

The second thing we can do to manage interfaces is to ensure that each interface has a single point of control. This is commonly done by creating some sort of interface definition document, assigning a single person responsibility for managing the document, and establishing some procedure for making changes in this document. A convenient way to do this in most companies is to use the engineering document control system. An interface document is managed with revision levels and change procedures so that everyone on the team knows what the current version of the interface is.

Third, we should have a mechanism for freezing or stabilizing the interface. We need a target freeze date for each of the internal interfaces in the design. This is a delicate issue because there are disadvantages to freezing an interface too early in the design process. However, when we freeze an interface, we free the designers of subsystems connected to this interface from worrying about the rest of the system. Now they must only worry about what is happening to the interface. As we mentioned earlier, this dramatically simplifies the communications for the subsystem design team.

The interface freeze should take place according to a predetermined schedule. A changing interface can cause massive rework in a design, because the interface forms the boundary conditions for subsystem design. It is the equivalent of the product specification for the subsystem. If the interface changes it can wreak havoc on the design work already accomplished on the module. A relatively minor change in an interface can force a subsystem designer to discard all his work and start over again.

As we mentioned earlier, there is a dark side to freezing interfaces. An early freeze locks in system-level tradeoffs. It makes it more difficult to do system-level optimization. For example, once we freeze the power supply interface we make it much easier for the power supply designers to get on with their work. They now have a fixed target for the voltages, currents, and regulation levels. However, the benefit to the power supply designer comes at a price for the other subsystems, which are now constrained by the values that have been determined in the power supply interface. System-level optimization becomes more difficult.

In complex systems, where system-level optimization is important, we need to build in some counterbalancing mechanism to ensure system-level optimization. For example, when we design an aircraft it is common to have weight budgets for each part of the system. Interfaces between subsystems are frozen and each subsystem has a specific weight target. However, there are often complex interactions between the weights of these subsystems. By removing one pound from the engine we may be able to reduce the weight of the wing by three pounds. If the engine simply has a weight budget the engine designer may be content to stay within this budget. We need some mechanism to recognize the system-level effect of a weight change. Typically, this is done by assigning a group with system-level responsibility for the critical parameter. For example, a weights and moments office may be responsible for optimizing overall weight of the system.

Let us consider for a moment how Rolls Royce approached the design of their Trent 800 jet engine. The design team was organized into subsystems, but management recognized that they had to have somebody worrying about system-level optimization. They provided an organizational focus for this by creating a chief weight officer, who had ultimate responsibility for the weight of the engine. This individual coordinated the optimization of weight at the system level, overcoming a key weakness of the traditional approach to engine design which establishes a cost and weight budget for each key subsystem. The Trent 800 team discovered that a high-cost manufacturing technology for turbine blades would reduce the weight of these blades. The lower-weight blades reduced the weight of the rotor. The lower-weight rotor reduced the weight of the housing. The result was a dramatic system-level multiplier effect on any weight reduction of the turbine blades. This weight reduction was so significant that it made sense to exceed the cost targets on the blades to exploit it. As a result, some versions of the Trent 800 engine are reported to have achieved a weight reduction of 12 to 22 percent over the comparable Pratt and Whitney and General Electric engines. Such an advantage is almost unheard of in a business that fights for each ounce of weight.

The fourth key to managing interfaces is to establish adequate design margins in the interfaces. This means that we must allow enough extra capacity in the interfaces to permit changes in the system to be contained within individual subsystem components. In other words, the subsystems must not be too tightly coupled to one another, or a change in one will force us to change everything else in the system. For example, consider our power supply. If the capacity of the power supply is exactly equal to the needs of the system we will have trouble dealing with change in the system. What would happen if one of the system elements needs more power? We would have to change the power supply. Now the new power supply may not fit into the package, so we have to change the package. Perhaps changing the package will create an electromagnetic interference problem with another printed circuit board in the system, so we may have to change this board as well. The rework in the system rapidly spreads far beyond the original element that changed. When this happens in a system, it is a sign that the interface margins are not large enough. We check for this problem by measuring the ratio of local to global rework in a system. This is a sensitive indicator as to whether we have created excessively tight interface margins.

We must be somewhat cautious because setting interface margins is not simply a question of providing generous margins between all system elements. Large margins can burden the system with high costs and poor performance. We must provide the "right" margin between system elements. In general, we reduce the value of the system when we loosen coupling by increasing the interface margins. In the extreme, with no coupling at all we have created a pile of components that does nothing. Tight coupling creates value, so we must use care setting interface margins. Certain modules should run tightly coupled and others loosely coupled. How do we decide which ones to couple tightly? A good rule of thumb is to loosen coupling around the risky modules of the system.

For a practical example, consider our power supply again. We have a new technology that we believe will be more compact than the old technology. Do we design the package to take advantage of this decrease in size, or do we design it large enough to hold the larger old-technology power supply? It depends on the risk associated with the new technology. If it is risky, we should leave enough space in the package to switch back to the old power supply. Otherwise, a problem with the new power supply technology could force redesign of the entire system. Another area that is commonly risky is the external interfaces of the system. Despite our best attempts to determine the user interface requirements, customers are likely to change their minds. Experienced designers recognize this, and leave extra capacity in this interface, making it easy to change. With early interface definition, clear accountability, a freeze schedule, and adequate design margins we will have made a big improvement in the management of interfaces.

SPECIFIC ARCHITECTURAL IMPLEMENTATIONS

Let us now look at how we can combine these principles to pursue specific economic objectives. We will return to our four key objectives: development expense, unit cost, performance, and schedule.

Low-Expense Architectures

We can take three key steps when our objective is to minimize development expenses. First, we should maximize reuse of existing designs. Second, we should displace customization outside the system boundary. Third, we should obtain nonstrategic subsystems from vendors. Let us look at each of these steps.

One way to lower development expenses is to maximize reuse within the system. Whenever we reuse a design solution we reduce the design and testing hours for the product. Such reuse requires that a module have enough inherent flexibility to be used in more than one product, which generally means it must be designed from the very beginning to have this flexibility.

Designing a module for reusability rarely occurs by accident, because it usually takes more effort and time to create a flexible module. For example, a French software company discovered that when they wrote software modules to be reusable the average size of the module went up by a factor of three. Since the size of a module can affect its memory requirements and processing speed, such reusable modules would have been a poor solution if the system had constraints in either of these areas. The extra effort would have been worth it if the modules were used more than three times. In actuality, each module was used an average of nine times, which lowered the effective cost of the module by 67 percent. This translates into a threefold improvement in productivity. Thus, reuse can cut development expenses substantially.

A second way to use architecture to reduce development expenses is to displace some of the customization task outside the system boundary. For example, consider the macro languages that are offered in some software packages. This is an interesting way to place the burden of customization on the customer rather than on the developer. The way we draw the system boundary has dramatic impact on our development expenses because anytime we push design work outside this boundary we reduce our workload.

A third approach to reducing development expenses is to increase the number of subsystems that are bought from vendors. The decision to buy out a subsystem should be based on two factors. The first is the relative importance of the subsystem to the competitive positioning of the product. For example, the input stage of most instruments is critical to their performance. An instrument company should normally try to control this strategic "high ground." If it buys the input stage from a vendor, then its products may achieve little differentiation. User interfaces are another area of key differentiation that most companies try to control. The second factor is the relative capability of the vendor and customer. For example, a power supply vendor may make millions of systems per year. Its customer, the instrument company, may use hundreds of units. In such a case it would almost never be cost effective for the instrument company to design its own power supplies. Scarce development dollars should be saved for the pieces of the system that can really create a competitive advantage. Purchasing nonstrategic sections of the system leverages scarce development resources.

Low-Cost Architectures

Our architectural approach will be different when we are trying to design very low-cost products. In such cases we can take three different steps. First, we tightly couple subsystems within the design. Second, we specify subsystems to minimize manufacturing costs. Third, we seek scale economies for key components.

The first step to achieving a low product cost is to reduce interface margins. This is equivalent to tightly coupling the subsystems, which leaves us vulnerable to the global rework we described earlier in this chapter. Such rework can be acceptable when the unit cost savings are high enough. Since every bit of extra capability adds cost to the design, we will focus on reducing the margins on the high-cost subsystems. We may even choose to reduce the modularity of the product if we feel that the cost burden of such modularity is too high.

The second way we can reduce manufacturing cost is to specify our subsystems explicitly to minimize manufacturing cost. This requires a tight fit between product and process, and demands very heavy manufacturing involvement early in the development process. We design the subsystem to fit the process rather than designing the process to fit the subsystem. For example, engineering will design printed circuit boards using components that can be automatically inserted instead of hand stuffed. These components might not be their first choice from a technical perspective, but the cost of hand insertion is so high that it is worth finding a way to use automatically insertable components.

To achieve this focus on design for low manufactured cost requires the direct participation of the experts on cost, such as manufacturing engineers and vendors, in key design decisions. The design engineer is no longer king. Instead, the power of manufacturing and vendors rises dramatically. For example, some appliance manufacturers are placing increased design responsibility on their component vendors. Rather than providing detailed part specifications they are giving broad performance specifications and tight cost objectives. They have the component vendor prepare a detailed specification. This results in a component design that is tightly optimized for the realities of the vendor's manufacturing process.

The third way that we can lower manufacturing cost is to search carefully for scale economies on key components. One computer peripheral company found that every one of its development programs was specifying a different power supply design. They were buying twenty different power supplies when all of their needs could be met by five or six standardized units. Interestingly, although the standardized unit was overkill for some of the designs, it was still cheaper than buying smaller quantities of more tailored versions.

It is important to place the job of finding scale economies outside the individual project team. The team has an incentive to locally optimize their specific program, and will rarely be trying to optimize the company-wide economics. It is also important to make these decisions very early in the development process. The most successful reuse occurs when the choices are made as part of the conceptual design process. In most situations reuse objectives for specific subsystems should be part of the original project plan.

High-Performance Architectures

Selecting an architecture for high levels of performance requires a different approach. Again there are several useful steps. First, we build the design around the key performance-limiting element. Second, we focus on system-level optimization. Third, we tightly couple subsystems within the design. We will discuss each of these in turn.

Our first key step to achieving high performance is to design the system around the characteristics of the performance-limiting element. Consider for example the prize-winning solar car, the Sun Raycer, designed by Paul MacCready for General Motors. A governing design factor was the weight of the car, since this determined its ability to climb hills effectively. By achieving a low dead weight a small power package could be used, which permitted a small frame and body. Every high-performance design will have an equivalent performance-limiting element.

An implication of this approach is that high-performance architectures will normally be designed in a very sequential process. By attacking the governing technical parameter first, we can then attack related subsystems in a logical sequence. The governing technical parameter can be identified by modeling the design, by analyzing competitor designs, or by sheer experience with the product. The latter method is by far the most common. To do this we must put this experience on the team or ensure good access to it. We have to use experts effectively when we are trying to operate on the cutting edge of technology.

A second step for maximizing performance is to focus on the problem of system-level optimization rather than subsystem optimization. This is important because, as we discussed in Chapter 5, a system cannot be optimized by optimizing each one of its subsystems. We must carefully manage the tension between local optimization and global optimization by having some of our effort focused on local optimization and other effort on the global optimization problem. For example, on an aircraft design program we might use a weight budget to force local optimization at the subsystem level, but at the same time use a weight czar empowered to make system-level tradeoffs to handle the global optimization problem. System-level optimization is critical when we are trying to achieve high performance.

A third step to maximizing performance is to tightly couple the design. In this case we are shaving our interface margins to maximize performance rather than to minimize cost. For example, when we are trying to run an electronic circuit at maximum possible speed we will often leave very little margin for timing problems. Such thin margins expose us to more testing and rework to tune the design, but they push the design right to its limits. When performance is the key to business success we can't afford to waste any opportunity to maximize performance.

Fast-Development Architectures

The final objective that we can use our architecture to achieve is development speed. This objective actually requires a fundamental shift from the approach that we used to achieve low expenses, low cost, and high performance. Each of those objectives was best achieved by using a sequential approach to design. In contrast, development speed is best achieved by using a concurrent approach.

To exploit such a concurrent approach we take several steps. First, we reuse subsystems. Second, we stabilize architectural interfaces early. Third, we place design tasks with high schedule variability off the critical path. We will describe each of these in turn.

Our first step is to focus on reuse of subsystems. Any time we reuse a subsystem we have eliminated a design activity. If the subsystem is already designed, it is automatically off the critical path. Reuse can have a dramatic effect on development speed, and such reuse is critically dependent on architecture. We can only get high levels of reuse when we use modular architectures.

The second step for improving development speed is to stabilize interfaces between modules early. In fact, the management of architectural interfaces is critical to achieving rapid development. As we discussed earlier in this chapter these interfaces need to be well-defined, clear accountability must be assigned, they must have a "freeze schedule," and they need adequate margins.

The last of these factors, interface margins, is very important for rapid development. Interfaces need enough excess capacity to absorb the inevitable changes that will occur during the design process. If we do not have enough margin in the interfaces, our modules will experience massive rework. This generous margin approach is the opposite of the thin margin approach that we used to maximize performance and minimize cost.

The third step for improving speed is to pull design tasks with high schedule variability off the critical path. In particular, we will try to use architectures that exploit known technology, because technology development typically has high schedule uncertainty. The process choice of decoupling technology and product development is highly appropriate for rapid development. In contrast, when we are trying to push performance or drive to minimum product cost we use the opposite approach and tightly couple our technology and our product program.

A key point of this chapter is that architectural approaches should be a response to economic objectives. An architecture is only "good" to the extent that it helps you to accomplish your economic objective.

WHO DOES IT?

A natural question to ask about architecture is who will do it? Is this the job of the team leader? Do we give it to a system architect? Do we get the entire team involved?

It has often been observed that the best architectures are the results of a single mind, or at most a team of two or three minds. This is probably due to the complexity of the decisions involved, and the strong demand for integration of the decisions. However, an individual or small group may have problems addressing architectural issues that have implications beyond the team level. We need a means to represent cross-project architectural interests.

This leads us to believe that good architecture is unlikely to come from a system architect alone, or from a team leader. Too many other members of the organization have vital information that is required to make the architectural choices. Some of the best product architectures arise from an understanding of the marketing and manufacturing implications of the architectural choices. For example, consider the modular structures described earlier which were used by Tektronix in their laboratory oscilloscopes. An engineer may have correctly argued that the interfaces in these structures would reduce the reliability and performance of the scopes. A manufacturing manager may have correctly argued that the interfaces added parts, which increases cost and complexity for manufacturing. Purchasing would have pointed out that the added parts were connectors, which are expensive and have long lead times. Finally, the marketing manager would have spoken. He would have explained to the team that a modular scope could be easily and cheaply upgraded by the customer. This would allow Tektronix to sell a replacement module at a high gross margin and still offer the customer a cheap alternative for upgrading his scope. He would point out that many businesses make more money on upgrade modules than they do on the original product. The marketing manager would prevail.

Let us look at another example, that of a suitcase manufacturer. The design team is working on a suitcase that has a combination lock on it. Marketing gets the idea that color accents on the suitcase would look nice and asks for colored locks. Engineering checks with the lock manufacturer and discovers that the locks are available in different colors for no change in price. Does this mean that the design is good? They check with manufacturing and the purchasing manager goes through the roof. She explains that the lock is sourced from Europe with a sixteen-week lead time. She says that she will have to hold at least sixteen weeks of inventory for each of the colors and points out that marketing has never been any good at forecasting which colors will be popular. She suggests that it might be better to use a snap-on plastic insert that is cheap and has a short lead time. Engineering tells her that it is bad design for manufacturing to use two parts to do the job of one. She glares at them and says it is even stupider to structure a product so that a high-cost, long-lead-time component is both non-standard and unpredictable in demand. Variability should never be put in a high-cost, long-lead-time component.

The point of these two examples is to illustrate that architecture is not simply an engineering problem. In these two cases marketing and manufacturing were important stakeholders in the decision. Some mechanism must be created to get them involved in the architecture process. I suggest creating an architectural review that is cross-functional, and that may even involve key vendors, if they can offer important recommendations on how to improve cost or lead times on key components.

SUMMARY

In this chapter we have explored the important interaction between the design of our product architecture and the design of our development process. We discussed three important underlying principles. First, modularity is a powerful way to achieve certain economic objectives. Its use should be driven by economics. Second, it is important to segregate variability within our architecture. Third, managing architectural interfaces is a critical activity. Unfortunately, most companies devote too little attention to this issue.

We then explained how we could apply these principles to the specific economic problems of maximizing each of our key objectives. This permits us to create low-expense, low-cost, high-performance, and fast-development architectures.

Finally we discussed why architecture should be a cross-functional and cross-program issue. It cannot be left to a technical architect alone, and it would be dangerous to optimize it on the level of the development team. There are too many other important economic interests that must be considered.

I want to reemphasize that architecture should be an economic decision, not a technical one. This is not to say that it should be left to the accountants, for technical factors are critical to assessing expense, cost, performance, and schedule. Technical experts are still likely to play the dominant role in selecting the architecture. However, they cannot do the job alone.

With the architectural context firmly in place we can now turn to a specific process step that has confounded many developers. Theories abound on how to do a good specification. In the next chapter we will systematically cover the process of creating a specification.

9

Get the Product
Specification Right

T he creation of a product specification is a critical subprocess,
which we will tackle in several pieces. We will begin by deciding how to choose a target market for our product. Then we
will discuss how we achieve an in-depth understanding of the customers within this target market. Both of these steps must take place
before we begin to prepare a specification. After this we will describe
how we create a specification and how we use this specification during development.

IT STARTS WITH STRATEGY

Our company strategy is a key context in which we do product development. Strategy determines which market segments we will compete in,
who we will compete with, and how we will compete. The single yard-
stick by which we measure our strategy is an economic one. Good
strategies make money, bad strategies do not. We need to understand
our internal economics, those of our distribution channels, and those of
our competitors to do a good job setting strategy.

The products we choose to develop are a critical piece of our strategy, but our product choices must fit with the rest of the strategy. For
example, one computer peripheral company tried to differentiate
their product on the basis of its performance advantages. Unfortunately, the channel of distribution they used were order takers who
had little technical knowledge and no ability to explain these benefits

to the customer. This channel sold products on the basis of price alone, which meant the company achieved no premium for its superior technical performance. It is quite common to see such misfits between the product and the distribution channel. The important thing to remember is that good products cannot fix bad strategies. We need to start with a well-crafted strategy to make money-developing products.

SELECTING THE CUSTOMER

The first and critical step in the specification process is to select a group of target customers. This step commences when we begin to create our strategy and continues as we formulate our product plans. The choice to serve less than 100 percent of the customers is called market segmentation. This is simply the act of dividing up the market with the goal of finding a group of customers that is more profitable to serve than another group. This difference in profit can result because the customers are willing to pay a higher price, or because the customers can be served more cost effectively.

Of course, there are an infinite numbers of ways to segment any market. Fortunately there is a very simple test to tell if you have a good segmentation scheme: look for a profit difference between the segments. This raises an interesting problem for the product developer. Can the marketing staff segment the market by themselves? Unfortunately not. Doing good segmentation demands a knowledge of both value and cost. Marketing can determine value by trying to assess what price different customers are willing to pay for the product. However, it is still necessary to know the cost of serving each group of customers to assess the segmentation scheme. This means that both manufacturing and engineering people must be involved to segment a market.

The results of the market segmentation step should be a definition of the target customer and a rough definition of customer needs that will be satisfied. These needs are normally described by stating the functions that the product will perform rather than the features that the product will have. At this stage you should have a rough idea of the size of the revenue stream that the product could generate and the gross margins that might be achieved. Having chosen an attractive customer segment, your next step is to understand the customer.

UNDERSTANDING THE CUSTOMER

If there is one weakness in most product specification processes it is that the design team does not achieve an adequate understanding of the customer. To produce a product that people will buy, we need to focus on three critical issues. First, what do the customers want? Most companies will ask this question. Second, why do they want it? This question is vital because it tells us how much value customers may attach to what they are asking for. Unfortunately, most companies lack information in this critical area. Third, how do customers make their decisions? We need to discover the criteria they use to assess whether the product meets their requirements. Since this decision is influenced by perception as well as fact, we need to probe deeply to understand the cues that affect perception. Except for strong consumer marketing organizations, most companies are very weak in this area.

In an attempt to offset this common weakness we will focus on three tools that have proved particularly useful: customer interviews, observation of customers, and focus groups. We have carefully chosen these tools because of the value that they provide in relation to the effort involved in using them. There are many other tools available and they all generate some useful information. However, many of them return a relatively small amount of insight for the time and effort invested.

Customer Interviews

Customer interviews are probably our most important single tool for understanding the customer. They invariably provide a lot of information in a relatively short period of time. They are vastly superior to questionnaires, because the interviewer can ensure a consistent interpretation of terms and can interactively probe into confusing issues.

Too often these interviews are viewed as the job of marketing alone. Sometimes they are foolishly delegated to a third party. These are dangerous traps. Having the entire team participate in the interview process has two key benefits. First, it dramatically increases the number of interviews that can be done in a given period of time. Second, it makes that entire team a much better consumer of marketing information. When team members see areas of confusion at the customer firsthand, they begin to understand which requirements are built on bedrock, and which ones are built on quicksand.

The customer interview process requires identifying who will be seen, setting up meetings, designing an interview guide, and performing the interviews. Let us look at some effective ways of performing each of these steps.

The people you interview should be your target customers. Target customers are not always the same as current customers. A common mistake is to talk to the people that are easiest to talk to, and those are usually your existing customers. For example, many U.S. companies do most of their customer interviews with easily accessible domestic customers and are surprised when their product does not appeal to global markets.

You are likely to get more learning done with a concentrated period of interviews rather than by stringing them out over the entire development process. Typically you should call customers a couple weeks in advance and schedule two weeks of interviews performing four interviews per day. Normally by the time you have interviewed thirty to forty customers you begin to notice consistent patterns in their answers. Research done by Abbie Griffin and John Hauser suggests that 90 percent of customer needs are revealed by the time you have done thirty interviews.

Field interviews are best done with two people, one to ask the questions and the other to take notes. The role of asking questions can be switched during the interview. Such an approach generates better documentation and protects against distortions caused by individual expectations. Most companies pair a marketing person and an engineer. When more than one interviewer is in the field it is a good idea to have them review key findings at the end of each day. Focusing on what was learned in each day's interviews will ensure that two interviewers do not hear two different things. You will also sharpen the questioning if you highlight areas where the responses can be interpreted in different ways.

Creating a good interview guide is an essential element of preparation. It should be composed of questions in the following areas:

1. Background information on interviewee and company
2. The purchase process
3. Buying criteria
4. Likely future purchases
5. Competitor evaluation

Background information is critical since it provides clues for refining segmentation. Any segmentation effort will test different ways of sorting the customers into groups. For example, you might ask the interviewees whether decision making is centralized at the corporate level or decentralized at the divisional level. If you discover a difference in needs between these types of companies you may have found a useful segmentation scheme. This background information may have to do with the role of the product, whose budget pays for it, its effect on company economics, and the like. As you progress through a series of interviews potential segmentation schemes will emerge. Once they do, spend more time probing in related areas of the interview guide. This is natural and appropriate. Remember, the interview guide is a tool designed to help you, not a rigid template that must be followed.

It is important to understand the purchase process because it is usually much more complex than "the best product wins." Typically you will find different players such as users of the product, financial decision makers, and technical decision makers. Sometimes you can interview everyone at once, but this is usually the exception. You get more more accurate information when you interview these different players separately. It is not unusual to find people claiming to make certain decisions who, on closer scrutiny, have exaggerated their role. It is usually a good idea to ask customers to describe a recent purchase, rather than having them describe a theoretical purchase process. You may discover that the actual process is different from both the way management wants it to work, and the way an individual might like it to be. As an interviewer you are most interested in what actually happens.

The first day of field interviews is critical, because the interview guide is always imperfect. You want to debug the interview guide so that you can focus the limited interview time on the most important questions. When there are multiple interviewers in the field it can be difficult to insure that their interview guides and questioning are synchronized. For example, if one question concerns the importance of reliability, you want to understand how each customer defines reliability. You may discover that for the typical customer reliability refers to system availability. If so, you may decide to have all interviewers shift to a more precise term. A useful way to maintain this synchronization is to have interviewers teleconference at the end of each day to compare notes. Keep doing this until the interview guide becomes stable.

The questions on buying criteria should be carefully structured. Most interviewers make the mistake of focusing on what the customer wants, since they believe the purpose of these interviews is to identify customer needs. In fact, there are two other important questions. We must find out why customers want certain characteristics and how they assess whether the product has them.

The question, "Why do you need this?" is critical because it allows you to determine the relative importance of different needs. This information is necessary to make tradeoffs between product functions, as you invariably will need to. Furthermore, it helps you to develop the model of application economics that we discussed in Chapter 2. Too often interviews teams return with a list of needs and no way of assessing the relative importance of the needs. Remember, you are trying to understand the customers, not simply to describe them.

The third key area of questioning is on how customers assess the product. For each identified need we must ask, "How do you know you have gotten what you want?" The answers to this question are usually quite surprising. Too often engineers and scientists believe that they must simply solve the customer problem. They fail to realize the critical importance of how the customer perceives the product. Let me illustrate with two simple examples.

A good friend who worked for a pesticide company told me an instructive story. The scientists back in the lab had invented a fabulous chemical that was 100 percent fatal to any known bug. They formulated it into a pesticide and sent it out for market tests. Disappointing results came back. Marketing said the pesticide was no good. The customers didn't like it. It didn't work. That's impossible, said the scientists in the lab. It will kill *anything*. What are those fools doing, forgetting to take the cap off the container?

A little further research answered the question. Customers were asked how they decided that the insecticide did not work.

"It doesn't kill bugs," said the customer.

"How do you know?" asked the interviewer.

"Well, I spray them and they just walk away as if nothing happened. Even when I soak them with the stuff they just walk away back inside the wall," said the customer.

"But, they've been poisoned. They are going to die!" said the interviewer.

"Well, they look pretty healthy to me."

"But, do you ever see them again?" asked the interviewer.

"I don't know," said the customer, "frankly, the bugs all look the same to me."

"What would I have to do to convince you it was working?" asked the interviewer.

"Well, when you get them with a *real* insecticide they roll over on their backs and wiggle their legs in the air."

It turns out that what typical customers want in an insecticide is not simply to kill bugs. They want to see the bugs die a painful death. You can produce a 100 percent fatal insecticide, but if it doesn't make the bugs roll over, you won't sell a can of it. The scientists had naively thought that the goal was to kill bugs. In reality, the product had to kill bugs and provide entertainment for the customer.

Here's another example. A scientific software company built a simulation program for aircraft design. It was a brilliant piece of software. The complex calculations took hours on even a powerful workstation. But customers complained that the software would keep locking up their computers. The company discovered that customers were turning off the program in the middle of its calculations, because they thought the system had shut down.

"How do you know it is shut down?" asks the designer.

"Well, it runs for hours and nothing is happening on the screen," says the user.

"But that's because the computer is doing its calculations," says the designer. "It will give you the answers when it is done."

"I see," says the user reflectively. "So I guess that means that the display looks the same when the program is working as it does when it is broken."

The designer finally realized that he needed to provide visible indications on the screen to show that the product was doing something. This actually slowed down the calculations, but it proved much more satisfying to the users, because they now could tell the program was still running.

The important thing to remember is that you have only done part of the job when you find out what the customer wants. You need to ask two more questions. You need to find out why they want it, and how they know that they have gotten it.

Meticulous Observation

The customer interview is a powerful tool. Many companies consider it the ultimate step in understanding the customer. However, other companies only view it as the first step along the path to customer knowledge. Why do they feel they must go beyond simply asking questions of the customer? Because they have discovered that customer interviews often produce distorted information. They have found that customers can be imperfect at articulating their thinking, behaviors, and experiences. They have found that, with effort, you can actually understand customers better than they understand themselves.

For example, if you asked the consumers of laundry detergent why they buy a certain product they would come up with a variety of explanations. It might appear that almost everyone was buying the product for a different reason. If you talked to the makers of laundry detergents they would have a far clearer view of the problem. For example, they would distinguish fragrance buyers from brightness buyers and explain how the perfumes that are added to appeal to one are different than the brighteners added for the other. They would explain that the naming and advertising of products is tailored for each type of buyer. The detergent manufacturer has a far clearer picture of why people buy the detergent than the consumers themselves have. *This is our goal: to understand the customers better than they understand themselves.*

How do we achieve such a superior level of understanding? To do so we must go beyond the mere information that the customer is reporting to us. The most powerful way to achieve this higher level of understanding is through meticulous observation of the customer and through the systematic collection of data. Let us examine these two techniques in more detail.

Meticulous observation requires scrutinizing the external behavior of customers during the purchase process and during the use of the product. The best tool for doing this is the video camera. The striking thing about observing videotapes of customers using the product is that we begin to notice things on the second viewing that were not evident on the first viewing. We begin to see even more after repeated viewing. Furthermore, the videotape provides a tool for quantitative analysis. We can accurately measure the time it takes to do certain tasks. One software company goes beyond simply videotaping the screen during product use. They also videotape the user's facial expressions. Transient facial expressions often convey information about the user's feelings that that user cannot consciously express.

One of the limitations of videotaping is that you are primarily observing external behaviors of the users and making inferences about the internal state of mind of the customer. It would clearly be more useful if we could get information about internal mental states. There are two techniques for doing this. One approach is to get users to articulate verbally what they are doing as they perform certain tasks. By getting users to provide a running dialog we get a better idea of what is going on in their minds. Another technique for doing this is to have the user view the videotape immediately after the taping and narrate it with what they were thinking about at the time they were doing certain things. Both approaches will generate more accurate information than simply observing external behavior.

Another technique for obtaining more accurate data is to embed data collection capability in the initial field test units. This is particularly useful in software products where the product itself can collect data about things like usage patterns. An example of this technique is reported in Michael Cusumano's book *Microsoft Secrets*. Microsoft produces instrumented versions of their software that collect actual data on the usage of certain product features. Such instrumented versions of the product can provide information that it is impossible for the customers to articulate themselves.

Focus Groups

A third technique for understanding customers is the focus group, a group of customers who are interviewed together. The event is typically videotaped, which is a big advantage because its findings can easily be communicated to people who were not present. There are several benefits to getting information from many customers at the same time. First, it saves time. You can easily talk to ten customers in two hours. Second, it encourages each customer to view more dimensions of the product and helps them use consistent terminology. What may appear to be conflicting views in one-on-one interviews can turn out to be very consistent when the same issue is discussed in a focus group.

There are four dark sides to focus groups. First, group dynamics will distort the data because groups of people behave differently than individuals. In particular, individual members can tend to conform to the opinion of the group, or to engage in silent dissent. As a result, the range of answers from a group will normally not be as broad as from the same people interviewed individually. In effect, groups will artificially distort their views to conform to the emerging norms of the group. For this reason, you should be very careful about relying on the data from a single focus group.

The second disadvantage of a focus group is that it does not engage the development team at a visceral level the way a customer interview does. If you want to get the team to live and breathe the customer, you need to send them out into the field with the customers. The mere fact that interviews will typically take place at the customer site will allow the interviewer to get information about the application that will never be visible in a focus group.

A third key disadvantage of focus groups is their cost effectiveness. Abbie Griffin and John Hauser have done interesting research on the relative productivity of focus groups and one-on-one interviews and suggest that interviews generate almost the same amount of information per hour of time invested. Since a one-hour interview is usually cheaper than a one-hour focus group, this would suggest that interviews can be more cost effective.

The fourth disadvantage is avoidable. Too often focus groups take a long time to set up. Teams wait months for the market research staff to design and coordinate the focus group. Much of this delay can be avoided if the logistics of arranging the group are decoupled from the design of the questions. There is nothing that prevents us from setting up the focus group months in advance and defining the questions to be asked twenty-four hours before the actual event. We certainly need to know the target customers to set up the focus group, but the questions can wait until later.

These advantages and disadvantages mean that focus groups should be used selectively. They are most useful to confirm information already obtained in field interviews and from customer observation. They can be extremely useful during an intermediate stage of the product development process to test design concepts and evaluate prototype units. In such cases, they can provide feedback on design choices without having to send a busy development team into the field for a couple of weeks.

I have deliberately ignored many other tools such as purchased market research, questionnaires, and Quality Function Deployment (QFD). In my experience these tools do generate unique and useful information. I would encourage you to try them and find out how well they work for you. Here we will restrict ourselves to the three tools that have given us the best results for the time and effort required to use them.

CREATING A GOOD SPECIFICATION

We now can get to the central issue in product specification, which is producing a clear target for the development team. To assess the specification we must be clear about the two roles of a specification. First, a specification is a critical input for the design process. It tells the design team which functions the customer is likely to value in the product. As such, the specification is the echo of the customer's voice that is heard in the design lab.

The second key purpose of a specification document is as a control device for the project. By setting a goal for the performance of the product we create a reference point from which to measure it. If we begin to deviate from this goal we can take corrective action. With such a reference point we can detect problems early and take corrective action while the cost of making changes is still small. This suggests that to be effective the specification does not have to control everything, but rather the "important" things. Let us take a careful look at this distinction.

The Minimalist Specification

The twin objectives of communications and control give us a clearer idea of what is required in a good specification. For example, let us look at the problem of communications using some of the ideas of information theory that we described in Chapter 4. We can consider the specification to be a message from the customer to the design team. In a formal sense, the information contained in this message is related to the degree to which it is surprising to a development team. Information that contradicts widely held beliefs is most important, and must be conveyed accurately. Requirements that are already common knowledge communicate little new information to the team. This suggests that we want to be particularly good at communicating a limited number of nonobvious or counterintuitive requirements; thus, the specifications should be brief.

Unfortunately too many developers consider a more detailed specification to be more desirable. There is a long tradition in development organizations of fighting for full definition of the product requirements. Many people think that the more complete a specification is, the better. Detail is viewed as an inherent good. For example, Fred Brooks, in his classic book *The Mythical Man-Month,* defines the specification as describing and prescribing "every detail of what the user sees." Such a philosophy can lead to very detailed specifications.

Let us contrast this with a different view. In the early years of Hewlett-Packard, the development team would begin test instrument design by writing the catalog page for the instrument. Their logic was that any feature important enough to mention to the customer in the catalog was important enough to mention to the designers. On the other hand, some features were so trivial that they would not be mentioned in the catalog. This was a sign that they had little influence on the actual purchase decision. Why should the design team be constrained on such an attribute? In fact, writing the catalog page was such a useful tool because it focused on communicating key product advantages to the customer. Scarce catalog space was only used for messages that were likely to influence the customer's purchase. This automatically focused the team on critical product attributes.

This focus on critical attributes is very important. A full definition of all product attributes usually does more harm than good. Each target attribute is another constraint for the designer, thereby complicating the design task. What is worse, many of the constraints are arbitrary, and can result in compromising a parameter that is really important to the customer. In reality, a specification that contains many constraints only dilutes the attention of the design team away from the things that really need to be optimized.

Surprisingly, it is much harder to produce a brief specification than a detailed one. Detailed specifications are easy to create because we simply copy every feature offered by every competitor. In contrast, to do a brief specification we need to make choices. We need to know which features are truly important to the customer. This takes much more profound knowledge of the customer.

A second key principle of producing a good specification is to indicate the relative importance of features. A designer needs to know what will happen as we deviate from the target value of the parameter in the specification. In fact, viewing the specification as a control system we would only want to constrain and detect deviations in those product parameters that are most critical for the economic success of the product. With limited resources, we must focus our control effort on the things that are important. This focus can be provided qualitatively by using methods that rely on having the customer assess the relative importance of product features. Many of these methods use systems of weighting factors but they are still essentially qualitative methods. These qualitative methods are most useful when perception of features is important, such as with consumer products.

The second way to provide focus is to use quantitative tools. Two such tools that we have found particularly useful are the application economic model that was described in Chapter 2, and the product performance benchmark. A product performance benchmark is typically a functional task that exercises multiple features in a product. For example, a performance benchmark for a VCR might be how long it takes to begin recording a TV show. We could improve this benchmark by making the motors larger so that the VCR starts faster, but this is an expensive way to solve the problem. A cheaper way to do this is to make the control electronics smarter. For example, we could assume that the users want to record the channel that they are currently watching and to start at the current time. This will simplify user interface tasks and improve the speed on the benchmark. The key value of a product performance benchmark is that it shifts the focus to quantified functional performance, which is usually the way the customer thinks about the product. It allows us to make tradeoffs between parameters to maximize a particular aspect of performance.

Whether qualitative or quantitative tools are used, we must always have some method to focus the team on important features. A list of 300 features with a target value for each is a prescription for an unsuccessful program.

A Product Mission

One qualitative tool for providing focus is so important that it deserves a separate discussion. It is the product mission, or what some would call the product's value proposition. This is the answer to the question, Why should a customer buy this product instead of the competitor's? If this question cannot be answered in a compelling way in twenty-five words, then there is a fundamental problem with the design of the product.

Some people would argue that the purchase motivations for the product are actually far too complex to capture in one or two sentences. Our experience after years of doing market research suggests the opposite. Most successful products have a clear and simple value proposition. Buyers typically make their choice between competing products on the basis of three or four key factors. Even for sophisticated products, where a technical buyer will consider many features, this buyer usually has to explain his choice to his manager, or to the CFO. Inevitably the reason for purchase has to be articulated in a very simple form. Whenever we make it hard for a potential customer to build internal consensus for our product, we are less likely to win the purchase decision.

When such a value proposition is articulated at the beginning of the design process it will guide the myriad tradeoff decisions that one makes during the design process. It becomes a compass for the design team, always pointing them towards true north. For example, when the design team knows that the product's key competitive advantage is weight then every tradeoff will be made in favor of lowering the weight. Thus, we achieve extraordinary alignment of many small decisions without having to control each one of the decisions.

Despite its obvious value, it is surprising how few design teams can clearly articulate the mission of their product. It is common to find five different missions in the minds of five different team members. This disparity leads them to make decisions in different ways.

A simple trick to force ourselves to create a clear mission is to write the advertisement for the product as one of the first team activities. This forces us to define a succinct message to communicate the key competitive differentiation of the product. We should have this advertisement posted on the wall of the team room throughout the program. This keeps the key competitive advantage of the product blatantly visible in the team room. Without this all features can appear equally important and the team will not stay clearly focused on gaining an advantage on a chosen critical attribute of the product.

A key test of the mission statement is its simplicity. It is an old adage that if the reason for the purchase cannot be conveyed to the customer during a sixty-second elevator ride you will not be able to sell the product. A second good test is to ask what the mission statement excludes. If you discover no customer, no application, and no feature has been excluded then the mission has no information content. We were working in the early 1980s with a supplier of personal computers on defining their mission. They were targeting home users, small businesses, large businesses, the government, and educational institutions. A perceptive VP of engineering commented that it might be easier to define who we were *not* trying to target, adding that the only segments that we had left out were the homeless and the unemployed.

The Specification Process

A third basic principle for creating a good specification is to use a good process to create it. Two key measures of this process are whether it delays the program and how intensely it engages the development team. The issue of program delay can actually be turned into a question of batch size. The central question is: How much of our specification do we need to start the design process? By starting without a full specification we can overlap development and specification, reducing our cycle time. Such a reduction is not free. It leaves us vulnerable to expensive rework, because we may have completed design work that will change later in the process. Thus, batch size is a tradeoff between development speed and development expenses.

When the potential rework cost is lower than the cost of cycle time we will overlap specification and design activities. A practical approach for doing this is called a progressive freeze of the specification. Using this approach we define a schedule for freezing different product requirements. For example, we might decide to freeze the number of buttons on the front panel thirty days after the start of the design process, but we might determine the color of the front panel ninety days later. The point is that we do not have to freeze all features on the same day. We can freeze them in increments depending on when the information is needed.

In using such an approach we must be careful that everything ultimately does get frozen. This means that we need a simple control system to ensure the complete specification is frozen early enough in the development process. The simple way of doing this is to assign a point value to each item in the specification and keep track of the total point value that has been frozen up to date. This gives us an indication of how close we are to achieving closure on the specification.

The second critical measure of the specification process is how broadly the team is engaged in developing the specification. Too often we find specifications that are developed solely by the marketing department, and mocked by engineers. This situation is easily aggravated when we break the specification into two different documents, as some companies do, a marketing specification and a technical specification. It is much better to use a single specification that is a joint work product owned by the entire team. Psychologists have found that participation in defining goals always results in greater commitment to these goals by those who have to carry them out.

From a practical perspective this means that most of the detail in the specification will be developed after the formation of the core team, rather than before the funding of the program. Product specification is a product development issue, not a product planning issue. Product planning produces a concept that we can fund. We do the product specification after the team is in place. The result is a more customer-focused design, because the designers do the customer interviews and internalize their needs. If specification is done by some other group, the designers may lack a deep understanding of the target customer and application. They may understand the product's technical dimensions profoundly, but will be missing insight into exactly how these technical characteristics are translated into value for the customer.

USING THE SPECIFICATION

Work on the specification does not end once we have created it. It is always a living document that should change during the design process as we learn things about the application and our technical solution. Having a performance target, our specification, increases the chance that we will be able to hit this target. Yet if the target market is constantly in motion, then our specification should also be in motion.

There is a core assumption embedded in the way a company uses its product specifications. Some companies may notice that every specification they have ever prepared in the history of their company has had to change during product development, but they attribute this to human error and lack of discipline. They deeply believe that they can produce a good specification if only they try hard enough. You may recognize this as the classic thinking of an open loop control system, as described in Chapter 5. Open loop systems try to set the perfect target and strive to hit this target with great accuracy. They do not use feedback.

There is another way to think about the problem of specifying the product. It starts with the assumption that the specification is inherently flawed. If we assume that the specification is probably bad, then its latent defects must be found as early in the development process as possible. Such a view dramatically changes our planned activities in product development in two ways. First, we will devote attention to detecting and correcting latent flaws. Second, we will look for alternate channels to obtain additional information on the "true" requirement. Let us look at each of these approaches in turn.

If we believe the specification contains latent flaws, our first reaction is to look for them. This is quite different from the traditional approach which assumes the specification is good. If we believe the specification is good, then marketing can release it to engineering and relax until the product is ready for sale. If we think the specification is inherently flawed, then we will work continuously during the process to try to detect these flaws. This means that we need to be continuously validating the requirements during the development process. This is actually a dramatically different approach from the philosophy of specification-driven development that we find in most companies. Figure 9.1 depicts the difference between a specification-driven process and a customer-driven process.

Most companies follow the upper process which focuses on conformance to specification as the goal of the design process. This process builds the feedback loop between the desired specification and the actual performance of the design. The feedback loop does not include the translation of market needs into specifications, so errors in this activity will be undetected.

The lower process in Figure 9.1 is common in many consumer marketing organizations. Instead of locking down specifications, they focus on creating buying preference at the point of sale. They check the design against the customer, not against the specification. At various stages through the development process the product is tested to estab-

FIGURE 9.1

Specification vs. Customer-Driven Process

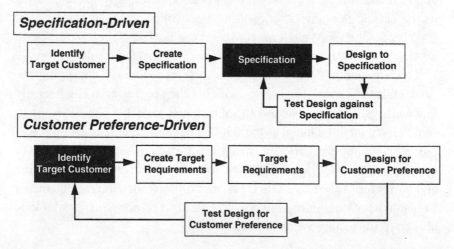

lish whether it generates preference over competing products. They are not concerned with whether the beverage has the right color brown, but rather with whether people will buy it. This larger feedback loop creates a much more robust process, but it requires more effort on the part of the design team. Its advantage is that customer-driven processes will almost never generate a product that nobody will buy. This contrasts strongly with the specification-driven process which can easily produce products that nobody wants.

When we structure the process to get feedback from the customer we need specific mechanisms to get quick, accurate feedback. The speed and accuracy of this feedback can be improved considerably once this becomes an explicit process design goal. For example, at an electronics company a new marketing VP asked one of his subordinates to get a quick answer on a specification issue for a product team. He was told it would take six weeks to arrange the focus group and it would cost several thousand dollars to answer the question. His previous company had maintained an advisory group of customers that they could call on short notice. He could get his toughest questions answered in two or three days. This was a twentyfold difference in response time. The value of this rapid response capability is extremely high. A design team cannot stop work to wait for six weeks until marketing comes back with an answer. Instead, they will make an assumption and continue work. In contrast, if customer feedback comes back in two or three days, they can afford to wait for the real answers.

We will discuss the importance of early market feedback on the specification in more detail in Chapter 12. For now, let us just emphasize that our marketing people are very busy throughout a customer-driven development process. Besides continually testing the specification, we develop alternative communications channels to bring the voice of the customer to the design team. There are three common ways to do this.

First, we can use customer partners. One manufacturer of telecommunications test equipment will not even undertake a project unless they have a customer partner to work with on the program. They have found that their success rate is dramatically higher with such a partner because customer partners provide a way to get quick answers on design issues. Certain requirements can be left undefined early in the design process and resolved later. They also provide a prearranged beta site for testing the product.

A variant of this technique is to put the names and phone numbers of three representative customers in the product specification. This provides a clear anchor point for the product. The customers are chosen to span the segment of the market that will be targeted. By using three customers we avoid locking in on the unique needs of a single customer. Using specific customers protects us from mistakes due to data aggregation in our market research.

A second common alternative communications channel is customer advisory boards or user groups. A carefully selected group of customers can act as a steering committee for the design. By arranging periodic meetings with this customer group we can validate initial product planning, get early feedback on conceptual design choices, and later get inputs on detailed design choices. Since the customers on these boards are usually strongly committed to the success of the company they are normally quite careful to respect the need for confidentiality. Feedback from such an advisory board member does not have to be restricted to formal meetings. Many companies arrange to have advisory board members available for short notice telephone consultations. This is a quick way to get feedback on a tough design choice.

A third alternative communications channel is using a proxy customer on the design team. One company that makes accounting software has accountants on its development team. These accountants think the same way the customer does, so they can provide very accurate advice to software designers on feature decisions.

No matter what tools we choose to use, our design process will always be more robust when we have alternative channels to communicate the customer's voice to the design team. *The specification should never be the only tool telling the design team what is important to the customer.*

SPECIFIC IMPLEMENTATIONS

Let us now consider how we must change our specification process when we are confronted with the four separate economic objectives: development expense, unit cost, performance, and schedule.

Our first economic objective is development expense. In most cases expense will be minimized by a careful and thorough definition of all requirements before we begin the program. This eliminates any rework that might come from a poor definition of the program objectives, but it places specification on the critical path of the project. The key to getting a good specification using this approach is to ensure that downstream groups, like manufacturing, participate in the process.

To control expenses we also need some means to change the specification as the project evolves. This is important because we may discover that a feature that we thought would be easy to design is actually very difficult. What made sense as a one-week design task may no longer make sense if it will take fifteen weeks to complete. If possible, this requirement should be dropped from the specification.

When we are trying to minimize development expenses we will be very strict at blocking changes that increase our design workload, and we will be very liberal about encouraging changes that decrease the workload.

Our second key economic objective is designing for low product cost. Low-cost products require eliminating all unnecessary elegance from the design. The cost of the product becomes the single most important design goal for the program. Such a cost goal should be broken down between subsystems and owned by the entire design team. We must get our experts on cost, the manufacturing people and vendors, involved in the creation of the specification. We are unlikely to get low-cost designs if the specifications are written by marketing and engineering alone.

Low cost also demands that we do very careful market segmentation and achieve a deep understanding of the truly critical needs of the customer. Often it is valuable to constrain only a few key features and allow the design team to make all other tradeoffs to minimize cost. Any feature that places a cost burden on the product must be carefully challenged, and this challenge should continue throughout the entire design process.

In such a process, specification changes to minimize cost will become a way of life. For example, consider a medical instrument project designing a product with a numeric display on it. The marketing people had specified a display with three-quarter-inch characters, believing that this was necessary for visibility in the operating room. The design team began work and discovered that they could provide a standard display with one-inch characters for about half the price of the three-quarter-inch display, which was a custom component. This was clearly a situation where a specification change during the design process would improve the product cost.

Such situations are common, because the cost data corresponding to certain design solutions, technologies, and components do not become available early in the design process. We are much more likely to optimize product cost by allowing noncritical design parameters to seek their low cost points. Figure 9.2 shows an example of a design change being made to optimize product cost.

For our third objective, high performance, we need intense contact with the expert on performance: the customer. We must focus on the technical parameters that the customer uses to assess performance and avoid compromising performance by chasing after minor features. This requires a simple specification focused on a few critical features. Quantitative tools such as models of application economics and performance benchmarks are used for making tough tradeoffs. The team must be closely aligned around the key performance parameters as a critical goal.

For high performance, we will benefit from a strongly customer-driven design process. We use customer partners, advisory boards, and put specific target customers in the specification. These sources can help us adjust our target as we better understand the technical challenges of meeting performance goals.

Finally, when we are focused on performance we will again find our specification undergoing changes. Important information about what is technically feasible will become available during conceptual design and early detailed design. We need to test our original decisions against this emerging information. When we discover our initial assumptions were inaccurate, we must change our plans. This means that we need a simple straightforward process for making changes in the specification.

For our last objective, speed, we must start the design before we have a complete specification. The techniques of progressive specifica-

FIGURE 9.2

Cost Optimization

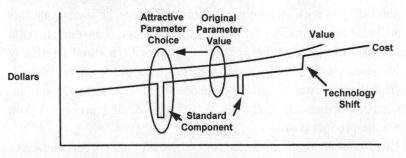

Performance Level

tion described earlier in this chapter are very useful. Such an approach becomes particularly important in two cases. First, we use it frequently with high complexity products, because full specification definition can take a lot of time. Second, we use it in rapidly moving markets because these markets create volatility in the requirement. It is pointless to push for meticulous definition if customer needs are evolving rapidly.

In such fast-moving markets it is also very useful to make the development process customer-driven rather than specification-driven. We use tools like customer partners, customer names in the specification, and customer advisory boards. By anchoring the project on the customer, rather than the specification, we will automatically detect changes in customer needs. Our fundamental reference point for control purposes becomes the actual customer, who is a moving target, rather than a specification document which is a static reference point.

SUMMARY

This chapter has focused on an essential subprocess in product development, the creation of a product specification. Certain critical activities that must precede such creation of the specification include the selection of the customer and understanding this customer. The three most important tools for understanding the customer are customer interviews, meticulous observation, and focus groups. Too often companies do a poor job at these front-end activities in the development process. They move rapidly to create a list of features without spending much time selecting and understanding their customer. Such actions only create the illusion of rapid progress; companies that shortcut these steps pay the price later.

Next comes the creation of the specification itself. We explored the need for a clear product mission and described the technique of progressive freezing of the specification. There was strong emphasis on the importance of a "thin" specification rather than a "thick" one. Use this approach with caution. It is the quality of the specification that makes it thin, not the thinness that makes it a high-quality specification. Brevity is a test of clarity and focus, not the cause of clarity and focus. I have seen brief but terrible specifications.

After creating a specification we must use it during the design process. We should assume that the specification is latently flawed and test it continuously during the development process to detect these flaws. Marketing must be very active throughout the design process, not simply at the beginning and end of this process. We called this approach a customer preference-driven process and contrasted it with the less robust, but more common specification-driven process.

We also emphasized the need to develop alternative channels for bringing the customer's voice into the design process. Three key techniques for doing this are customer partners, advisory boards, and proxy customers.

Finally, we described how these principles could be implemented for each of our four key development objectives. It should be obvious that there is no single approach to doing specifications that meets the needs of all four objectives. Thus, there is no "best practice" for doing a product specification. Instead, we always return to our economic objectives and use them to point us towards the answer that is right for our individual situation.

10

Use the Right Tools

In this chapter we will discuss how technology can help us to achieve our critical development objectives. After introducing some general principles about how technology can help, we will outline four key areas of technology and follow this with a discussion of how tools can help in particular situations.

THE USE OF TECHNOLOGY

Technology impacts development processes in three ways: it accelerates information flows, it improves productivity, and it reduces delays. Let us look at each of these factors in turn.

Accelerated Information Flow

The first major impact of technology on the development process is its ability to accelerate information flows in the design process. This means that valuable information can be produced earlier and distributed much faster. As we discussed in Chapter 4, information has more economic value the earlier it is received. By providing information early we can increase the speed of the design process and thereby reduce its expense.

For example, some companies doing clinical testing of pharmaceuticals will place their test data in an on-line database that can be accessed throughout the trial. Trends towards success or failure become visible quickly. This contrasts with a traditional approach which would wait for the entire trial to be complete before analyzing the data and assessing success. If you know that the drug is likely to succeed you can safely lay the groundwork for the next phase of clinical trials with little financial risk. This improves both the speed and financial risk of the project.

Another factor that accelerates information flow is the emergence of computer databases and telecommunications systems. Physical proximity is no longer essential for the quick exchange of information which can now be be communicated across the world in minutes. One semiconductor company uses design centers in Europe and America to extend the number of hours per day that are spent working on the design. With design activities concentrated at one center and analysis and simulation at the other, designers can have test results by the time they return to their desks the next morning. The more we can eliminate waiting for test results, the faster we can do the design.

This rapid information flow translates into quick feedback cycles for the design team. As we observed in Chapter 5, closed loop systems tend to go rather far off course if feedback is slow. Let us look at an example of applying this principle. In the book *Microsoft Secrets* Michael Cusumano discusses the rapid feedback cycles that have been achieved on programming projects at Microsoft. Some programs have daily build schedules, which means that they integrate all the modules together once a day. It is very valuable for programmers to get quick feedback on the quality of their design while the design choices they made and the logic of their code are still fresh in their minds. If they have to wait months for feedback they will have worked on many other tasks in the meantime, making it hard to pick up old code. These rapid feedback cycles translate directly into higher productivity for the design team.

Improved Productivity

Although each project is different in some respect, some design activities are still repetitive. Design automation tools take these repetitive steps and automate them. A finite element model calculated manually is a boring and unrewarding activity. Design tasks that are rich with repetitive calculations are ideal candidates for automation which improves both speed and accuracy.

Interestingly, such automation does not always translate into a savings in design time or expenses. Many computer-based tools have a "steep learning curve." Productivity is low at the start but improves quickly as you gain experience. Expressed another way, there is a very high fixed-cost component, in time and expense, when using many of these tools. In some cases a quick manual calculation can produce an answer faster and more cheaply than the sophisticated tool.

The second reason that savings may not appear is that we often find ourselves doing more calculations with our new tools. When calculations were manual we were quite stingy about only calculating those things that needed to be calculated. When a tool comes along that makes it much easier to do a calculation, we apply the tool to everything. The growth in calculations can often outstrip the productivity improvement added by the tool.

On the positive side, the computer also can eliminate many routine tasks like checking design rules and checking for interference between mechanical parts. These tasks seldom excite a design engineer and often get less than full attention. In contrast, the computer is a tireless worker that treats each calculation with equal enthusiasm.

Reduced Delays

There are two ways that technology can reduce delays in our process. We have already talked about one of them, which is the acceleration of information flow. The second impact is a bit more subtle: technology reduces process queues. To understand how technology does this we need to think back to some of the ideas we discussed earlier.

In Chapter 3 we pointed out four general methods for dealing with queues: adding capacity, reducing demand, reducing variability, and using control systems. Technology acts primarily to increase capacity and reduce variability. When capacity increases, and if we are smart enough not use up this capacity by overloading the organization with new projects, we will see a decrease in development queues. Unfortunately, most companies use productivity increases as an excuse to start new projects and their queues remain the same. You can avoid this problem by monitoring the right metrics, which we will discuss in the next chapter.

Technology also helps us to reduce queues by reducing the variability of design activities. Technology drives "art" out of the process and substitutes "method," which has less variability than art. Since variability in task duration is a major cause of queues, technology will help us reduce the size of these queues.

IMPLEMENTATION PRINCIPLES

There are two important principles to follow when introducing technology into a process. First, if we want to use technology to its potential then we will have to change our development process. We can implement technology without process change, but we can never fully exploit it without changing our process. Second, we should adopt technology based on its economics, not simply for the sake of having new technology. Many technologies are pushed for their own sakes. Avoid this trap because there are abundant opportunities to find technologies that do achieve handsome payback.

Technology Changes Process

Let us begin by looking at the interaction between process and technology with the example of implementing computer-aided design (CAD) within a company. Such an implementation would commonly go through three stages. In the first stage, the pre-CAD dark ages, engineers with slide rules would be doing analysis and preparing some rough overall drawings for the design and drafting group. This group would be working with traditional vellum and pencils to create the final engineering drawings for the product. They would typically be located in the same area as the engineers that they were working with, so a close relationship would develop between the two groups. The draftsmen would even make minor design decisions based on their experience, so the engineer would not need to specify everything. Still, an engineer would ultimately have to sign off on the acceptability of a drawing.

In the next stage CAD would be introduced. When CAD systems first emerged they were expensive, slow, and hard to use. No engineer wanted to be waiting two minutes for the screen to redraw. Few engineers had the patience to learn the complex user interface of the system. Even if they learned it, a CAD seat for every engineer would have been too expensive. The logical response to these pressures was to centralize the CAD resource in a single group. This group provided services to the engineers. Thus, a new technology changed the economics of the process, and we responded by changing the process.

Once we made this process change we would notice some interesting organizational impacts. The centralized group was typically located in a different area because they often needed an air-conditioned computer room for their equipment. They didn't have nearly as good communications with the engineers as they did in the old days. This affected their responsiveness and it also hurt design quality. Being in different locations decreased informal information flow. The draftsmen did not talk as much to the engineers, and the engineers did not get as much feedback from them. Because the draftsmen were a major repository of knowledge, when the communications link with them was weakened we lost valuable feedback, reducing the quality of our designs.

In the third stage of CAD it became attractive to make CAD seats available to the engineers. This occurred because user interfaces became easier, system speed increased, and the cost per seat came down. However, again this required changes in operating procedures. The CAD stations were moved back into the engineering area and the engineers were trained to use them. Many of the detailing activities formerly done by the drafting group were now done automatically by the CAD system. Design rules could be embedded in the software instead of being carried in the heads of the draftsmen. The number of draftsmen went down, and the engineers began to see what they were designing much earlier in the design process. By seeing the design emerge as they created it they could make changes much earlier.

The important point behind this example is that the way we organize both our process and our people will be influenced strongly by the technology. If we are not prepared to change these dimensions as we introduce the technology we will not get our money's worth out of the technology.

Pay Attention to Economics

The second important implementation principle is to be guided by economics. This is the one reliable compass that we have to point us to true north. The choice of technology should always be driven by its effect on the economics of the development process.

This point is critical because most companies have many resource needs competing for scarce budget dollars. You may want better CAD systems, better instrumentation for your designers, improved capabilities in your test facility, more general purpose PCs available to a larger portion of the department, a new parts database to encourage reuse of components, a product data management system, and on and on. How do you decide where to spend the money? You must have some rational way of selecting between potential investments. The solution lies in the analysis that we discussed in Chapter 2. Remember, the overall development process has four key economic parameters: development expense, unit cost, product performance, and speed. To change any of these four process parameters has economic impact. Whenever we evaluate a potential investment we must ask how it will change each of these factors.

You may notice that this approach is radically different from the traditional focus of the accounting department on only one of the four factors: development expense. That narrow focus is dangerous because development expense is rarely the most important economic leverage point.

For example, let us consider a new CAD system. Our analysis may show us that engineering design is on the critical path for a very small portion of the development process, whereas testing may consume a lot of time on the critical path. If critical path time is expensive, then it would generally be smarter to work on the testing process than to work on making design activities more efficient. We need to spend our dollars on the things that pay off best. Of course, such analysis can be subtle because technology can impact economics in a complex way. For example, expensive engineering changes late in the design process may originate from poor tools being used early in the design process.

Let us look at how we could use a business model to analyze the effect of adding another seat in the CAD area. If a CAD seat cost us $100,000 and it reduced the queue in the CAD area from fifteen days to an average of five days, the total cost of ownership per year of a $100,000 piece of capital might be $35,000, including depreciation and maintenance.

Now let us look at the cost of delay. Ten days of extra queue in the CAD area may affect ten products introduced in the course of the year. The average cost of delay for these programs may be $500,000 per month. This means that the business-level cost of delay for this company is $166,000 per day of queue. The total delay cost impact of not adding the seat is $1.66 million.

Compare this to the annual cost of adding the seat. We break even on the extra seat in eight days. Figure 10.1 illustrates the economics of this decision.

You will note that this analysis depends on having a business-level cost of delay. If you do not have a business-level cost of delay, approved by the finance department, you have little chance of doing this analysis.

FIGURE 10.1

Adding a CAD Seat

Annual Benefit	Annual Cost
Queue Reduction = 10 days	**Annual Expenses = $35,000**
Cost of Queue = $166,000/day	
Total Benefit =$1.66 Million	**Total Expenses = $35,000**

Net Benefit $1.63 Million
Profit Payback 8 days

TECHNOLOGIES

There are four general categories of opportunities for technology to affect the way we do product development. First, there are tools that automate design computations and decisions. Most CAD systems fall into this category. Second, there are technologies that improve the effectiveness of testing processes. These include rapid prototyping and test automation systems. Third, some tools can improve communications within our organizations. Telephone systems, networks, and videoconferencing fall into this category. Finally, there are tools that simplify information storage and retrieval. We will discuss each of these areas in more detail.

Design Automation

The automation of design computations and decisions has had a huge impact on most companies' design processes. It is not unusual to see productivity increases of 10:1 in areas that are susceptible to automation. Calculations that used to take twenty days are being completed in twenty hours. Many modern products like microprocessors could not even be designed without these tools.

Design automation tools provide four economic benefits. First, they reduce the time it takes to do our design analysis. For example, the productivity of a designer doing integrated circuit (IC) design has increased by at least a factor of 100 in the past ten years. We can design circuits today that would have been impossible in the past. Second, the tools reduce the expense of doing this analysis. This benefit comes along with the time savings. Third, the tools systematize our design process by doing things like embedding design rules into the computations. They can allow us to produce higher quality designs than we could achieve manually. Finally, they make it possible for us to consider many more alternative solutions, which can enable us to find a more optimum low-cost solution.

It is not necessary to describe these tools in detail because they are marketed diligently by their vendors. If you have use for such a tool and can afford to buy one it is likely that a salesperson is already knocking at your door. I will simply offer two observations.

First, while many very successful designs have been done with very simple tools, you are operating with a significant handicap without good tools. Oversold though they may be, these tools are critical for a modern design process. The financial payback on design automation is usually very compelling.

Second, design automation should not be restricted to standard packages that are sold by vendors. Many design tasks can be automated with simple tools like spreadsheets, databases, and math programs. For example, one electronic component company reduced the cost of bidding on new designs by a factor of 100. They simply created a database of the hundreds of existing custom designs they already had. Then, they developed a simple way to interpolate between the designs in the areas where they did not have an existing solution. Since the existing designs were well-documented and tested, they achieved significant savings in documentation and testing. The result was that most of their quotations could be done in less than a day.

Prototyping and Testing

The second major category of tools allows us to test products earlier, faster, and more efficiently. The tools in this category include prototyping technologies and all varieties of test automation. Testing is a highly attractive area to automate because its work is inherently repetitive and usually on the critical path of programs. Unfortunately, many companies that invest aggressively in design automation are living with twenty-year-old tools in test automation.

When we look at prototyping we can distinguish between cheap prototyping technologies and rapid prototyping technologies. Both enable us to test earlier in the development process and get answers from customers much faster. Cheap prototyping approaches are those that leverage the cost of the prototype. We can use our existing product or even a competitor product as a tool for prototyping. One printer company used a Digital Equipment printer, the LA-120, as the testbed for their product. They wanted to test a new electronics concept before their own mechanism was ready. By using the LA-120 mechanism they quickly found that their electronics concept was sound, so they could finish the rest of the design. As we will discuss in Chapter 12, a carefully focused technical testing strategy can dramatically reduce the cost of early prototypes.

Rapid prototyping technologies are equally valuable, but their value comes from their speed. They generate information for us early in the design process when we can correct problems cheaply. This can be helpful in reducing market risk and technical risk. For example, tools such as stereo-lithography may enable us to get a visual model of the product early in the process. Too often we delude ourselves into thinking that we can visualize things accurately from a blueprint. Not everyone can. For example, a VP of marketing at a telecommunications equipment company saw the first physical prototype of a new product and said, "You know, I really thought that it was going to be smaller than that!" Blueprints and artists' renderings never communicate as much as a full-scale physical model.

In addition to prototyping early, we can automate our test processes, producing major benefits in both testing costs and testing speed. Once we have automated a test facility we can run it twenty-four hours a day, seven days a week. This greatly shortens the time it takes to do some tests—particularly reliability testing. We will discuss this topic in more detail in Chapter 12 when we look specifically at the testing process.

Communications

A third major category of tools are those that improve communications on a team. Since product development has high uncertainty, and uncertainty can only be resolved with information, we have a great need to communicate information during the development process. In fact, as we discussed in Chapter 1, since the primary output of development is information, we are more concerned with how we handle information than how we handle physical product.

The good news is that tools for communications have been improving quickly. (Perhaps almost as fast as we are increasing the complexity of our projects.) These tools affect the speed and cost of exchanging information. Consider, for example, an electronic product developer who is working with a supplier in Taiwan. The supplier is doing tool design. Drawings used to be sent via courier with several days of delay. Now data files are sent electronically in less than an hour. This means that changes are flowing much faster. A further advantage of such electronic information exchange is that data does not have to be reentered into the system, reducing unnecessary data-entry errors.

Many companies today are adopting videoconferencing technology, which can enhance the flow of information. Videoconferencing seems to work very well when you already know the people on the other end and have worked with them. You are more likely to be comfortable with a person you have eaten lunch with than someone you have only seen on a TV monitor. Videoconferencing appears to be very useful when you need to get a bunch of busy people to make a decision. For example, one company uses videoconferences to link their foreign sales offices into their domestic marketing department. When they need feedback on a design they get regional managers from all their regions on the same video link and reach a decision. There is no need to wait until everybody can gather at headquarters.

E-mail systems are the best value for the money of any communications tool available today. For less than $20 a month you can exchange information with people on the other side of the world. Furthermore, E-mail has an exceptional advantage over many forms of verbal communications and videoconferencing: it provides a permanent textual record of the communications. This textual record can be searched for key words or transferred into other documents. It is likely that E-mail will become as ubiquitous as the telephone for most development teams.

We have even seen companies invest in tools as simple as pagers to improve team communications. If a buyer who supports a team is not able to attend the team meetings, she can be paged when her input is needed, and either resolve the issue over the phone or come to the team room to resolve it.

The communications tools mentioned above are transforming many development teams. They are inexpensive compared to many of the other technologies that we have talked about.

Information Storage and Retrieval

Technologies used for information storage and retrieval are important because they eliminate wasteful overhead and encourage reuse. On a complex project much time is wasted because people do not have a single reliable source of information. Computers and data communications give us a very powerful tool to fix this. Complex databases can be implemented with sophisticated information management systems, but useful solutions can also be as simple as a bill-of-material maintained by one person and available on a network. What is essential is that the latest change is instantly available throughout the organization, and that there is a sole authoritative source for the data. Computer technology has given us a better way to do this than any manual tool.

A key area where improved information storage and retrieval easily pays off is in design reuse. We discussed the importance of module reuse in Chapter 8. But information reuse goes far beyond the reuse of modules in the system. We can reuse specifications, test plans, market studies, and a vast array of information. This reuse will occur when it becomes easier to retrieve the information than it is to recreate it. There are many product data management systems and groupware products that make this easier to do.

Earlier in this chapter we discussed a component design process that took six months to complete. Much of the time was spent in doing custom design work and testing the design to see if it would work. The company had a large number of similar designs but was doing a unique design for every order. The problem was retrieving the information on the old designs. When this problem was solved they discovered that most of their custom orders could be handled by interpolating between existing solutions. All that was needed was an easy way for the designers to access the various solutions. The average design lead-time dropped from about six months to about six days. It is worth noting that this thirty-fold improvement in cycle time occurred without investment in CAD systems or design automation. It simply required creating an easy way to access information about existing design solutions and indexing it in a way that was useful to the engineer doing the next design.

SUMMARY

This chapter covered the impact of technology on our development process. We explained how technology can improve our process by accelerating information flow, improving productivity, and reducing process delays.

However, this technology can only be fully exploited when the development process is changed to take full advantage of it. Each change in technology forces us to reconsider the design of our development process.

We also described how the economic analysis techniques of Chapter 2 can be applied to evaluate investments in these technologies. Many companies make the mistake of considering only the expense impact of using the new technology. This is a shortsighted way to view the technology since it only considers one of the four key economic parameters, and one that is usually not very important.

Finally, we described four key areas of technology that are impacting product development. Design automation is probably the most visible area for most managers, and it is certainly one that has compelling justification. But this is only one area of opportunity. A second key area is prototyping and test automation. Testing can easily consume half or more of the development cycle. It represents a very attractive area to improve both cycle times and efficiencies. The last two key areas are communications, and information storage and retrieval. These technologies are having substantial impact because the tools are often quite cheap compared to the benefits.

In closing this chapter, we must once again stress the need for a balanced approach to technology that carefully evaluates the economics of the chosen investments. The complexity and cost of many of the potential investments are rising to the multimillion-dollar level. They are too important to be treated with a quick qualitative justification. Any tool that is worthwhile will show attractive economics as long as you consider the *full* economics of the tool. This means that you must quantitatively estimate development expense, unit cost, product performance, and cycle time impacts and convert these to profit dollars. Otherwise, you will either miss the opportunity to invest in a good technology, or you will waste money on a marginal one.

11

Measure the Right Things

I n this chapter we will discuss how to control a process. We will begin with some general principles in the design of control systems. Then we will cover the implementation of controls at a project level which are focused on particular economic leverage points. Finally, we will look at business-level controls focused on the same leverage points.

GENERAL PRINCIPLES

We must begin our discussion of controls with some general ideas regarding the design of our control systems. We will explore how economic analysis can help us with the problem of process control. Then, we will discuss the concept of the control triangle, which is a simple but powerful tool for thinking about control strategies for multidimensional control problems. Next, we will consider where we want to put control points in the organization. Finally, we will talk about some strategies for the selection of metrics.

Drive Metrics from Economics

The first question is, why control the process? When we know *why*, it almost automatically clarifies *how* we must control the process. Is a controlled process inherently better than one that has more uncertainty? No. Since the purpose of our process is to make money, it would follow that the purpose of controlling the process must be to influence economic outcomes. There is *no* other reason to be interested in process control.

This is a critical concept. Control and reduction of variability are only valuable if they impact our economics. Ask yourself if you would be interested in controlling the process if your profits were guaranteed by an insurance policy. If they were, most people would see no need to control their process.

Now if, in fact, our underlying goal in controlling the process is to influence the economic outcomes, this points us clearly to one of the central issues in process control. We must focus our control effort on parameters that have the greatest impact on economics. Fortunately, we have a highly effective way to determine this, which is the economic analysis that we discussed in Chapter 2. If our business-level analysis suggests that most of the economic leverage is in schedule, we should focus our control effort on schedule; if we discover most of the economic leverage is in cost, we should focus on cost. We can only determine where to focus our control effort by finding out which parameters most influence the economics of the project.

This simple concept is perhaps the most frequently violated principle in control system design for product development. If you look at the project controls in a typical company they are intensely focused on the control of expenses, whether or not this is a leverage point. For example, one electronics company VP of engineering pointed out that he needed approval from his boss to take office supplies out of the storeroom even though he was authorized to make multimillion-dollar decisions on vendor contracts. This focus on expense control probably comes from the fact that our control specialists, the accountants, have very well-developed systems for controlling expenses. Our largest control system gaps are in the area of controlling unit costs, product performance, and development speed.

The Control Triangle

Although we may choose to focus our control effort on the parameter that has the most economic impact, this will not give us the luxury of ignoring other project parameters. If we leave these other variables unconstrained we could be in for unpleasant surprises. Instead, we need a rational approach for applying constraints to programs.

A powerful tool for doing this is called the control triangle, which is

FIGURE 11.1

Project Control Triangle

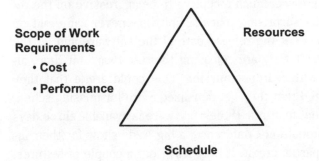

Scope of Work Requirements

• Cost

• Performance

Resources

Schedule

shown in Figure 11.1. We can think of each project as having three primary constraints. The first constraint is the scope of work. This is determined by the level of product performance and the unit cost we are trying to achieve. The second constraint is the amount of resources that we allocate to the program. The third constraint is schedule or the duration for which we apply these resources. In essence, we must make the resources times the schedule equal to the required scope of work; otherwise the program will be incomplete. A convenient way of showing this relationship is by depicting these three constraints as a triangle.

As we discussed in Chapter 1, one of the interesting things about product development is that it has variability in it. This means we cannot constrain all three sides of the triangle. Instead, we must consciously choose which side of the triangle will bear the project's inherent variability. We will constrain two sides of the triangle, and variability will be driven into the third side.

In most companies the choice of which sides to constrain is made unconsciously. If there is a standard approach, it is to constrain the scope first, then the resources. This will then drive the variability into the schedule axis. Such an approach is so common that most companies use it without even thinking about it. This approach is embedded in standards like ISO 9000, which insists on defining all design inputs first and then identifying the resources required to do the project. It is embedded in the Software Engineering Institute model, which defines requirements first. Yet, for the thoughtful product developer it is not the only alternative. Let us consider two other approaches.

One alternative is to constrain schedule and resources and let scope function as the safety valve. This is an increasingly common technique, particularly with software products. For example, vendors of CAD software used to define a new release of software and announce a release date in advance. There was much incentive to be aggressive on the release date. It was not surprising that the software never came out on time. Now, companies set the release date of the software and let the scope vary. As a result they are releasing their software on time, although sometimes with features missing. One could argue that they have finally recognized that they get penalized more for missing schedule than for leaving out features. If their software is available three days after the Design Automation Conference, a big trade show for their industry, they get no partial credit. If they leave out a couple of features, they still get most of the benefit from the product introduction. Therefore, they have made the correct business choice by using scope of work as the relief valve on the program.

What would happen if you were developing implantable heart valves? Would you want to give the team a schedule and a budget and tell them to do the best they could at meeting requirements? Not too smart. In this case, partially fulfilling the requirements would be an expensive mistake. At the same time, variation in schedule is expensive because time-to-market is critical in the medical products industry. In this case, the best strategy is to constrain requirements and schedule and to use resources as the relief valve. This is perhaps one of the most difficult approaches to manage because resources are a very "sticky" control factor. In practice, we almost always have to overresource the program from the very beginning, because it is usually difficult to add resources late in a program.

In both of the above alternative approaches you see companies constraining the sides of the triangle where variation will do the most damage. This is a very fundamental principle of project control. The choice of what to constrain is not simply one of philosophy and tradition, it should be grounded on economics. For example, if our economic analysis shows that expense variation has low overall economic impact, we put our variation there. We never adopt the traditional sequence of constraining scope and resources and driving variation into the schedule unless the economics make this sensible.

Decentralizing Control

The third key choice in control system design is how decentralized to make the control. To make this choice we need to distinguish between three types of control events that take place during the operation of a closed loop control system. The first is the adjustment of actual performance in response to a control signal. For example, the heater comes on because the room temperature is too low. This control event occurs very frequently. The second control event is the setting of the control setpoint, in this case, what temperature to keep the room at. This second event occurs much less frequently. The third event is the choice of control system. For example, should we use an open or closed loop system to control temperature? Should we control the temperature in the middle of the room or the temperature by the doorway? This is the least frequent choice. Figure 11.2 shows these three types of events.

Since Level One events occur frequently and in large numbers, we want to control these events at low levels within our organization. Thus they can be handled rapidly and at low cost. Level Two control events involve the adjustment of the setpoint. In many cases, we can afford to place these decisions at intermediate levels in the organization because they occur infrequently and they have a great impact on system performance. At times it is even useful to push control of these decisions down to the team if it has a better understanding of the system-level consequences than higher levels of management. For example, the development process may develop a control rule which says we begin using external production to supplement the prototype shop whenever the queue for prototype parts is greater than two weeks. It may be better to let the VP of engineering decide on whether two weeks is the correct number than to let the CEO make this choice.

Level Three control events refer to control system design. They generally should be made jointly by middle and upper-level management be-

FIGURE 11.2
Levels of Control Events

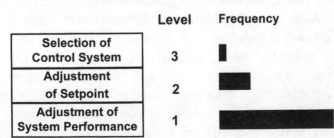

cause of the broad and lasting impact of such decisions. It is important to get the users of the control system involved in control system design because we want them to "own" the control system. When the users participate in the design of the control system they understand its goals better, can minimize its non-value-added activity, and are more likely to happily use the control system. Furthermore, if they have participated in the design and selection of the control system they can detect when the control system has outlived its usefulness because they understand the underlying assumptions behind its selection.

An interesting example of this control strategy occurred on the Boeing 777 program. The weight of the plane was critical to the success of the program. Boeing would have to pay the excess fuel cost for the life of the plane if it was overweight. There was an enormous economic incentive to hit the weight target of the plane. Management recognized that a control system for this parameter was necessary.

A classic management response might be to have the program manager control all decisions associated with weight. Such an approach is pulling the Level One control event to a high level in the organization. The danger in this approach is the enormous delays it adds because so many decisions must be approved.

A more sophisticated approach, and one that is very common in the aerospace industry, is to establish a weight budget for each subsystem and to track how subteams do at meeting their weight budget. Such an approach pulls the Level Two events to a high level of the organization and leaves the Level One events at a relatively low level.

Boeing used an approach that was even more sophisticated. They determined the economic cost of missing the weight objective and then deployed decision rules down to the worker level. Reportedly, an individual designer could make design decisions to take weight out of the plane, spending up to $300 per pound with no required approval. The designer could go to $600 per pound with the approval of his or her supervisor, and to $2,500 per pound with approval of the program manager.

Such an approach has great advantages over the traditional budgetary controls. In a weight budget system, if you were working on an assembly that was within its budget you would not work any harder. If you were over budget you might resort to expensive choices to try to get back to budget. This might mean that the wing team might buy weight for $3,000 per pound while the engine team was neglecting opportunities that cost only $300 per pound because they were still within their budget.

This example illustrates two alternative designs for the Level Two control rules for the system. In the first case, using a weight budget was deploying specific targets to the team; these targets drove local optimization of the weight of each subassembly. Such local optimization of subassemblies does not always lead to global optimization of the system. In the second case decision rules were deployed. Decision rules are powerful because they optimize at the system level, avoiding the problems of a locally optimal, but globally suboptimal decision.

Selecting Metrics

A fourth principle of control system design is to choose metrics that are well-suited to the control objectives. We normally look for three characteristics. First, they should be simple. Second, they should be relevant. Finally, they should focus on leading indicators.

We like simple metrics because they are easy to generate and easy to understand. We increase the value of a metric by making it easy to understand. A "sales-weighted mean R&D profit throughput index" is likely to mean nothing to anyone except the person who thought it up. Measures like the total project spending are easy to understand. We also get more accurate and timely information when we make it easy to generate the metric. The ideal metrics are self-generating in the sense that they are created without extra effort in the normal course of business.

The second characteristic we look for is the relevance of the metric to the desired objective. Many things that are easy to measure are not very relevant. For example, we could measure, as one company did, Fedex expenditures per project. They placed tight control on this activity because of exploding costs in this area. Yet this cost element is not likely to have much effect on overall program economics. One could argue, as the company did, that focusing on this visible cost area was of symbolic value, raising cost consciousness. But the symbolic effect could have been achieved by focusing on any one of many other factors, all of which would have been less damaging to the development process. The problem is that people use Fedex because some things are time-sensitive. By placing prior approval requirements on a time-sensitive activity we eliminate the advantage of using Fedex. It would have been far smarter to communicate the heightened interest in cost effectiveness by something like using cheaper rental cars.

One test of relevance is whether the metrics focus on things that are actually controllable by the people being measured. Psychologists have found that when people think that they can control something, they are more motivated to control it. Measuring people on things they cannot control simply causes stress, dissatisfaction, and alienation. This creates an interesting tension between the need to be controllable and the need to be comprehensive in our metrics. Our interest in controllability will cause us to focus on local parameters. Such local focus can create globally suboptimum decisions. In contrast, when we focus on global parameters, then the people being measured may feel that they cannot control what they are measured on. This argues for a blended strategy where we focus most of our metrics on controllable, local factors with some counterbalancing metrics on global parameters.

A third characteristic of a good metric is that it is focused on leading indicators. As a general rule accountants like metrics that are lagging indicators because they provide more accurate information. An accountant likes to get the monthly shipments accurate to the penny, even if it takes three weeks to close the month. A manager, on the other hand, prefers an imperfect forecast of the future to a perfect report on the past. Let us look at some real life examples. In a testing department, for example, we can measure productivity in terms of the number of test hours per product. This will give us some feel for whether testing is efficient or not, but it is a lagging indicator. On the other hand, consider a metric like personnel turnover in the test area. A high turnover rate among testers can lead to a lower productivity level in the future. The turnover in this area can be a powerful leading indicator of future productivity problems.

Another example of a leading indicator is process queues. As we saw in Chapter 3, a process queue gives a very early warning of cycle time problems. Thus, it is better to measure the size of the test queue than it is to measure the processing times of individual tests because test queue size is a leading indicator of future delays in test processing.

A leading indicator of schedule problems is the manning level on the team. If we compare planned manpower versus actual manpower we often discover that the team is not operating at full strength early in the program. This is dangerous because this is when the most critical design and architecture decisions are made. Figure 11.3 shows how we can track the percent of authorized manning early in the program.

The specification freeze metric that we discussed in Chapter 9 can

FIGURE 11.3

Planned vs. Actual Manning

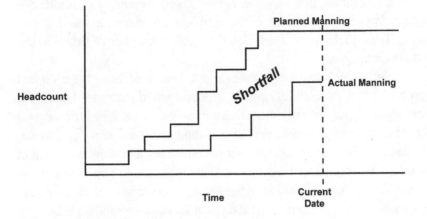

also be a strong leading indicator of rework in the process. If half of the specification is still not frozen, we will commonly see expensive downstream rework. Process capability or Cpk is often tracked throughout the development process because it is a leading indicator of cost and quality problems later on. It alerts us to manufacturing problems long before the design reaches the factory floor. In contrast, engineering changes after manufacturing release of the product serve as a powerful diagnostic tool, but are a lagging metric.

In summary, there a few basic principles that we should keep in mind when we structure our control systems. We should focus our metrics based on the economics of the program. We should consciously decide where to permit variability to develop in the project, driving it into a parameter that will do the least economic damage. Control should be decentralized as much as possible by placing the most frequent decisions at the team level. Finally, we should look for simple, relevant, leading indicators of future problems.

PROJECT-LEVEL CONTROLS

Let us now look at how we might apply these principles to the design of control systems for each one of our four critical objectives: development expense, product cost, product performance, and development speed. We will begin by looking at project controls and then move to process controls.

Expense-Focused Controls

There are three primary methods for controlling project expenses. We can limit delegation, use expense budgets, and do piecewise funding of projects. We will discuss each of these, which are shown in the first column of Table 11.1. We will refer to this table a number of times in the next several pages.

First, let us look at limiting delegation. This is perhaps the simplest approach. It forces justification and approval when expense dollars are being spent. While limited delegation can be effective, it has the side effect of forcing a lot of justification of spending decisions, and typically delays these decisions significantly. Most companies avoid the approach of having managers approve every decision in advance. The primary exception lies in capital spending, where many companies will carefully review each attempt to spend capital against an existing capital budget.

A second method for controlling expenses is to establish expense budgets. This approach is used in almost all companies. An initial spending budget is established for each area. To exceed the budget, people must get approval. Since most decisions will fall within the budget, they can be made quickly.

One challenge in using a budget approach is the amplification of variability that we discussed in Chapter 5. Anytime we decompose an ag-

TABLE 11.1

Economically Focused Controls

Expense	Unit Cost	Performance	Speed
Limit Delegation	Limit Delegation	Limit Authority	Control Schedule Changes
Expense Budgets	Cost Budgets	Performance Budgets	Time Budgets
Piecewise Funding	Design Reviews	Design Reviews	Schedule Review Meetings
		Decision Rules	Use Priority Systems
		Design Defect Tracking Systems	Monitor Queues
		Customer-Driven Process	

gregate top-level target into pieces we will increase the variability of each of those pieces. This means we will see noise that increases the more pieces that we divide the budget into. Therefore, though we divide the budget into lots of little pieces, we should not try to control these little pieces. If we do, we will spend all our time trying to chase down random variations in spending. It is much better to control at a higher level of aggregation.

A third technique for controlling expenses is to do piecewise funding of the program. This is perhaps the least common approach in large businesses, but it is very common in venture capital–backed start-ups. Most start-up companies are not funded with all the money they need to design their products. Instead, they get an initial round of funding and work until they begin to run out of money. If they have done something useful with the money, then they get more money at an attractive price. If not, they either get no money or pay dearly for it. This approach ensures that good money is not invested in a failing project.

This approach contrasts strongly with the one-shot funding approach used in most corporations. In some companies moneybags come in two sizes, big and empty. Because it is a long painful process to get a big bag of money, you ask for as much as you can get. You produce wonderfully detailed forecasts of the future, with high profits and huge sales. Management scales these back, but eventually decides to give you the money. Once you have the money you never give it back, no matter how bad the project becomes.

Cost-Focused Controls

The three primary methods for controlling the unit cost of the product parallel the approaches we use to control expenses. They are limited delegation of authority, using cost budgets, and design reviews. (See the second column of Table 11.1.)

Limited delegation of authority for decisions that influence unit costs takes many forms. Which decisions we control depends on whether more cost comes from outside purchases or internal manufacturing activities. To control outside purchases some companies provide approved parts lists and approved vendor lists that designers are encouraged to use. The "encouragement" is that you avoid the daunting paperwork that it takes to get a new part into the system. Other companies will encourage engineers to design for existing processes, preventing them from designing a part that cannot be made by the existing manufacturing process.

In general these explicit limits of authority tend to be quite cumbersome. They are very common in defense-related companies, many of which are not known for producing cost-effective products. Often engineers are forced to use expensive, nearly obsolete components and processes because they are the ones that are already approved. In practice, it is unclear whether limiting authority for design decisions is actually effective at producing low-cost products.

In contrast, the second method to control unit costs is effective and frequently used. Cost budgets are established for key modules, allocating a portion of the total cost of the product to each module. Then, the cost of the actual design is tracked throughout the development process. This is a powerful technique because it provides a clear objective without controlling, and delaying, every engineering decision.

The third method of control is to do design reviews explicitly focused on the achievement of cost objectives. Called design for manufacturing (DFM) reviews, these take place throughout the development process. Manufacturing experts critique the design, pointing out process limitations and highlighting design decisions that will raise manufacturing cost. These reviews are most productive when made during the first 20 percent of the development cycle when specification and conceptual design decisions are being made. Such decisions determine most of the product cost.

Performance-Focused Controls

Six controls focused on product performance are shown in the third column of Table 11.1. First, we can limit authority to change performance. Second, we can use performance budgets. Third, we can use design reviews. Fourth, we can use decision rules. Fifth, we can use design defect tracking systems. And finally, we can use a customer-driven process.

The first method is to limit the authority to deviate from a performance target. It is typical to use the product specification as the control document when we do this. For example, if we had a team designing an implantable heart valve, we would not give them autonomous control of product requirements. Instead, we would formally approve the specification at the beginning of the program and put it under configuration control. Then, any future changes would need approval by the same people who approved the original specification.

In general, though such rigid controls over every feature in the specification may look attractive, they are unwieldy. They dilute attention by trying to focus on everything instead of on the "decisive" features. There are a couple of pragmatic modifications we can make to this approach. First, we can use a "sacred features" approach. For example, we might consider the product logo and the color scheme to be a "sacred" feature. Though they may be arbitrary, they are carefully constrained and cannot be changed without the approval of the program funders. Ordinary features can be decided by the team itself. This approach works well because it can focus the control effort around the most important features. A second way to implement specification control is to use functional requirements instead of features. A functional requirement should be something the product does. For example, the car must accelerate from 0 to 60 in ten seconds. Functional requirements give designers freedom to alter individual features while still constraining overall performance.

A second tool to control performance is the performance budget. This budgets a key performance parameter among various elements of the system. For example, for aerospace systems the weight budget is very important. For radar systems bearing error is a key performance parameter, so such systems have an error budget which is allocated among system elements. In integrated circuit design it is common to have a target size for a chip, because the size of a chip has an enormous impact on the number of good chips that you can get from a wafer of silicon. Chip development programs commonly allocate a chip "real estate" budget among the various subsystems so that the total system will hit its die size target.

A third tool for controlling performance is the use of design reviews. These reviews evaluate chosen design solutions to determine if they are the best possible solution to the design problem. To provide an independent point of view these reviews use people who are technically knowledgeable but who are not members of the project team. Such independence is important because the project team will become committed to the solution that they have invested the most effort in. These reviews can be done both informally and formally. Formal reviews are a requirement for quality procedures like ISO 9000, and are valuable and necessary. However, some companies choose to supplement these formal reviews with informal sessions where a couple of engineers from other teams are gathered to look at a tough problem and the proposed solution. The advantage of informal reviews is that they require less preparation time and less documentation, so that the focus can be almost exclusively on problem solving.

A fourth tool for controlling performance is the use of decision rules. An excellent example of this approach is the decision rule for weight that was used on the Boeing 777 program. This example was discussed in more detail earlier in this chapter.

A fifth tool for controlling the performance is an effective tracking system for design defects. These systems log each defect into a database and classify it in terms of importance and status. Defects progress through several stages. After a defect is detected, it is analyzed to determine a root cause. Then a solution is identified, and the solution is designed. Finally, the solution is implemented and tested. Not only is such a tool a powerful way to track individual defects, but the aggregate data coming from such a database give enormous insight into the development process. For example, whenever we find defects at a faster rate than we fix them the quality of the product is out of control. Eventually we reach a critical point at which the defects are being fixed faster than they are being found. At this point quality starts improving. By monitoring the rate at which defects are being found and fixed we can align resources appropriately to each stage of the process. It makes little sense to be generating a large queue of waiting problems if our bottleneck is in fixing these problems.

All of these first five tools are based on a specification-driven design process. The final tool for controlling performance is using a customer preference-driven process, as shown previously in Figure 9.1. The key to this alternative approach is that it uses customer preference as the reference point against which we measure the design. Such a reference point creates a feedback loop that compensates for both errors in formulating the specification and those caused by shifting customer requirements. It ensures that the performance meets the customer requirements rather than simply those that were imperfectly captured at the time that we wrote the specification.

Speed-Focused Controls

We also have a range of choices available when we have to control schedule. First, we can put tight controls over deviations from schedules. Second, we can create a time budget for the program, which is simply a detailed schedule for the program. Third, we can use schedule review meetings to detect deviations and plan remedies. Fourth, we can establish a priority system. Finally, we can monitor work queues in our process. These approaches are shown in the fourth column of Table 11.1.

The first tool to control speed is placing tight controls over deviations from schedule. At one company the CEO said that he wanted to be personally informed whenever his pet project deviated from schedule. The project moved like lightning to the head of every queue. Needless to say, it was completed in record time. This is a powerful way to keep an individual program on track, albeit at the cost of other programs. When we constrain schedule we must be careful to create some other relief valve for the process. We cannot constrain budget, scope, and schedule at the same time.

A second tool to control speed is a time budget. This is simply a detailed timing plan for the project activities. Such schedules are best developed by those involved with the work. An aggressive schedule usually comes from a three-step process. First, management provides overall guidelines in terms of target completion date, acceptable risks, and permission to challenge the fundamental procedures where they do not make sense. Next, the team builds a bottom-up schedule using these guidelines. The third step is for management to review the bottom-up schedule and modify the rules if necessary.

As we mentioned in Chapter 5, when we design a schedule by grouping individually variable activities this affects the variability of the overall schedule. The variability of the total package will depend on how the individual components are combined, as Figure 11.4 shows.

When activities are combined sequentially, and the variability in each individual activity is independent of each other activity, then the total variability is proportional to the square root of the sum of the squares of the variability of each activity. What this means in a practical sense is that activities combined in series will have less variability on a percentage basis than any of the individual activities. Thus, we magically reduce uncertainty when we combine uncertain things. In contrast, when we combine activities in parallel the total variability is driven by the variability of the worst case activity. Highly concurrent activities have inherently higher variability than sequential activities.

Variability does some other interesting things to our schedule when combined with the expandable character of development work, a prop-

FIGURE 11.4

Variability and Schedule Design

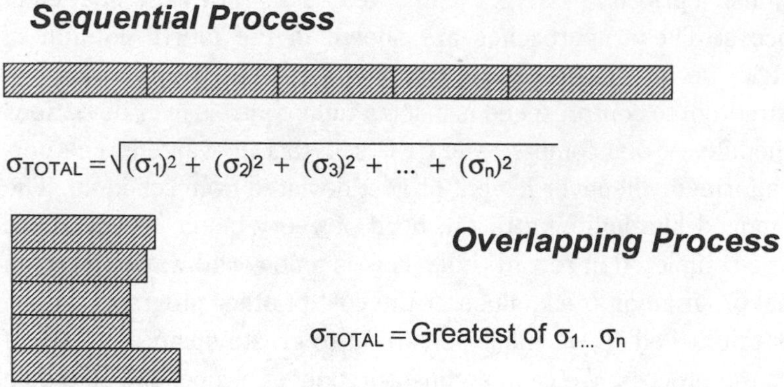

Sequential Process

$$\sigma_{TOTAL} = \sqrt{(\sigma_1)^2 + (\sigma_2)^2 + (\sigma_3)^2 + \ldots + (\sigma_n)^2}$$

Overlapping Process

$$\sigma_{TOTAL} = \text{Greatest of } \sigma_{1\ldots}\ \sigma_n$$

erty that we talked about in Chapter 1. We are sometimes tempted to believe that preparing schedules, and rigorously enforcing them, teaches people how to plan better. This only works to a limited degree. If we try to get developers to produce high-certainty schedules, we force them to leave margin in each individual activity that they estimate. This margin gives us a high confidence estimate but it virtually guarantees slow development, because inevitably the margin will be used to refine the design. We normally find it is best to use two schedules on a project. The team works to an aggressive schedule and a high confidence schedule is published to the external world. Both schedules are official project schedules. The normal margin between the internal and external schedule is about 20 to 30 percent of project duration. The project team should monitor the safety margin between the two schedules to ensure it does not erode too early in the program. This need for two schedules is almost unique to the highly variable world of product development. Were it not for variability and expanding work we would be able to use a single master schedule for the project.

A third tool to control speed is schedule review meetings. These are analogous to design review meetings except they are focused on future activities rather than what has already happened. These meetings review the immediate future activities to identify changes in the critical path of the program, problem activities, and needs to reallocate resources. Depending on the pace of the program review meetings should take place weekly or monthly. Occasionally, they will take place daily.

A fourth tool to control speed is the use of priority systems to determine the sequence with which competing jobs will be handled. Such systems are particularly important when there are queues in a development process, since these queues are a major source of delay. Priorities should be set for projects on the basis of their cost of delay, calculated as explained in Chapter 2.

A final tool to control schedules attacks the problem of queues directly by monitoring them. As we discussed in Chapter 3, measuring process queues gives us the same information about the health of the process as we can get from measuring cycle times, but it gives us this information much faster. The easiest way to find process queues is to ask the development team. It is very common to find queues in drafting, procurement, prototyping parts, and testing. By measuring and managing these queues we can attack the key determinant of cycle time, process queues.

BUSINESS-LEVEL CONTROLS

Up to now we have focused at the level of the individual project. There are analogous controls that we can place at the level of the overall business. These controls measure the functioning of the overall development process. Again, the controls should be focused on our four key economic objectives.

Expense-Focused Controls

Expense-focused controls measure the relative efficiency of our development process. They tell us how good we are at converting R&D dollars into products. We can measure ourselves either against our own products or against competitor products.

For example, a typical measure of efficiency is R&D expense per product introduced. If one of two comparable products costs twice as much as the other one, something went wrong with the development process. If it costs us more to develop a product than our competitor, we have a less efficient development organization.

Of course, one weakness of cost per product is that some products generate much more revenue than others. This points us toward a more refined measure of efficiency, which is dollars of sales generated per dollar of development spending. In a crude sense, this number is simply the inverse of a common financial ratio, which is R&D spending as a percent of sales. A more accurate version of this number will relate the spending on a particular product or product family to the revenue produced from this product or product family. We should note, however, that as we move away from simple measures like spending per product, it becomes harder for us to get competitor information to measure ourselves against.

Finally, we can further refine our measures by looking at gross margin dollars generated per dollar of R&D. This metric gives us more credit if our product produces higher profits. The metric can be computed either on a period by period basis, or on a product by product basis. If we look period by period we get a quick answer, but an inaccurate one due to the mismatched timing of R&D spending and gross margins. If we look on a product by product basis we get accurate numbers but we must wait several years to get a clear picture of gross margin. A useful compromise is to measure gross margin generated by the product during a limited window, such as the first two years after introduction. This gives you fairly quick feedback with good enough matching.

Cost-Focused Controls

There are two basic ways to measure the unit cost achievements of the development process. The first is internally focused. It measures the cost-performance ratio of the product. For example, integrated circuits may improve at a rate of 20 to 30 percent per year. If we find our designs are failing to improve in cost-performance ratios, then our design efforts are not producing economic benefits.

The second way to measure unit cost is against equivalent competitor products. This is generally done by a type of reverse engineering, which carefully calculates the manufactured cost of the competitor design. Some of the cost advantage will be due to manufacturing capabilities and some of it will be due to design decisions. A careful analysis will show us how much of our cost advantage is due to each and can be used to focus improvement efforts in the area of greatest leverage.

Performance-Focused Controls

As you may recall from Chapter 2 on economic analysis, we normally measure performance by looking at the revenue stream associated with the product. This means that a performance advantage should be measured in terms of market share gains, sales growth, or price premiums in the marketplace.

At times we can also use technical measures of performance to track our improvements, but this should be done carefully. For example, a power supply vendor might look at the watts per dollar that he can provide to his customers. We would suggest caution whenever using such technical measures, because they can lead companies to chase a single product metric instead of paying attention to all of their customers' needs. For example, at a time when most of the disk drive industry was focusing exclusively on the cost per megabyte of their disk drives, Conner Peripherals spotted a niche in the laptop computer market where low power consumption was the key driver. As a result they dominated this profitable segment of the market while the companies that focused only on cost per megabyte had to struggle with cutthroat commodity pricing.

Speed-Focused Controls

The central issue in measuring development process speed is to define a cycle time metric for the development process. Companies have experimented with a variety of metrics, as shown in Figure 11.5.

First, let us look an internally oriented metric. We can break the overall process into several smaller chunks and measure each piece separately. This allows us to more easily troubleshoot cycle time problems and gives us faster feedback regarding improvement. Three logical chunks are the fuzzy front end, the development process itself, and the

FIGURE 11.5

Cycle Time Metrics

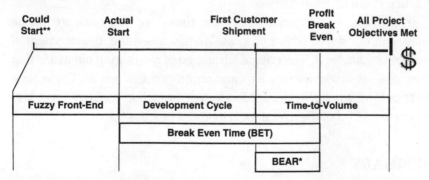

Note:*BEAR = break even after release; **Could Start requires existence of technology and product need known by customer.

volume ramp of the product. There are a variety of ways to define the markers for each of these intervals. We normally begin to measure the fuzzy front end when we receive a project proposal which contains an idea that could justify triggering the business planning process. Our normal criterion for deciding the fuzzy front end has begun is if technology exists and a customer need is known. This forces us to separate technology development from product development, which is generally a good practice as described in Chapter 7. The fuzzy front end is over when we open a charge number for the program. This marks the beginning of the development process itself. The development process ends when the first revenue unit of the product is shipped to the customer. This also marks the beginning of the time-to-volume stage, which measures the time between the first revenue unit and when all program objectives are met. Such objectives may include unit cost, manufacturing yield, product availability, warranty failure rates, and the like.

Another variant for measuring the development cycle is break-even time (BET), which was introduced by Hewlett-Packard. It measures the time from the first dollar spent until the development investment has been recovered. A portion of break-even time, called break even after release (BEAR), measures the time from first shipment until profit break even.

An alternative way to measure cycle time is to adopt an externally based measure. Such a measure focuses on whether a product introduction arrives in the market ahead or behind those of important competitors. From a business perspective this measure has more significance than an internally oriented measure. It does not matter if we run faster than the competition as long as we win every race. We can do this by starting running before they do.

In addition to measuring our cycle times we can measure queue lengths in our development process. We discussed the measurement of queues in Chapter 3. The critical advantage of monitoring queues is that they give us instantaneous information on process health. Cycle time metrics have a much longer feedback cycle, which in turn results in less effective control of the overall development process.

SUMMARY

In this chapter we began with some general principles for the design of metrics. We emphasized the need to drive metrics from economics to ensure the control effort focuses on project and business parameters that really make a difference. We also discussed the concept of the control triangle and how the unconstrained axis of the triangle will act as a relief valve for the inevitable variability involved in doing something new.

We made a distinction between what we called Level One, Level Two, and Level Three control decisions. We discussed the importance of decentralizing the highly frequent Level One control decisions and controlling Level Two and Level Three decisions at higher levels of the organization. A typical strategy for doing this is to provide decision rules, rather than performance standards, for the team. We closed our discussion of general principles by suggesting three practical criteria for selecting metrics: simplicity, relevance, and acting as a leading indicator.

In the remainder of this chapter we discussed specific control tools that could be used at the project level and the business level. These tools were focused on our four key economic goals: development expense, unit cost, product performance, and development speed. The key message of this chapter is that allocation of scarce time and attention to project control must be done with a keen understanding of the underlying economic leverage points. Don't spend resources controlling things that don't influence the overall economics of the business.

12

Manage Uncertainty and Risk

I n the previous chapter we explained that the only reason to control uncertainty was to influence economics. We seek to control those things that might prevent us from achieving our economic objectives. We can depict a simplified version of this problem using what management scientists call a decision tree, shown in Figure 12.1. For example, let us say we have a choice between using a new technology or the old one. If we use the old one we have the same costs we have today. If we use the new technology and it works, we might save $1 million. Let us say it will cost us $100,000 to develop and test the new technology. Our payoff is the probability-weighted savings of the new technology less the cost of developing it. This is $1 million less $100,000 times the chance that the new technology will work. Our downside is that we waste money developing a new technology that does not work. This is $100,000 times the chance that the technology does not work.

When we talk about risk we focus on the downside. To reduce risk we must reduce either the magnitude of the downside or the probability that it will occur. The most obvious way to drive all risk out of the process is to always choose the old technology. Unfortunately, this means that we can never enjoy the benefits of new technology. I make this simple point lest you think that I am only interested in eliminating risk. I am not. As we saw in Chapter 4, if we eliminate all chance of failure, we have eliminated all information generation from the design process. In reality, we want to "manage" risk in the specific sense that

FIGURE 12.1

Quantifying Risk

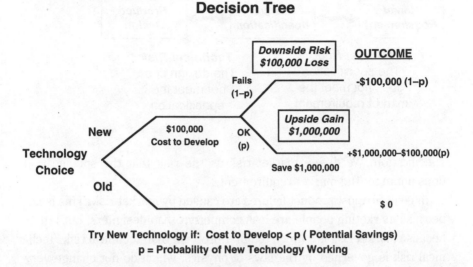

Decision Tree

Try New Technology if: Cost to Develop < p (Potential Savings)
p = Probability of New Technology Working

we are willing to take rational risks. This means that we will accept the downside from a decision if the payoff is high enough.

This also means that there are three factors that can make a risk more attractive. First, we can decrease the magnitude of the downside. Second, we can reduce the probability of the downside. Third, we can increase the magnitude of the upside. Usually we find the biggest opportunity to control risk in product development lies in decreasing the magnitude of the downside, rather than reducing the probability of failure.

In this chapter we will discuss a useful model for thinking about risk, which is to segment it into market and technical risk. Then, we will discuss how each of these risks can be managed. After this we will dig deeper into the problem of managing testing, which is a major leverage area for most development processes.

MARKET AND TECHNICAL RISK

As Figure 12.2 illustrates, the overall risk that we are trying to manage is the risk that the product design will not meet the market requirements. We can divide the risk of product failure into two components using the product specification as the dividing line between them. We define technical risk as the risk that the design does not the meet the

FIGURE 12.2

Types of Risk

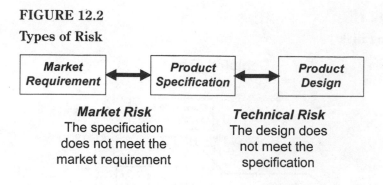

specification. We define market risk as the risk that the specification does not meet the market requirement.

In general, most product failures are caused by market risk. This is not because marketing people are less competent than designers, but rather because market risk is a much tougher problem than technical risk. Technical risk is governed by the laws of physics, which do not change very frequently. In contrast, managing market risk means capturing the requirements of what may be a diverse group of users. As we discussed in Chapter 9, these people may have differing needs, they may have trouble expressing these needs, and their needs may be changing with time. This makes market risk a more formidable challenge than technical risk.

We can even attempt to put some measures on how well companies do on different aspects of risk. Companies like Motorola report doing a six-sigma job of getting their designs to meet their product specifications. This means that the design will fail to conform to its specification at a defect rate of 3.4 parts per million. In contrast, we might look at how successful companies are at meeting market requirements. Most companies would be delighted to have 50 percent share of their market. This would correspond to less than one sigma defect rate. For most companies overall risk is dominated by the market risk.

Ironically, although market risk dominates, most companies focus the majority of their risk reduction effort on technical risk. They spend millions of dollars testing to determine if their products meet their technical specifications, and resist spending hundreds of dollars to assure that their specifications actually meet market requirements. When it comes to managing risk the major opportunity for most companies lies in controlling market risk. This is true even when we find abundant opportunities to manage technical risk better.

FIGURE 12.3

Risk Management Steps

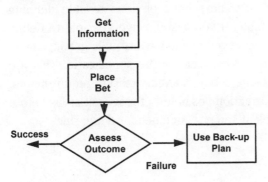

To manage risk from an economic perspective we need better information on the upside, downside, and probability. This will enable us to place intelligent bets. In general, we will be better off if we receive this information early because this will decrease the downside and raise the upside. For example, if we are experimenting with a new shielding technology for our electronic circuits we would like to know whether it will work as early as possible. If it works better than expected, we can use it more if we know this early. If it doesn't work, we would also like to know this early, while the cost of changing the design is still low. If we place what we think is an intelligent bet and it does not pay off, then we need to have some alternative approach, or back-up plan.

This means that our risk management strategy usually has three pieces. First, we must obtain information so we can place intelligent bets. Second, we must determine if the bets have paid off. Third, we must have some sort of back-up plan in case we have lost. These three steps are shown in Figure 12.3.

Let us look at the process of managing market and technical risk in this context.

MANAGING MARKET RISK

As we discussed earlier, market risk is determined by how well the product specification meets customer requirements when we introduce the product. Two factors that increase this risk are that customers often do not know what they want, and that their requirements may change during the development process.

Our first step in managing market risk is to assess which areas of the product specification are at risk. These can either be overt areas of disagreement or areas where customers have obvious trouble defining their requirements. For example, if you asked a five-year-old to define the requirements for a video game you would have trouble getting a useful definition. Risk areas can also be areas of the specification that are known to be vulnerable to change due to changing market requirements. We must obtain the best information possible in these risk areas before we place our bets. Let us look at some techniques for doing this.

Use a Substitute Product

A consumer products company looked at an attractive higher-priced niche in their market. A competitor had dominated that niche with a premium product formulation. The company wondered if it should design a product for this niche. The development would have cost millions. The wise old R&D manager said, "Perhaps there is another way to approach this problem. Do we really have to develop the product?"

Instead of developing and test marketing the product they created some new packaging concepts and a dummy advertising campaign to position the product. They put the competing product into their own new package and tried it on a focus group. The results were fascinating. They discovered that their customers perceived them as always offering low-priced products and were unwilling to pay a higher price for the premium formulation. The company could have spent millions on product development only to discover in test marketing that they would not have been able to realize the necessary pricing in the market.

This highlights one of the most powerful techniques for resolving market risk early in the design process. We don't need our own new product to resolve market risk; we can use a competitor product, or a modified version of one of our old products.

Simulate the Risky Attribute

An equipment manufacturer wants to introduce a new piece of machinery. The only problem is that it makes a different kind of sound than the old product which made a steady hum. The user is likely to be sensitive both to the loudness of the sound and the type of sound. How much sound dampening is really needed? One approach might be to build multiple prototype units with different levels of sound dampening to assess which one has the highest acceptance. However, the answer will come late in the development process, when it is expensive to change things. An alternative approach is to recognize that we are trying to test a particular attribute. We do not have to test the entire product. A tape recording with a volume control could be used to find out what level is acceptable. This alternative test is more precise and can be done earlier, because it does not require a completed design.

If the risk of a bad specification is centered around certain product attributes, they often can be tested independently very early in the design process. We do not need to complete the design process to find out what the customers really want. By conducting early testing of particular attributes we find out whether our bets will pay off early in the design process.

Make the Design Flexible

A third way to control market risk is to avoid committing ourselves to a single market segment. This is equivalent to making the back-up plan part of the design itself. For example, consider a software product where some of the market wants the icons on the top of the screen and some of them want the icons on the bottom of the screen. One way to deal with this problem is to do careful market research to choose the preferred alternative. An alternative approach is to offer both options and let the users select their preference.

We must add such flexibility with care because it can raise cost and complexity. Nonetheless, products that have enough flexibility to be adapted to the needs of individual customers can be big winners.

Move Fast

In markets that change rapidly market risk is inherently high because the requirement evolves so quickly. As we saw in Chapter 7 this risk rises exponentially with the length of the development cycle. Thus, *if we shorten our development cycle we dramatically reduce market risk.*

At one communications company a team leader who had just completed a record-breaking six-month development program remarked, "We did the program so fast that marketing did not have a chance to change their minds." Another way of looking at this is that they did it so fast that marketing did not *need* to change their minds. The faster we develop the product the more stable the requirement becomes.

MANAGING TECHNICAL RISK

Let us now turn to technical risk. This is the risk that the design will not meet its specification. Since the specification sets goals for cost, performance, expenses, and schedule, a negative variation in any of these creates technical risk.

Technical problems arise when we have inadequate resources to accomplish the required design tasks. Sometimes this comes from incorrectly estimating the work required to do the design. Such incorrect estimates can come from poorly defined design tasks, from optimism, or from management's adjustments to the original estimate. We will focus on this estimating problem. A second cause of technical problems occurs when we do correct estimates, but fail to resource the program adequately to support these estimates. In such cases we can shift our focus to tracking the actual application of resources to the program versus the plan. As we discussed in the last chapter, a manpower or expense budget for a project is a good tool for doing this.

Inadequate staffing during the early stages of a project is a chronic complaint of development teams. They find that the key technical players, who are needed to start the current program, are still fighting fires on the last program. We avoid this problem by creating some downtime for key technical people between high priority programs. Scheduling a month or two of lower priority work can provide a buffer to absorb the potential variability of the previous program. This work can consist of investigating new technologies, evaluating process improvements, or any potentially deferrable task. It allows us to start the next project with all members ready to engage the task fully, which plays an important role in team dynamics.

We must stress that the problem of following through on manpower plans is simply one of management priority. When new product development truly has priority in an organization we see few problems. When the daily actions of management demonstrate that manufacturing and customer problems always take priority, then resources will constantly be stolen away from the product development teams and these projects will suffer. To prevent this management should track whether new product programs actually receive the planned resources early in the program. This can be done by talking to project managers, attending team meetings, and looking at actual timesheet data. It cannot be done by asking who is assigned to the team, because as all project managers know, being assigned to a project and actually working on it are two different things.

Let us now shift our attention to the problem of getting good estimates of things we have never done before. As with market risk we have three issues. First, we must obtain the information required to place intelligent bets. This allows us to take sensible risks. Second, we must determine if these bets have paid off. The earlier we find this out the easier we can react. Third, we must have some sort of back-up plan in case we lose the bet. It is better to pre-plan this reaction than to improvise it. As we address these issues we must focus our attention on the areas of greatest technical risk.

How do we find these areas of high technical risk? The biggest technical problems will show up in two areas. First, we can have problems with particular high-risk technologies. These problems can show up at any stage of the program. Second, we can have problems with the overall integration of the system. This problem usually shows up near the end of the design process when we begin system integration. I would strongly recommend that you look at actual failure data for your own projects to determine the relative importance of these two failure modes.

Our experience suggests that for most products the majority of failure modes relate to integration, which means they lie in the interfaces rather than in the modules. This occurs because the number of interfaces in a system increases much faster than the number of modules, as shown in Figure 12.4. In most projects technical risk will be dominated by system integration risk.

Controlling Subsystem Risk

Let us start with the first source of technical risk, the high-risk subsystem. Which subsystems have high technical risk? To assess this we must first perform our project-level analysis to determine how each program objective (expense, cost, performance, and speed) will impact profits. Then we assess each subsystem to determine how it might impact each of these factors. The easiest way to do this is to use a team meeting in which members estimate the downside risk for each subsystem in

FIGURE 12.4

Interfaces and Modules

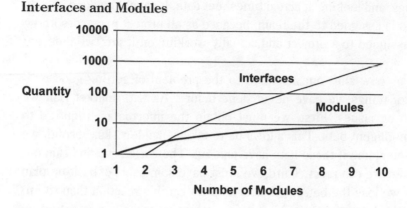

terms of magnitude and probability. This can be done by having each member assess risks independently, having a discussion on why different team members have rated risk differently, and then having team members reassess risks. The output of such a meeting is a surprisingly good understanding of project risk. Contrary to the common view that unknown risks are most important, most teams are surprisingly aware of where they are likely to fail in a program.

Once we have determined the location of subsystem risk we must develop a strategy to deal with it. The two best techniques are to avoid the risk entirely, or to quickly resolve the uncertainty and use a back-up approach if the original approach fails.

We should avoid risk when the payoff of taking the risk does not offset the downside. For example, we may have the potential to incorporate a new technology in the design to achieve a substantial cost savings. Doing this may delay the program from one to three months, depending on the problems that show up. On the surface, delaying the product may seem to make sense because of the cost savings. A more careful analysis might reveal that the same cost reduction could be made after manufacturing release. This would occur early in the product life before many units are shipped, allowing us to capture 95 percent of the cost savings without any possible delay. Shifting subsystem risks to later product introductions frequently makes economic sense.

If taking a risk is economically justifiable, we should not try to avoid it. Instead, we try to resolve the uncertainty and create a back-up plan in case the risky approach fails. Normally, there are two ways to resolve the uncertainty. First, we can resolve it analytically by creating a computational model or simulation. This is an increasingly powerful technique, particularly when the cost of a prototype is high. Second, we can construct a focused technical test early in the program by prototyping the specific high-risk subsystem.

Such highly focused prototypes can resolve very complex technical problems early in a program. In fact, the notion of doing design on paper without any physical models or prototypes is a relatively new approach in engineering. You may wonder how great works of architecture were built properly the first time without any of the analytical tools that exist today. What was the secret of the ancient architects? They commonly constructed a large scale model before they built the actual structure.

When the first nuclear submarine was built Admiral Rickover insisted on having a cardboard and wood full-scale model built. He believed that this was the only way to ensure the maintainability of the engineering plant. Submarine design requires that equipment be packed in very close proximity to get good volume utilization. This permits the hull to be smaller, which gives it less drag and thus makes it go faster for a given size power plant. The best way to safely push to the limit on volume utilization is to build a physical model.

The key in these models is that they are highly focused on answering specific questions. If you want to assess the interior layout of a submarine you don't need to build it out of steel—cardboard and wood work fine. The purpose of the model is to resolve a limited number of technical issues.

There are two side benefits to building such models and prototypes early in a program. First, they often resolve market risk at the same time as they resolve technical risk. People react much more faithfully to physical models and working prototypes than they do to artists' renderings and engineering drawings. Second, these models have a strong energizing effect on the organization. The psychological reality is that we are more likely to be convinced that a project is making progress when we see something physical than when we see images on paper.

There is a delicate balance to be struck between the perfection of the model and the effort required to achieve this. If the model is too imperfect it can give inaccurate results and can actually demotivate the organization. Observers may prematurely decide that the project has no chance of success. If we spend too much effort in making the model perfect we can build an excessive commitment to the chosen design approach. The more effort we have put into creation of the model, the more likely we are to resist design input from other sources, such as the customer. Nonetheless, it is usually smart to worry about the appearance of any model, even those focused on technical issues. This appearance often has an important impact on people outside the team, and it can be difficult to reverse initial impressions.

Once our models have resolved whether a particular approach works, we know whether to use it or use a back-up plan. Such back-up plans are best developed ahead of time. In many cases, if the risk is high enough we may partially implement the back-up plan to improve our reaction time in case we have to use it.

Controlling System Integration Risk

The second key source of technical risk is system integration risk. For most programs this is the greatest source of technical risk. Four strategies to reduce system integration risk are outlined here: we can increase the reuse of interfaces; we can provide extra design margin in the interfaces; we can increase the amount of subsystem testing; and we can force system integration to occur earlier in the project.

Our first strategy to reduce system integration risk is to reuse interfaces. We do this because most system integration risk lies in the interfaces. As we discussed in Chapter 8, when we reuse an interface we have a stable, tested interface to act as the design criterion for the design of an individual module. For example, integrated circuit design will often use existing submodules, called library modules, as building blocks of design. Since these existing modules have already been manufactured on another product, we are reusing the interface between the circuit design and the manufacturing process. This eliminates many potential problems regarding the fit between the circuit design and the manufacturing process.

A second strategy to reduce system integration risk is to provide extra design margin in the interfaces. As we discussed in Chapter 8, this margin allows performance problems in individual modules to be contained locally within that module. This margin needs to be carefully allocated to buffer risk around the riskiest modules of the system.

A third strategy for reducing system integration risk is to increase subsystem testing. By creating a robust subsystem test environment we can identify many of the problems that we traditionally find in a system test. A good way to do this is to analyze the defects from system testing and ask if they could be found in an earlier test stage. For example, we may discover that a subassembly that works in the lab does not function in a harsher field environment. We can reduce this problem by doing environmental tests earlier at the subsystem level.

A fourth and final strategy is to force system integration to occur earlier in the design process. Companies are increasingly moving away from "big bang" integration at the end of the design process to what many companies call "piecewise" integration. They are recognizing that you can begin to exercise interfaces between subsystems as soon as you have more than one subsystem complete. An example of this early system integration is the design approach now used by Microsoft, as reported by Michael Cusumano in his book *Microsoft Secrets*. Microsoft often begins the integration process in the first third of the development process, doing daily builds, or integrations, of the code from this point on. An interesting feature of this process is that one individual on the team is appointed to be responsible for the daily build of the code. He or she is called the "build master." The build of the code is a lengthy process and the build master is usually up until late at night. You get this duty if you submitted the code that didn't compile on the previous night, or as the programmers say, "if you broke the build." This makes everyone work hard to submit clean code.

Back-up Plans

Our back-up plans protect us against failure on a key economic parameter. We normally seek to offset damage in one area by compensating with one of the other three parameters. For example, we may exceed our development expense if our design is more difficult than we expected. There are three ways to react to this. First, we could relax our unit cost goals on the project. This might permit us to reuse existing but higher cost subsystems from other projects and thereby save some design time. It could also reduce the degree of refinement that was necessary in the design, which would also save design time. Second, we could relax our performance targets. We might drop some features or lower the performance goal on other features. This can be reasonable even when it means the product will become unacceptable to some customers. It simply means that we will experience a lower market share or receive a lower sell price in the market. Third, we could slip the schedule, moving to a more sequential design process, with a smaller team working longer. Such teams are more efficient. Which of these approaches we would choose will depend on the results of our economic analysis which tells us the compensation technique with the least economic impact.

In a similar manner, we can look at strategies for reacting to risks that affect unit cost, product performance, and schedule. Figure 12.5 summarizes some of the strategies we can use to deal with different types of technical risk.

In the development of these back-up plans, many of the same principles apply that were used in developing the original plan. The back-up plan should be written down or we risk having different team members with different understandings of what we will do. The back-up plan should be prepared by the people who may have to execute it, because we need both their knowledge and their commitment. Finally, the back-up plan should be prepared in advance, because we will do a better job of weighing alternatives when we have time to reflect on our choices and consider dissenting points of view.

WORLD-CLASS TESTING

We now turn to one of the primary tools for resolving both technical and market risk, our testing processes. Too often testing is viewed as a necessary evil in the development process. It only exists because we make mistakes. If we made fewer mistakes, we would not need to do all this testing. We should spend our money on "designing in quality" instead of finding defects by testing. The result of such an attitude may be a test department that is underresourced and undermanaged. Unfortunately, by viewing testing as a problem, rather than an asset, we miss the opportunity to capitalize on the extraordinary improvements that can take place in product testing.

Let us start by putting testing in perspective. The elapsed schedule time for product testing is typically 30 to 60 percent of overall development cycle length. This is not another minor activity, it is a *major* design activity. Furthermore, during most of our design process we are doing paper design. Our tests tell us whether our paper models accurately represent the real world. Without tests we are operating in the abstract world of theory. The mismatch between the physical world and the world of theory is often unexpected. This means, as we saw in Chapter 4, that test results have inherently high information content.

FIGURE 12.5

Back-up Approaches

Compensation Approach	Risk Area			
	Expense Overrun	Unit Cost Overrun	Performance Shortfall	Schedule Delay
Expenses	■	• Reengineer High Cost Subsystems	• Reengineer Low Performance Subsystems	• Increase Program Resources • Pay for Priority Service
Unit Cost	• Relax Unit Cost Goals • Reuse Subsystems	■	• Relax Unit Cost Goals • Use More Expensive Subsystems • Reuse Subsystems	• Accept High Initial Costs • Reuse Subsystems
Performance	• Relax Performance Goals • Drop Some Features • Resegment Market • Use Two Step Introduction	• Relax Performance Goals • Drop Some Features • Resegment Target Market	■	• Relax Performance Goals • Drop Some Features • Resegment Target Market • Use Two-step Introduction
Schedule	• Slip the Schedule • Reduce Team Size • Use Cheap but Slow Services	• Slip the Schedule • Fine Tune the Design • Wait for Costs to Improve	• Slip the Schedule • Wait for Technology to improve	■

In fact, testing is usually the stage of design process that generates the greatest amount of information. Thus, since our goal in the design process is to generate information, we should be very interested in our testing activities.

One of the key reasons that most companies misunderstand the role of testing is because they fail to distinguish between design testing and manufacturing testing. This is natural, because both types of testing may use the same testers, doing the same tests, using the same equipment. The similarities are easier to see than the differences, yet the differences are fundamental. Manufacturing testing is done to identify defects in the manufacturing process. A good outcome from a manufacturing test is no failures. The key measure of a manufacturing test is its efficiency. Design testing is very different. Design testing is done to generate information about the design. A good outcome is high information generation early in the design process. As we saw in Chapter 4, this means that we want a failure rate close to 50 percent. We also want to get this information as early as possible. For example, we are willing to increase testing costs by duplicating tests at different stages of our development process because any information we can get early is extremely valuable. Thus, in contrast to a manufacturing test, the key measures of a design test are its information generation rate and when it generates this information.

We can look at test process design using the same concepts of subprocess design that we discussed in Chapter 7. A test process can be optimized for expense, for unit cost impact, for performance, or for speed. Since we use different approaches for each, we need to be clear about our goal. As usual, the economic analysis of Chapter 2 provides our sense of direction. Let us look at how we might do testing differently to optimize different objectives.

Cheap Testing

The first objective is minimizing testing expenses. This is an appropriate objective for a manufacturing test, but rarely the most important objective in design testing. When it is, we find that there are four key techniques for reducing the expense of testing. First, we can eliminate duplicate testing. Second, we can test at the most efficient subsystem level. Third, we can automate many testing processes. Fourth, we can avoid overtesting the product.

Many times designs run through the same battery of tests over and over again. By eliminating duplicate test coverage we reduce our testing expenses. To use a simple analogy, most word processor users will spell check their document at the end of the editing process instead of doing it ten times along the way. This gives the same output quality with less time spent spell checking.

Use this technique with caution because it may increase other design expenses at the same time as it reduces testing costs. Tests done late in the development process often identify defects when they are very expensive to correct. Thus, all the money we save by late testing can be wasted doing expensive design changes.

A second technique for reducing testing costs is to test at the level in the product structure at which we can find defects most efficiently. Most commonly this is at the subsystem level because we can exercise subsystems more thoroughly, cheaply, and quickly by testing them directly. For example, a copying machine consists of a mechanical mechanism and control electronics. The electronics monitor the mechanism to detect things like misfeeds and mechanical component failures. One way to test the electronics is to test the copier at the system level, waiting for a mechanical component to fail to find out if the electronics are not working. An alternative is to isolate the electronics and test them as a subsystem. Now we can simulate the signals that might be generated by the misfeeds and failed components. By simulating these signals instead of waiting for real-world failures we can fully test the electronics a thousand times faster than we could at the system level. This is an enormous savings in time and expense.

A third technique, automating the test process, can dramatically reduce testing expenses. When we automate testing and data collection associated with the test we can shift from doing testing forty hours a week to doing testing continuously, 168 hours per week. Labor costs go down substantially and testing equipment works twenty-four hours per day.

A fourth technique is to avoid overtesting the product. Many times companies perform tests that waste testing resources. For example, a series of ten tests may be ordered on a prototype. The engineer reviewing the early test results discovers that the product failed the second test and will have to be redesigned, yet the remaining eight tests are run anyway, even though the data they generate are of little value. The problem is that the test department has been trained to run the whole pack-

FIGURE 12.6
Branched Test Plans

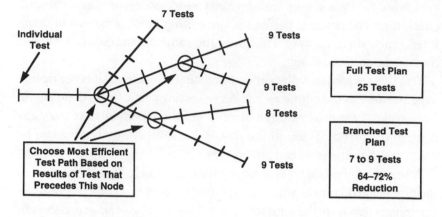

age of tests every time. The use of branched testing plans, as shown in Figure 12.6, is a practical solution to this problem.

With such a plan if the product fails certain tests we can follow a different branch. This can dramatically reduce the total number of tests, usually cutting testing expenses by at least 50 percent.

Low Unit Cost Impact

The next economic objective is to reduce the unit cost impact of testing. Again, we rarely find that this is a critical objective for most projects because testing adds little to unit costs. When we find this is important, we have two techniques to achieve it. First, we can eliminate product features that have been added solely to make the product easier to test. Second, we can use testing as a tool to fine tune product costs.

The first technique works better in theory than in practice. In theory, we reduce unit costs by eliminating product features that have been added for testability alone. For example, designers may put in test points or add connectors to a design to facilitate testing. Software programmers may add special sections of code to facilitate debugging of the product. Eliminating these features may lower costs. In practice, these features usually add little cost and they often only add the cost temporarily. Once design testing has been completed, it is usually easy to delete these features as a cost reduction of the product. We rarely find ourselves forced to carry the burden of extra unit cost for the entire shipping life of the product.

The second technique is more practical. Testing can be used as a very effective tool to fine tune the design. Our paper models are always approximations in some respect. In some cases they will cause us to overdesign the product, raising the unit costs. For example, many electronic circuits can product EMI, or electromagnetic interference. There are standard design solutions to this problem which involve reduction of source levels and shielding the source. Unfortunately, these solutions usually cost money. One company that designs computer equipment in a very price-competitive segment uses testing to keep unit costs low. They prototype the design and only add shielding when it is absolutely essential. Their designs never work the first time, but after several tests they have a working solution that is much cheaper than it would have been with a conservative, do-it-right-the-first-time design. When we use such a strategy to reduce unit costs we find ourselves testing extensively early in the design process.

Maximizing Performance

Our third key objective is product performance. As you remember from Chapter 2, we measure this with the life-cycle revenue of the product. We maximize this revenue when the product fully meets the customer's requirements. To test for this we must verify full functioning of the product. There are two ways to focus our test process on maximizing performance. First, we try to maximize test coverage. Second, we try to enhance the validity of the tests.

Our first strategy for maximizing performance is to increase our test coverage. This term refers to the percent of potential failure modes that are detectable by the tests. It may come as a surprise to some readers that 100 percent test coverage is an impossible goal for most products. The number of permutations and combinations that need to be tested can be staggering. For example, consider a personal computer that might run a single program with one hundred different monitors, one hundred different video boards, and one hundred different printers. It would require one million tests to validate all possible combinations. Now assume that there are one hundred possible operating system configurations, and the user might install only three of five hundred different programs on the machine. We now have to test over 124,000,000,000,000,000 combinations. If we could test one thousand configurations per second it would take almost four thousand years to run all the tests. And even if we did run all the tests, we would be testing trillions of possible configurations that will never occur in reality, which is a waste of time and money.

To deal with this problem most complex products are not 100 percent tested. Instead, smart developers carefully analyze their testing plans to ensure that product testing is focused on probable applications and configurations. This means that we must have a keen understanding of the actual application of the product to design such a test plan. We need much more than a simple list of product features.

This points us towards a second tool for improving performance. We need to enhance the validity of our tests. Our testing should generate the same type of failures that are showing up in the field. For example, if we are discovering that our products overheat in the field, but not in our testing lab, we need to understand why this occurs. Users may not be locating the equipment properly or they may be using it at higher temperatures. If we want to detect these failures before they show up in the field, we need realistic test processes.

We frequently see a lack of realism in test processes. Tests can be too loose. For example, when a company's product is connected to the well-regulated voltages that come out of a typical U.S. wall receptacle there may be no problem. But when the same product is sold in the third world where power regulation can be almost nonexistent, that product may have high failure rates. Tests can also be too strict. One company put their consumer product through a demanding series of tests only to discover failures that never showed up in the field. They kept redesigning their product to eliminate failures that never were likely to occur. One way to check the validity of our test processes is to test products that we know are successful in the field, ours and those of the competition. When we find that successful products fail our internal tests it is likely that our tests are not valid.

Fast Testing

An increasingly important economic objective for many companies is to optimize development speed. There are four techniques we can use to decrease testing time. First, we can increase the amount of parallel testing. Second, we can use reliability prediction. Third, we can decrease testing batch sizes. Fourth, we can monitor and manage queues in our test processes. We will discuss each of these in turn.

The first technique for decreasing testing time is to increase the amount of parallel or simultaneous testing. This will shorten the critical path of the project because a test off the critical path costs us no cycle time. For example, let us say we are trying to determine the proper strength for a particular component. If our low-strength design does not work we will use the higher strength design. When cycle time is important we should perform tests of both designs in parallel. That way the high-strength design is already pretested if we need to use it.

A second technique for shortening testing cycles is using reliability prediction. One technique for doing this is called the Duane method. This method of measuring reliability growth plots the cumulative failure rate on a logarithmic scale as a function of cumulative operating hours on the product. Such a plot is shown in Figure 12.7. When the failure rate is tracking downward as a straight line our fault correction process is functioning properly.

The power of this technique is that it allows us to predict when we are likely to achieve the targeted reliability of the product. When we get close we can begin downstream activities before we have reached our reliability target with minimal risk. For example, it is common for manufacturers of general aviation aircraft to test the plane's wings to make sure they will not fail due to fatigue. Such testing takes a long time. They do not wait to complete such tests before they begin selling the plane. Instead, they test the wings to a certain number of cycles and then begin to sell planes. They are confident that they can put test cy-

FIGURE 12.7

Reliability Growth

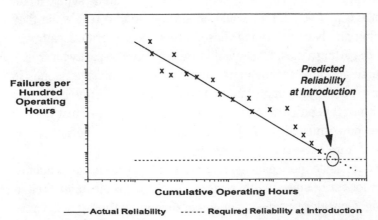

Failures per Hundred Operating Hours

Predicted Reliability at Introduction

Cumulative Operating Hours

————Actual Reliability   ------ Required Reliability at Introduction

cles on the product faster than any user will, finding any problem years before it will be a safety risk in the field.

The third technique we can use to improve testing speed is to reduce the batch size in our testing processes. By now you should be familiar with the relationship between batch size and cycle time. It should be no surprise that we can improve the speed with which we generate test results by decreasing the batch size of our testing processes. It should also be obvious that the path to doing this lies in decreasing the "fixed cost" per test, since this makes it economical to test in smaller batches.

Most companies have not taken advantage of small batch sizes in their testing processes. Instead, they fall into the same trap that we fell into in the pre-JIT factory. They try to amortize the fixed cost of setting up and performing the test over as large a test as possible. The natural outcome of this approach is that tests last a long time and make us wait a long time to get results. "Big-bang" system integration at the end of the development process falls into this category. In contrast, daily build-test cycles in software reduce batch size significantly. This smaller batch size gives us a very important advantage in refining our design quickly. Because feedback is so quick, the designers are still immersed in that particular section of the design. When testing isn't done until months after the act of design, it is hard to remember the details of the design, so that correcting defects is slower and less efficient.

The path to smaller batch sizes lies in reducing fixed cost per test cycle because such reductions make small batch sizes feasible. When we do this we can get some surprising benefits in other areas. For example, one company had dozens of test stands for testing a motor-operated system. They discovered that 30 percent of available test-stand hours were being consumed in setting up the equipment on the stands. With some simple modifications in the test stand, they could be setting up one test while they were running another one. Doing these setups off the critical path was equivalent to getting almost 50 percent more test-stand capacity for free.

The fourth and final technique is to measure and manage queues in the testing process. This important metric is one of the prime indicators of the health of this process. As we discussed in Chapter 3, test queues are a more powerful indicator than testing cycle times because they alert you to future cycle time problems before they occur.

Testing queues do more damage than we think. In some cases queues beget even longer queues; in other cases they cause projects to circumvent testing. Consider two design engineers planning their tests.

Design Engineer 1 (DE1): How is the test plan coming along?

Design Engineer 2 (DE2): It's almost done.

DE1: How many tests are we asking for?

DE2: We'll need the test department to do ten of them.

DE1 (looking at plan): It looks like they'll only run one noise test.

DE2: Yeah, I think we should pass easily.

DE1: But what if it is too noisy? We'll have to put some damping on it and test again.

DE2: Yeah, but that's not very likely.

DE1: I know, but the test department has an eight-week queue. If we fail a test, we will have to wait eight weeks before another test stand becomes available.

DE2: Maybe we better ask for another test on a unit with extra damping.

(Later)

DE1: Well that about does it.

DE2: Yeah, let's see, we'll request twenty-two tests from the test department.

DE1: Well, that's a lot of testing, but at least we won't get in their queue twice.

The moral is that queues can actually increase workload. In other cases, they may decrease it when engineers are too impatient to wait for the test. Instead, they will find some other way avoid risk, for example, by overdesigning the part to prevent failure. This is likely to be much more expensive than a more aggressive and well-tested design.

Continuous Improvement

Before we leave the topic of testing we should examine one more chronic problem. This is the failure to continuously improve test processes. A well-managed company should be as interested in improving testing processes as it is in improving any other business activity. In fact, if we believe that testing is a core competence, it should be a higher priority.

Unfortunately, the average company does tests the same way it did five years ago. The primary reason for this is that management has not asked for any changes in testing quality, cost-effectiveness, or cycle time. We have no objective, we have nobody responsible, we have no plan, we have no resources allocated, and we have no schedule. This is a pretty good way to accomplish nothing.

The solution is fairly straightforward. We need explicit objectives, specific people assigned to accomplish them, a plan, resources, and a schedule. For example, at one electronics company they began taking resources to start automating their test processes. Over about a ten-year period they put semi-robotic automation in the testing area and automated data collection. They were able to reduce a thirty-day test process to one that took less than twenty-four hours. They now have the ability to introduce their product in several European markets simultaneously, instead of using their traditional phased approach. Engineers get feedback on their design so much faster that productivity has improved enormously.

SUMMARY

This chapter covered the problem of managing uncertainty and risk. We made a distinction between market risk, which is the risk that the product specification does not meet the market requirements, and technical risk, which is the risk that the design does not meet its specification. We noted that most companies do much worse at managing market risk than they do at managing technical risk. We stressed the importance of thinking about risk quantitatively in terms of the potential downside and the probability of this downside occurring. From this perspective the most important risk to the program can be to any of our four objectives: expense, cost, performance, and speed.

Then we explored several ways to manage market risk. We examined how to use substitute products to validate the requirements and how we could simulate a key product attribute. We discussed how we could keep the design flexible on an uncertain product attribute and how shorter development cycles act to reduce market risk. Then we turned to technical risk and explained the two key strategies of controlling subsystem risk and controlling system integration risk.

Finally we addressed the problem of managing testing processes, and optimizing these processes for any one of our four objectives. Which objective we choose depends on our project and on business-level economic analyses (discussed in Chapter 2). Here, too, approaches that work well to achieve one objective may be the opposite of what we want to do to achieve another objective. There is no best practice in testing, but rather practices that help us achieve certain economic objectives.

As we close this chapter we must point out that too many companies do a poor job at managing testing. They fail to recognize the critical role that design testing plays in generating information. Instead, they fall into the trap of treating it like manufacturing testing, which has totally different objectives.

We have now completed our discussion of the tools used in the Design Factory. It is time to encourage you to use them.

Part Four

NEXT STEPS

13

Now What Do I Do?

We have covered a lot of material in this book, some of which is new for many readers. Now it is time to begin putting these ideas into action. The recommendations I am about to offer are directed at senior management, because any successful attempt to transform the organization requires their involvement.

Rather than review the ideas of the book we will identify some modest first steps that senior managers can take to get the train moving. Overcoming inertia is usually a more difficult problem than accelerating the train once it is moving.

DO YOUR MATH

Understanding the economics of your development projects and processes is the only way to select the "right" course of action. The central theme of this book is that we have a variety of choices that are each appropriate for certain economic objectives. The appropriate course cannot be selected without a compass, and the only reliable compass we have found is economic analysis. You have wasted your time reading this book if you continue to believe that there are "best practices" that are universally appropriate for all development environments.

If you believe that product development is about developing products, you have also missed the core idea that our real objective is profits, not products. Since economic analysis is the foundation upon which every other profit-seeking decision depends, we must begin by doing the economic analysis described in Chapter 2 to create decision rules.

If these decision rules are to be useful throughout the organization, the finance department must be involved in these analyses. Otherwise, the numbers will not be viewed as official or credible. Yet the busy finance department is unlikely to get involved unless they are required to do this by senior management. Thus, a good first step is to assign a financial analyst to support every development team and ensure that each team has acceptable economic models to guide their day-to-day decisions. Once you have project models in place, you have the foundation to progress to business-level models, which are essential for development process design.

USE DECISION RULES

The economic analysis will be worthless if you do not use it to make day-to-day decisions. If managers ignore the economics and rely on their intuition to make decisions, they will make bad decisions and they will send the wrong signals to the organization. If you wish people to make decisions on the basis of facts rather than intuition, you must model this behavior yourself.

This does not mean that there is no place for intuition. We desperately need this intuition to create effective forecasts of the future, but the intuition should be applied to model inputs, not in creating assumptions about the outputs. We find that arithmetic works better than intuition for financial calculations.

A good second step, then, is to insist that important decisions are framed as economic tradeoffs and made on the basis of facts. If your intuition says the answer is wrong, then track the problem back to the flawed assumptions and correct them. Do not send a signal to your organization that rational decision making is ignored at the top of the organization. The more you frame decisions as economic choices, the more your people will adopt the same method.

PAY ATTENTION TO CAPACITY UTILIZATION

We frequently encounter managers who have a poor understanding of the relationship between capacity utilization and process queues. As a result, they load their processes to very high levels of utilization and are surprised that projects are late. As we pointed out in Chapter 3, we cannot load a process with variability to 100 percent utilization without large queues.

The primary way to break out of this mindset is to grasp the economics of queues. This is possible once we have a way to assess the cost of the queue, which is provided by our economic analysis. Furthermore, our understanding of queueing permits us to identify the key areas of the process that require extra resources. These are activities on the critical path that have high levels of variability. Thus, the third step is to take a careful look at your key process queues and quantify whether you have made the right tradeoff between the cost of capacity and the cost of the queue. We stress that this is a quantitative problem, and that simplistic approaches like overresourcing all projects will have less impact than applying this resource at the true bottlenecks.

PAY ATTENTION TO BATCH SIZE

Deeply embedded in the development process of most companies is the assumption that large batch sizes are appropriate for product development. It is not at all uncommon to find phased development systems where 100 percent of work is transferred to the next phase on a single day. Throughout this book we have provided many examples of how large batch sizes damage the speed, efficiency, cost, and performance of development processes. Changing to a small batch size model requires as much of a fundamental shift as JIT caused in manufacturing. It is unlikely that such a shift will come from the lowest level of the organization. Instead, it must be initiated by senior management.

There are two powerful ways to drive the process to smaller batch sizes. First, we can explicitly measure batch sizes and reduce them. This works particularly well for specific processes, like testing. The second technique is to measure the levels of design-in-process inventory (DIP). We should note that this is not a type of inventory that appears on the balance sheet, but rather a useful construct of management accounting. It is a useful tool in much the same way that a computed cost of quality is useful, even though it too is not present in our financial statements. The fourth step, then, is to begin measuring batch sizes or design-in-process inventory as a tool to drive down batch sizes.

RESPECT VARIABILITY

Too many managers think that the key problem with product development is the surprises. They try to eliminate all variability from the process. By now you should understand that it is the uncertainty that creates the information, and the information that creates the value of product development. This means that it is foolish to try to drive out variability from the development process.

We would propose an alternative solution. We need to create processes that continue to function in a world with variation. Fortunately, there are abundant tools to do this. The primary obstacle to using them is the belief that product development is or should be deterministic. It is time to discard this notion and use the right tools. It is time to recognize that the emperor has no clothes on, and that he never will. We need to treat development as a process with inherent variability. The fifth step is to approach development process design with the objective of making the process tolerant of variability as a key design objective.

THINK CLEARLY ABOUT RISK

In most companies you can take any risk you want as long as you are successful. This two-faced attitude towards risk is dangerous and confusing. We need to treat risk taking as a process of placing rational bets on the future. This means that a risk-taking action is viewed as appropriate, not based on its success, but based on whether it was sensible at the time the bet was placed.

The biggest obstacle to instituting such an attitude is the tendency to punish failures. This stigmatization of failure prevents us from communicating these events, which contain very high information content, and increases the chance we will have to learn the same lessons over and over again. The sixth step should be to celebrate and publicize the failures that occurred as a result of prudent risk taking. These failures generate new learning and are a key source of valuable information. They should be treated as such.

THINK SYSTEMS

We have stressed in many sections of this book that systems cannot be optimized by optimizing each one of their subsystems. Unfortunately, in most organizations managers below the level of senior management have specific responsibilities and explicit incentives to fulfill these responsibilities. Thus, they are encouraged to suboptimize the overall system. For example, manufacturing management may be measured on gross margin dollars generated each month. When they have to choose between building a prototype part to support product development and a part for a customer order, they will invariably choose the customer order. They do so because the prototype part generates no gross margin. We must deal with these dysfunctional incentives if we want to get systems thinking.

Senior management is usually the only group in the organization that has a clear picture of the overall system-level effects. As a result, it is critical for senior management to maintain the focus of the organization on the system-level objectives. This will often require setting aside incentive systems that encourage parochial optimization of local fiefdoms. A useful seventh step is to reevaluate the current incentives to ensure that they do not obstruct system-level thinking.

RESPECT THE PEOPLE

There has been a dangerous tendency in the quality movement to attribute all problems to the system rather than the people. While the intentions of this approach are good, its side effects are dangerous. If you believe that the primary determinant of outcomes is the system, this is where you will focus your time and attention. You will try to create a system that can be operated by fools.

An alternative view is that success is equally dependent on creating a workable system and populating this system with excellent people. This approach requires careful selection and development of people to ensure that the system will work as desired. Instead of complaining that "our assets walk out the door every night," we must welcome the chance to transform people into critical business assets rather than interchangeable cogs in a mind-numbing system.

If we truly believe that such an attitude toward people is correct and profitable, we will devote our scarcest resource, management time, to developing our people. This is a consistent characteristic of the best development organizations. The eighth step is to shift our management attention to making people a key asset of our process.

DESIGN THE PROCESS THOUGHTFULLY

It should be clear that the design of a development process requires both an economic objective and a number of careful design choices. Most of the efforts we encounter to reengineer development processes are hopelessly misdirected, focusing on things like process maps and the elimination of "waste," which is always assumed to be evil. By now you should understand that what may be labeled as "waste" may be serving a very different purpose in the product development environment. For example, duplicate testing early and late in the design process generates information early, when it is most valuable. Yet it looks like waste to the naive process reengineer. Excess capacity in the prototype shop may look like waste, yet it is the key to eliminating queues. An internal publications department may look cost-ineffective compared to outsourcing these services, yet the cycle time impact of such a department may far outweigh its development expense impact.

If we wish our people to adopt a more thoughtful approach to process design we need to be less tolerant of shallow thinking. This reduced tolerance does not require punishing simplistic solutions but rather encouraging deeper analysis and careful design. This is perhaps one of the most challenging recommendations, because busy senior managers are constantly bombarded with new slogans and themes begging for adoption. But if senior managers do not become more thoughtful consumers of management ideas it will be very hard to make entire organizations more thoughtful. The ninth step is to ensure that development process design is approached with the same methodical rigor with which we would approach our product design.

PAY ATTENTION TO ARCHITECTURE

It is too common that development organizations pay insufficient attention to the architecture of their products. Yet these architectural decisions have a huge impact on expenses, schedule, performance, and costs. They are too important to be left to the system architects alone, because other functional departments have important interests to be represented.

It is unlikely that architecture will be treated as a business-level issue unless senior management decides that it is important. Once architecture is legitimized as a business issue instead of a technical one, we will be able to get other functions to play a role in these choices. Our tenth step is to ensure that all product architectures obtain cross-functional reviews before they are adopted.

DEEPLY UNDERSTAND THE CUSTOMER

While there has been a wonderful increase in the number of companies that have decided to become "customer-focused," too often this stops at understanding *what* the customer wants. It is far more important to understand *why* the customer wants things, and to respect the fact that customers may have limited knowledge of their own requirements.

The implication of this is that we have to spend much more time understanding the reasons why customers want certain things. Tools like models of application economics provide a strong test of your knowledge in this area. Getting high percentages of your development teams out in contact with customers is also vital. Unfortunately, financial and organizational obstacles often discourage this broad contact with our customers. The eleventh step in our sequence is to constantly test whether your organization understands *why* customers require certain product characteristics and to remove any obstacles that stand in the way of obtaining such knowledge.

ELIMINATE USELESS CONTROLS

Too much of the control effort at most companies is directed at factors that have no economic significance. Thoughtful workers are constantly astonished by this senseless bureaucracy. The solution is not to discard controls but to make them relevant by focusing on factors that truly impact economic outcomes. The only reliable way we have found to do this is to ground them on the economic analysis. Getting prior management approval to remove a box of pencils from the storeroom makes little sense in any development environment.

This is an issue of emphasis, since budgets will almost always be required in some form. The question is really how much of the time of our talented people will be devoted to feeding data into senseless control systems. A useful twelfth step is to specifically review the time invested in supporting various control systems and ask whether this is aligned to the true economic importance of the controlled variable.

GET TO THE FRONT LINES

In my personal management experience I learned a lesson twenty-five years ago as a young naval officer on nuclear submarines. My department head pointed out to me that a division officer belongs in his spaces, not in his office. Throughout my management career I have been struck by the pronounced differences between great organizations like Hewlett-Packard, who practice this philosophy on a daily basis, and those that do not.

Behavioral congruency, or what is known as "walking the talk," is essential for good communications. For most people, how a leader spends his or her time will be the most important sign of what is truly important to the organization. Management demonstrates its interest in product development by the time it spends in the development organization. This is a critical tool for getting timely and accurate information about what is really happening.

Many senior managers appear to be reluctant to spend time in the middle of the development laboratory because they worry that this will demonstrate their lack of understanding of product technology. This is rarely a concern of the engineers in the lab. Mere presence in the laboratory has extraordinary benefits. My final recommendation is that senior managers get out to where the work is being done, to get a view from the ground level. With the possible exception of recruiting and selecting people, there is no better way to spend management time.

AVOID SLOGANS

I am aware of the wonderful irony in a slogan that advises avoiding slogans, but I could not resist it. We are now at the end of this book. Let us recap for a moment the central underlying theme of this book. Rather than arguing that there are best practices that confer upon their users certain automatic advantages, I would argue that managing the Design Factory requires a much more thoughtful approach. It is the economics of the business that ultimately determine which process parameters must be optimized. Once we know what we are trying to optimize we have the design objectives for our process. This enables us to make choices that are targeted at optimizing these objectives.

A wise man once said, "Wisdom is the art of knowing what is important." It is unlikely that there is any shortcut to wisdom; however, some routes are more direct than others. The most direct one we have found is careful observation and reflection on these observations. Curiously, it is only by assuming that your observations are inaccurate and your reflections are simplistic that you will improve their accuracy and penetration. Good luck.

Selected Bibliography

Alexander, Christopher, Sarah Ishikawa, and Murray Silverstein with Max Jacobson, Ingrid Fiksdahl-King, and Shlomo Angel. *A Pattern Language, Towns Buildings Construction*. New York: Oxford University Press, 1977.

Allen, Thomas J. *Managing the Flow of Technology*. Cambridge, MA: MIT Press, 1977.

Argyris, Chris, and Donald A. Schön. *Organizational Learning II: Theory, Method, and Practice*. Reading, MA: Addison-Wesley, 1996.

Brooks, Frederick P., Jr. *The Mythical Man-Month, Essays on Software Engineering*. Reading, MA: Addison-Wesley, 1982.

Clark, Kim B., and Steven C. Wheelright. *Managing New Product and Process Development, Text and Cases*. New York: The Free Press, 1993.

Cusumano, Michael, and Richard W. Selby. *Microsoft Secrets*. New York: The Free Press, 1995.

Griffin, Abbie, and John R. Hauser. "The Voice of the Customer," *Marketing Science*, Vol. 12, No. 1, Winter 1993.

Hall, Randolph W. *Queueing Methods for Services and Manufacturing*. Englewood Cliffs, NJ: Prentice Hall, 1991.

Kuhn, Thomas. *The Structure of Scientific Revolutions*. Chicago: University of Chicago Press, 1970.

Lorenz, Christopher. *The Design Dimension: The New Competitive Weapon for Product Strategy and Global Marketing*. Oxford, UK: Basil Blackwell, 1990.

O'Connor, Patrick D. T. *Practical Reliability Engineering*. Chichester, UK: John Wiley & Sons, 1991.

Ohno, Taiichi. *The Toyota Production System*. Cambridge, MA: Productivity Press, 1988.

Pahl, G., and W. Beitz. *Engineering Design: A Systematic Approach*. London: The Design Council, 1988.

Patterson, Marvin. *Accelerating Innovation*. New York: Van Nostrand Reinhold, 1993.

Petroski, Henry. *Design Paradigms: Case Histories of Error and Judgment in Engineering*. New York: Cambridge University Press, 1994.

Pierce, John R. *An Introduction to Information Theory: Symbols, Signals & Noise*. New York: Dover, 1980.

Porter, Michael. *Competitive Strategy: Techniques for Analyzing Industries and Competitors*. New York: The Free Press, 1980.

Rechtin, Eberhardt. *Systems Architecting: Creating and Building Complex Systems.* Englewood Cliffs, NJ: Prentice Hall, 1991.

Rich, Ben R., and Leo Janos. *Skunk Works: A Personal Memoir of My Years at Lockheed.* Boston: Little, Brown, 1994.

Seaston, J. A. H. *Improving the Competitive Weight of Large Turbofan Aero Engines.* Conference Paper C482, International Conference on Design for Competitive Advantage. London: Institute of Mechanical Engineers, 1994.

Shingo, Shigeo. *Non-Stock Production: The Shingo System for Continuous Improvement.* Cambridge, MA: Productivity Press, 1988.

Simon, Herbert A. *Sciences of the Artificial.* Cambridge, MA: MIT Press, 1981.

Smith, Preston G., and Donald G. Reinertsen. *Developing Products in Half the Time.* New York: Van Nostrand Reinhold, 1991.

Thomke, Stefan H. *The Economics of Experimentation in the Design of New Products and Processes.* Ph.D. thesis, Massachusetts Institute of Technology, February 1995.

Index

About the Author

D onald G. Reinertsen is president of Reinertsen & Associates, a consulting firm specializing in the management of the product development process. Before starting his own firm, he had extensive consulting experience at McKinsey & Co., an international management consulting firm, and operating experience as senior vice president of operations at Zimmerman Holdings, a private diversified manufacturing company.

His contributions in the field of product development have been internationally recognized. In 1983, while a consultant at McKinsey & Co., he wrote a landmark article in *Electronic Business* magazine that first quantified the value of development speed. This article has been cited as the McKinsey study that indicated that "six months' delay can be worth 33 percent of life cycle profits." Since then, he has gone considerably beyond this early work. He has worked with companies ranging from Fortune 500 Baldrige Award winners to small venture, capital backed, start-ups. He has developed a number of innovative analytical techniques for assessing the product development process.

Reinertsen holds a B.S. degree in electrical engineering from Cornell University and an M.B.A. with distinction from Harvard Business School. He is a member of the IEEE, SME, and ASQC and is co-author of the book *Developing Products in Half the Time: New Rules, New Tools.* He writes and speaks frequently on techniques for shortening development cycles and teaches a popular executive course at California Institute of Technology entitled "Streamlining the Product Development Process." He has trained thousands of product developers in more than a dozen countries on product development techniques.